D1503580

EDITOR

By the same author

THE BRITISH PUBLIC AND THE GENERAL STRIKE

FRENCH LIBERAL THOUGHT IN THE EIGHTEENTH
CENTURY

LOW'S RUSSIAN SKETCH BOOK (with David Low)

THE MAGIC OF MONARCHY

PROPAGANDA'S HARVEST

THE PRESS THE PUBLIC WANTS

HAROLD LASKI, A MEMOIR

CRITIC'S LONDON DIARY: From the *New Statesman* 1931–56

THE CROWN AND THE ESTABLISHMENT

THE TRIUMPH OF LORD PALMERSTON: A Study of Public
Opinion in England before the Crimean War

FATHER FIGURES: A First Volume of Autobiography
1897–1931

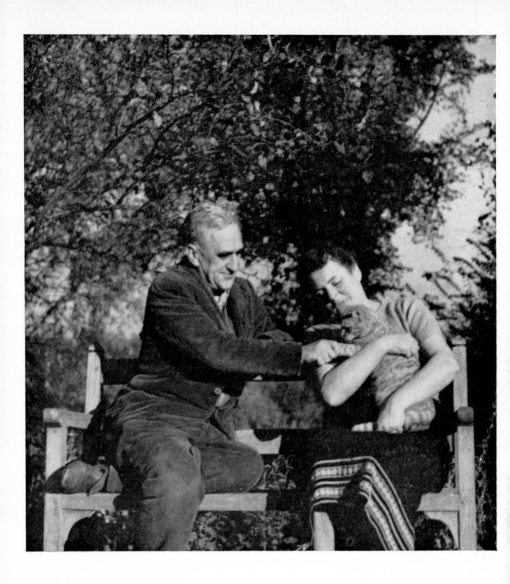

In the Essex garden

EDITOR

KINGSLEY MARTIN

*a second volume of
autobiography
1931-45*

HUTCHINSON OF LONDON

HUTCHINSON & CO (*Publishers*) LTD
178-202 Great Portland Street, London W1

London Melbourne Sydney
Auckland Bombay Toronto
Johannesburg New York

First published 1968

© Kingsley Martin 1968

*This book has been set in Bembo, printed in Great Britain
on Antique Wove paper by Anchor Press,
and bound by Wm. Brendon, both of Tiptree, Essex*

09 086040 3

PN
5123
M35 A32

Eggheads of the world unite, you've nothing to lose
but your yolks.

Adlai Stevenson

228184

CONTENTS

ILLUSTRATIONS

LINE DRAWINGS BY LOW

ACKNOWLEDGMENTS

For permission to quote, the author wishes to thank Victor Gollancz Ltd. for the extract from C. R. Attlee *The Labour Party in Perspective*; Michael Ayrton for the extract from a letter; the Trustees of the Beaverbrook Foundation for the letter from Lord Beaverbrook; Victor Gollancz Ltd. for the extract from H. N. Brailsford *Property or Peace?*; Cassell & Co. Ltd. for the extract from W. S. Churchill *The Gathering Storm*; Frederick Muller Ltd. for the extract from Hugh Dalton *The Fateful Years*; Lady Elliot for an extract from a letter from her husband, Sir Walter Elliot; Mrs. Aldous Huxley for a letter from her husband; Oxford University Press for extracts from Tom Jones *A Diary with Letters*; the executors of Maynard Keynes for extracts from his letters; Beaverbrook Newspapers for the letter from Earl Lloyd-George; the *World's Press News* for the extract from 'Malcolm Muggeridge's Viewpoint'; the *New Statesman and Nation* for material originally appearing therein; Beverley Nichols for a letter; Mrs George Orwell for the extract from her husband's letter; D. Kilham Roberts for extracts from the letters of his father, Harry Roberts; Earl Russell for extracts from letters; the Public Trustees and Society of Authors for extracts from the letters of G. B. Shaw; Mrs. Wickham Steed and Miss Joan Stevenson for the extract from a letter from Wickham Steed; the Clarendon Press, Oxford, for the extract from A. J. P. Taylor *English History, 1914–45*; Mrs. William Temple for two letters from her husband; Eyre and Spottiswoode for the extract from Hugh Thomas *The Spanish Civil War*; Professor W. A. Robson for extracts from the diaries and letters of Beatrice Webb, and, in the case of the letters, also the London School of Economics, which has the originals in its care; George Philip Wells and Frank Wells for extracts from the letters and writings of H. G. Wells; Leonard Woolf for two letters from Virginia Woolf; and M. B. Yeats and Macmillan & Co. Ltd. for the extract from 'The Second Coming', included in the *Collected Poems of W. B. Yeats*.

For illustration material, the author would again like to thank the

New Statesman and Nation, in which the majority of the line drawings in this volume originally appeared, and in particular Lady Low for permission to use the drawings by her husband, Edmond Kapp for allowing the use of his League Personalities, Miss Flora Twort for her portrait of Harry Roberts, the London School of Economics for permission to reproduce the portrait of Sir William Nicholson, and Macmillan & Co. Ltd. for the photograph of Maynard Keynes.

FOREWORD

I am not obliged in this book to make the usual protestations of frankness. I really have not much alternative, because I was editor of a paper which is still on file for all the world to read, and I have, to guide me, not only my *Diary*, published every week, but also many letters, memos and private diaries (never long maintained) on which I have drawn freely. I have not amended these first-hand sources by the hindsight of innumerable other books since published about the thirties; I have endeavoured to let the contemporary record speak for itself. This is how the fight against war and poverty appeared to me in the thirties and if it sometimes seems ridiculous now, that cannot be helped.

I am particularly grateful to Sir Gerald Barry and Paul Johnson, the present editor of the *New Statesman*, who have made so many helpful comments and suggestions. I owe thanks, too, to those who have checked my memory of events; in particular to Margaret Cole, Mabel Brailsford, Frank Woodhead of the London School of Economics, Sylvia Scaffardi, a staunch worker on the National Council of Civil Liberties in the thirties and Nigel Calder. Mrs. A. G. Dowdeswell has been invaluable to me, both as secretary and research assistant. Miss Edith M. Horsley of Hutchinson's has again done more for me than an author has a right to expect.

CHAPTER ONE

The Staggers and Naggers

I

I CAME to London in the autumn of 1930 to seek my fortune. In this book I want to record something of the mental climate in which I found myself immersed and to describe its problems, as they appeared to me at the time. Many books are published about the thirties, but they seem concerned mainly to show how feeble, absurd and misguided we all were. These are the characteristics attributed by each generation to their parents' generation. I want rather to show why we failed, and, above all, to explain our struggles to prevent the Second World War.

Horror of war was shared by almost everyone in this country, whatever his class or creed. The more thoughtful realised that to find a way of preventing war was the obligatory task of our generation. We failed, and the fact that when war came Britain was on the winning side was comparatively unimportant. In 1914 we had gone into the slaughter, some cheering, almost all without warning. In the thirties our eyes were open, yet the Gadarene swine found no agreement about a stopping-place as they plunged down the steep place into the sea. Einstein has warned the generation of the 1960s that nuclear war presents a prospect that is 'apparently inexorable. Each state appears as the inevitable consequence of the one that went before. And at the end, looming ever clearer, lies general annihilation'. In the thirties we saw war as an increasing menace, but not as inexorable, and we assumed we had personal responsibility for preventing it. Of course Einstein could be wrong, and, though the slope is steep and much more perilous today, it is possible that the present generation will find a stopping-point which we could not find. Anyway, I should like to record our conflicts and struggles in seeking a place where we could stick in our hooves, and why we failed.

B

I was just thirty-three when I came to London; I had no job, nor prospect of one. I was not in the least surprised when the Scott family did not renew my three-year contract on the *Manchester Guardian*. They saw that I was unsuited temperamentally and politically to be a leader-writer on their paper. I knew they were right, but no one likes failure.

I was glad to leave Manchester, where I made only a few friends. My neighbours, Kit and Malcolm Muggeridge, had revolted earlier. Kit had hung her pyjamas out of the window as a flag of defiance and Malcolm, a colleague on the paper, had announced that he was a Communist and gone off to Moscow, where, of course, he quickly came to detest its bureaucracy and poverty even more than he had disliked the boredom and complacency of the only Manchester he knew. We both had powerful Nonconformist backgrounds, but while Malcolm was in revolt against his, I was still dominated by my father's example. Unlike Malcolm, I had immense respect for the *Guardian*, but, like Malcolm, I did not enjoy sitting on so many fences and ending so many articles with 'it is greatly to be hoped' when it was obvious that the hope would be disappointed. I wanted responsibility and to speak my own mind. I had come frequently to my home in Finchley or to stay with friends in Bloomsbury, so that I was not wholly out of touch with London. I used to return to Manchester apparently confident, but really with my heart in my boots, knowing that I had no one with whom I could really discuss politics there and that I was leaving my roots behind me.

I had not much reason for self-confidence, however good a face I put on it. Before Manchester I had been for four years assistant to Harold Laski at the London School of Economics and had enjoyed the company of what was then a wonderfully talented staff. Like many other people, I had been almost in love with Eileen Power,[1] a sparkling and delightful woman who died suddenly from a heart attack; I had been lucky enough to be on intimate terms with both Harold Laski and R. H. Tawney, and I had many good friends among the junior staff. But I had been at violent loggerheads with Sir William Beveridge, the director, and with the secretary of the

1. Author of *Mediaeval People*, etc.

school, Mrs. Mair. Beveridge had naturally disliked a short and satirical book I had written on the General Strike, which had included an attack on the Coal Commission of which he had been the most influential member. I had tried my hand at W.E.A. lecturing, which I could have done well if I had had the modesty to realise that imparting knowledge to the ignorant requires at least as much, if not more, solid preparatory work than lecturing to the sophisticated. Before that I had been for four years to Cambridge and had spent a year at Graduate College, Princeton, New Jersey, and, although I had taken a One-one in my Tripos at Magdalene, I was not elected to a fellowship at any of the colleges which had nibbled at me. I knew this was really my own fault; I had been tactless, conceited, doctrinaire and opinionated. I realised when I came to London again that I should have to begin afresh, whatever job I took. I might still have gone back into academic life and should, I suppose, some day have become a professor. Such jobs were proposed to me, but it so happened that the editor of the *New Statesman* had drunk himself out of the chair and I was invited to step into it. In a previous volume[1] I have described how, after my appointment to the *New Statesman*, Maynard Keynes, the chief proprietor of the *Nation*, seized the opportunity to arrange an amalgamation between the two papers and how, a few years later, Gerald Barry's already doomed *Weekend Review* bequeathed to us its title and goodwill. He became a member of the *New Statesman and Nation* Board.

I am conscious that in relating my earlier life I have said nothing about my personal story in the twenties. I have described how, as a result of my puri anical upbringing, I was sexually retarded. I never fell in love, in any serious way, till I was twenty-six, and I was still sexually inexperienced when I made a foolish marriage two years later. She was an *artiste manquée* and I an ambitious extrovert. We spent a baffling seven years together, never unkind to each other, but never at one, and not believing in amateur psychoanalysis, I do not propose to write more about our relationship. In the earlier thirties I discovered happiness with Dorothy Woodman, and this continued for more than thirty years and still continues. One of the reasons for

1. Kingsley Martin, *Father Figures* (Hutchinson, 1965).

our success together was that we were both of us absorbed in our
own work and carried on our separate jobs, which were fortunately
complementary. I recall one early incident which illustrates our
relationship. We travelled on the same train to a Labour Party
Conference in Scarborough. We had to change at York in the
middle of the night, with some two or three hours to wait. We
had neither of us been there before and Dorothy at once went to a
telephone booth and rang up the police. Would they mind telling us
—it was a moonlit night—the way to the Minster? They were
charming, and at intervals while we walked about the city she rang
up the constable on duty, explained where we had got to and asked
his advice about the next sight which would be worth seeing by
moonlight. No one else I had ever met could have so profit-
ably and amusingly avoided passing the small hours in a dreary
waiting-room. I realised that with Dorothy life would never be
tame.

I was, of course, pleased and excited when I found myself in charge
of the *New Statesman and Nation*, which became popularly known as
the 'Staggers and Naggers'. To an almost frightening extent I was
responsible only to myself. I instinctively began with a sustained
attack on the National Government, which was formed a few
months after I took over. Perhaps it was at this time that I acquired
a reputation for being cocksure. Actually, I often found it difficult
to make up my mind. As a historian, I was quite sure what Lord
Palmerston, for instance, ought to have done in 1850. What ought
to be done in the thirties proved less easy to decide. In private I
laughed at myself for my crises of conscience. I used to mutter
Laurence Housman's verses about a small girl who 'turned round
and round till she fell giddy on the ground'. Her Victorian aunt,
after waiting quietly until she reached this disagreeable climax, said:

> 'You cannot look at life all round,
> Or all the facts that life may show
> Combine to give you vertigo.'

That was my difficulty. I had a not-quite-paralysing capacity for

The Editor at work

seeing seven sides to every question and foreseeing all the dangers of
any course of action.

Some of our problems would be decided, at least for the week,
every Monday morning at an editorial conference. We moved soon
after my arrival on the paper from the original *New Statesman*
premises (which have now altogether disappeared) at 10, Great
Queen Street. Now we were at 10, Great Turnstile, overlooking the
flowering cherries in the gardens of Lincoln's Inn—much more
convenient, even though reviewers might have to climb an outside
flight of iron stairs or go through the housekeeper's flat to get to the
literary department. After our conference in my room, we used to
adjourn for lunch to an oak-panelled restaurant in Red Lion Square.
It was a Georgian house, later destroyed in the Blitz, though for
many months the front door remained intact, inviting you in to a
heap of rubble.

At lunch there would be our very small political staff, which
always included H. N. Brailsford, about whom I shall have much to
say later, and Aylmer Vallance, an intriguing character who grew a
pointed beard and looked like the sea-captain in *Under Milk Wood*.
He had done many jobs in his time; fought duels with revolvers in
the Himalayas as a Secret Service agent in the First World War, and
been editor of the *News Chronicle* and on the staff of the *Economist*.
He wrote a number of books ranging from one on cathedrals to one
on finance; he was an excellent cook and his politics could be guessed
from the fact that he called his eldest son Tito. At one time he rented
a castle in the south of Scotland and used to drive up there in a fast
car on Friday nights and return in time for the conference on
Mondays. Perhaps his favourite subject was fishing, but he could
write with the greatest facility on almost anything. A contributor
who came regularly to lunch was Olga Katzin, who, under the
name of *Sagittarius*, contributed a brilliant satirical poem every week
for twenty years. I think this is something of a record in the history
of journalism. I sometimes met her on her way to a private room she
rented in Covent Garden, where she could work without any
domestic disturbances. She summarised, in brilliant satirical verses,
much that we had said in our editorial conversations, very much

as Vicky did in his cartoons after the war. It was not until he was invalided out of the R.A.F. that Norman MacKenzie joined the paper; I should rate him as one of the most reliable, conscientious and industrious journalists I have known.

At our lunches after the editorial conference the managing director, John Roberts, was always present, and so was Ernest Willison, who looked after our advertising and became one of my closest friends, as well as a world authority on sweet peas. One or two of our literary staff usually joined us at lunch, Raymond Mortimer perhaps the most often. He was the sort of literary editor with whom I scarcely ever wanted to interfere. He was more a Liberal and less a Socialist than I was, but he looked out from the same wide window and shared my forebodings about the world. He made it his job to help young writers and is as much the father of many literary reputations as Cyril Connolly became a few years later. I greatly regretted it when Raymond left us for the *Sunday Times*; the reason, I think, was not financial, but Raymond's need of a less exacting way of life than literary editing. After all, he could write reviews on a wide variety of subjects from France or Italy and was able to travel widely in all the five continents. V. S. Pritchett was often with us; he, like David Garnett (who was for a short time literary editor), was already famous, not so much as a novelist as an admirable short story writer and a superb and, above all, underivative literary critic and I have always been proud to regard him as my greatest literary discovery. Another unusual writer was G. W. Stonier, who never seemed to belong to the world in which the rest of us lived, but who, when challenged, wrote eccentric, unexpected and clever prose; the time came when he really turned his back on this civilisation and took a Land-Rover into the wilds of Africa.[1] And then there was Cuthbert Worsley, who became our dramatic critic after Desmond MacCarthy had left us. A famous actor told me that at one time Worsley was the only critic worth reading, because he alone talked helpfully about the

1. Stonier's originality as a writer is perhaps best seen in *Shaving through the Blitz* (1943) and *Round London with the Unicorn* (1951): his African adventures are recorded in *Off the Rails* (1967).

technique of acting as well as about the interpretation of the play. He left us eventually for the *Financial Times* and has earned fame for himself by his autobiographical book *Flannelled Fool*, in which, incidentally, he tells us that he became really happy, for the first time in his life, on the *New Statesman and Nation*. I don't think any weekly ever had a better coverage of the Arts than when Stonier was dealing with films, Desmond Shaw-Taylor with music, T. C. Worsley with the theatre and, very frequently, Raymond Mortimer with the visual arts.

I have left out two personalities who both had a powerful influence on the policy and character of the paper. The first was Leonard Woolf, who in the early days used frequently to lunch with us. He had been literary editor of the *Nation*, to which I had often contributed in the past. I had known him and Virginia Woolf ever since the end of the First World War, and found him, as I still do, the most companionable of men. He was always ready to advise me and became, I think, something of a Father Figure to me. No one was ever so ready for argument and, I may add, so obstinate and lovable.

Dick Crossman, now, as I write, Leader of the House of Commons, wrote for the paper several years before he became my principal assistant in 1938. We did not always agree; it may have been good for the paper that our differences were sometimes apparent. He is, I think, the very epitome of an intellectual; that is to say, his opinions are more founded on reason than those of most people. If they are rooted in emotion, they at any rate appear to be deductions from facts. If he seems changeable and uncertain in judgment, that is because he is almost desperately honest, reaching new positions when new facts are set before him, apparently forgetful that yesterday he held the opposite opinion. In this, he resembles Maynard Keynes, the only one of my friends whom I should put above Dick Crossman in intellectual power. In both cases, if you wanted them to change their minds, you had to provide them with new premises; you would then find them reaching the conclusion you desired much more quickly than you had done yourself. This is not the recipe for success in politics, and it explains why Dick's brilliance has not yet led him to be Foreign Minister or Premier.

The mass of the electorate is moved by instinct and by interest, not by argument. Stanley Baldwin was a successful Premier because every conventional Englishman knew that he shared his prejudices and represented his interests. Ernest Bevin made mincemeat of Dick in public controversies, not because Bevin was right and Dick was wrong, but because every trade unionist knew that Bevin understood his interests and would fight for them to the end.

A member of the House of Commons, Crossman was not present to argue about the final decisions of the paper, and found it necessary, perhaps too often, to explain that he was not personally responsible for all our editorial views. He wrote the best signed reviews that I have ever read in any paper and his leading articles have the qualities of his speeches. He modelled them on those of Joseph Chamberlain—never rhetorical, carefully thought out, powerful, pungent and persuasive. There were occasions at our lunches when we were mildly embarrassed by the scintillating and masterful part which he took in our conversations. Some distinguished guest would be present, a British Ambassador, for instance, who expected, no doubt, to be respectfully treated. He would be cross-questioned by Dick in the not-always-vain hope of extracting information about our foreign policy or behaviour in some outlying part of Asia or Africa. The unfortunate guest would leave, with the glare of Dick's eyes still penetrating his soul, wondering whether during his unexpected appearance in the dock he had acquitted himself with adequate discretion. Dick Crossman has now quite overcome his handicaps as a politician; he would have been the most formidable ever of Q.C.s.

A small difficulty that cropped up in the early days of our lunches was that Princess Bibesco, a daughter of Asquith and the wife of a polished Rumanian diplomat, regularly invited herself to lunch. She had been a great buddy of my predecessor, Clifford Sharp, and felt that she had a right to be on the inside of the paper. She was a continuous and entertaining conversationalist who, so far as I can remember, differed from Macaulay in never having 'brilliant flashes of silence'. Her wit took after Margot Oxford's, but she talked too much about herself, describing on one occasion, for example, how the exiled King of Spain had called on her in her Paris hotel bedroom so unexpectedly that she hadn't even time to put on a clean nightdress. I used to shut her up, rather brusquely, so that our serious talk about politics could get a chance. Perhaps for this reason she ceased to come to our lunches after the first year or so.

There was often an interesting outsider present at these lunches; I am sorry that in those days I did not keep a record. Once Jawarhalal Nehru was a guest, and important people came to meet him. It was a larger lunch than usual, and I went over the names of those present with Noel Brailsford. We could not remember who had occupied one of the places at table. Later, Noel rang me up to say 'I've just remembered who was our other guest. It was Clem Attlee, the leader of our great Party.' This was characteristic. I have never known anyone with Attlee's deceptive capacity for not being noticed—which no doubt explains why Churchill thought him in 1940 'a decent, modest, little man, who of course has a great deal to be modest about'. He had learnt better when Attlee was Premier after the war and scored over a disgruntled Churchill. 'I thought the little fellow got the better of you today,' said a Conservative MP to Winston, to which Winston replied in one of those brilliant, care-fully-rehearsed repartees for which he was famous, 'Feed a grub on royal jelly and it may become a queen.' One may find in such anecdotes a useful clue. Attlee himself was a considerable wit; if you search *Hansard* you will find memorable phrases in many of Attlee's speeches, but when Churchill made a witticism he carefully prepared the way for it, did an effective stutter and then brought it out, so to speak, on a silver salver. Everyone remembered it and it hit the headlines; Attlee addressed any witticism to his boots.

My own part at such lunches was mainly that of a chairman who summarised the varieties of opinion. It became obvious, if it had not already been clear at the editorial conference, who should write the leader for that week and what, in general, we should say. I would be picking up ideas and stealing stories from everyone to put into my *London Diary*, which I began in 1931 and did not leave off writing until 1961. For a time, in my first year, Leonard Woolf often collaborated with me and later various friends such as Raymond Mortimer, R. H. S. Crossman and W. R. Hewitt (*C. H. Rolph*), used to provide me with valuable paragraphs, but it was always my personal *Diary*. I wrote five-sixths of it and rewrote to my own liking any paragraphs submitted to me by others.

I think one reason for the wide interest in my *Diary* was that I was curious about everything and enjoyed talking about unimportant events that struck me as comic or ironic. I would begin with a paragraph or two about peace or the class struggle or unemployment, but go on to write about cats and gardeners and sex and crime and odd characters and events I had witnessed. Everything was grist to the *Diary*, and I took no end of pains about the writing of it, often drafting twice as much as I wanted and working at the paragraphs over and over again till they said a lot in a little space. You have to work very hard to achieve simplicity. I was always careful to write about the various small, progressive societies which would otherwise get no mention in the papers. I placed the 'This England' column, which we took from the *Weekend Review*, after the *Diary*, and I think in years to come people will read the extracts we chose for it— they were sent in by contributors—in order to illustrate the sort of place England was in a period which now seems remote. Scores of entries were submitted every week; we selected them, not always because they were funny, but because they illustrated peculiar Anglo-Saxon attitudes. We made collections of these extracts and published them as Christmas Specials. Reading them today, I realise that we produced really useful social documents and I find them historically as interesting, as well as more funny, than old volumes of *Punch*.

Picked at random, I don't know that I could find a better illustration of one common attitude of mind in the thirties than the following:

Speaking as a total abstainer, Lady Montgomery-Massingberd said it would help a great deal if people who did not care for alcoholic drinks would 'take the pledge'.

'Those of you who go to sherry parties and cocktail parties,' she added, 'finish what is in your glasses. Do not let it go away to be drunk in the pantry by someone who, perhaps, has not taken it before, or has not acquired the taste.'[1]

1. 'This England', 1937.

It is commonly supposed that an editor will always quarrel with
his printers, and I will not deny that there were rare occasions when
the Cornwall Press did not agree with us about what was fit to print.
I recall for instance that Leonard Woolf wrote a scathing parody of
a *Times* leading article which the printer refused to publish until I
altered *Times* into 'Britain's leading newspaper'—a change which
did not seem very important to me, since everyone knew which
paper we were satirising. Leonard, however, was furious with me
for giving way to the printer. In general, I got on admirably with the
printing staff who were responsible for bringing us out. Particularly,
I was friends with Mr. Wicken, who was proud of looking after the
New Statesman and Nation, rather than one of the many technical
papers for which the Cornwall Press was responsible. Of course,
everyone had to be rather patient with me because I was a devil for
correcting and rewriting. In the thirties we went to press on Thursday mornings, writing, correcting and passing for press the last notes
during the lunch hour. The leading article I commonly wrote late on
Wednesday nights. I had a theory, which it is easy to hold when you
are young, that I always should do everything I enjoyed doing first
and leave till the last minute the things I knew were compulsory.
Every journalist knows that you waste time if you start work too
early: the frantic deadline may bring out the best in you. I would
finish the leading article, maybe by one or two in the morning. I
would then send it by Post Office messenger who, in those luxurious
days, was obtainable day and night. I would discuss the make-up
with Mr. Wicken on the telephone and very likely decide that
previous decisions were wrong and that the paper had to be torn to
pieces and re-made. In the morning, when the page proofs arrived,
the staff was often surprised to see what it contained and, sometimes,
to read what it said.

In some ways, the thirties were the great age of the weeklies. All
the young writers who wished to make a reputation as literary
figures or even as budding politicians looked to the weeklies as the
natural place in which they could establish themselves. There was no
competition from the Sunday magazines or television. We had
several competing weeklies which seemed equally likely to exercise

influence or grow in circulation. In those days, *Time and Tide* made a good bid, with Lady Rhondda as editor, but it was too much a woman's magazine and was politically uncertain. The *Economist* was too much a technical journal to be considered as a competitor, but everyone took it for granted that the *Spectator* held the leading place. It was a very old-established journal and assumed a somewhat superior air. Once when Lord Cecil tried to arrange for the *Spectator* and *N. S. & N.* to collaborate in some League propaganda, it refused to be associated with us. I was on good enough terms with the editor, Wilson Harris, but I cannot deny that I was pleased when we forged ahead and could show a larger audited circulation. Not that we wanted the *Spectator* to do badly, but that we wanted to do better. In fact, it was to our interest for the whole class of weeklies to thrive. We wanted the habit of reading this category of journal to increase and we were all in a far stronger position to appeal to advertisers if we could prove that the weekly journals of opinion had a joint circulation of several hundred thousand. Agencies could then be more easily persuaded to write the special kind of 'copy' that would appeal to our type of reader.

Of course, we were at a disadvantage with advertisers. John Roberts and Ernest Willison worked with enthusiasm and success to overcome the advertisers' resistance to making use of a Left-Wing journal. On this matter, which might so easily have led to the kind of friction that is always supposed to exist between the editor and the manager of a paper, we never quarrelled at all. I did not interfere with the business side of the paper and John, who must often have cursed our editorial views, refrained from trying to influence my politics.

The relation of advertising to editorial policy is much misunderstood. I was shocked when the Royal Commission on the Press, held immediately after the war, pretended that advertisers do not influence editorial policy. It is true enough that except in the case of some small, local newspapers, advertisers do not attempt to bully editors. Great business concerns do not ring up Lord Thomson or Lord Rothermere and tell them to 'lay off' this or that line of policy; they do not need to. You need not blackmail a millionaire in order to make him into a Conservative. I have known cases where important groups of advertisers have brought pressure to bear on national papers; there was the extraordinary case of Lord Northcliffe's attacks on Kitchener in 1915, when for some days *The Times* was suddenly half its size because of the withdrawal of advertising. It was often said that advertisers induced the first Lord Rothermere to abandon his support of Mosley by threatening to boycott his newspapers. But such cases are very rare and in general it is true that no special advertising pressure affects editorial policy. Yet the whole tenor and attitude of the national Press is influenced by advertising. In the case of Left-Wing papers, advertising agencies do not say that they refuse their support on the ground that the journal is republican or atheist or socialist, but papers that do advocate such views have to fight much harder for advertisements than their more conventional rivals. A vicious circle can easily occur: where there is less advertising there will be less money and the paper that is short of advertising will find it harder to compete with its rivals in size or quality. It says much for John Roberts, who had started to build up the *New Statesman* before the First World War when it was a small Fabian organ, that he so far succeeded in overcoming sales resistance to a Left-wing paper that it at last became a paying proposition.

The *New Statesman and Nation* had never been run with the idea of profit, and certainly I never imagined making a financial success of it. All I had to prove was that it was a myth that you need be bankrupt or a crank if you were a crusader for unpopular causes. As it was, we began to make a profit after our amalgamation with *The Weekend Review* in 1934, and our Board, which consisted of old Fabians like Edward Whitley and Glyn Williams, and former *Nation* proprietors like Keynes and Arnold Rowntree, could hardly believe their eyes when, instead of forking out to meet an annual deficit, they began to declare an annual dividend. Between them, they must have paid out £100,000 or so to meet the needs of the old *Nation* and *New Statesman*; now before 1939 we were making a reasonable profit, which greatly increased during the war, but which was then snaffled by the Government's excess profits tax. For my part, the importance of financial success was the complete independence that it guaranteed for me and which made it easier to maintain the position of a national institution which the paper had somehow acquired.

Journalists in those days were prepared to work for salaries which sound today extraordinarily meagre. In fact, if the pound sterling was worth four times as much in the thirties as it is today, our payments were not particularly stingy. I certainly did my best to save money in the days before we were prosperous and I expect I was too slow in adjusting salaries and payments per thousand words when we began to be able to afford more. Anyway, Robert Lynd ('Y.Y.') never complained about seven guineas for his weekly essay, nor did Desmond MacCarthy ask for more than six guineas for his famous dramatic criticisms. Ordinary articles were paid for at 4 or 5 guineas; I calculated that we paid about £5 a thousand words throughout the paper. Our literary editor would make £700 or £800 per annum by contributing as well as editing, and G. D. H. Cole, who never failed to supply an economics article as well as two or three editorial notes, only received £350 per year in the thirties. Clifford Sharp in a mood of insobriety had promised £1,000 a year to Ellis Roberts, who was literary editor when I came to the paper, and I was given £1,050 a year in order to differentiate between us. Before the war I was given a bonus calculated on the profits of the paper, but I never received as much as £2,000 a year until after 1945. It never occurred to me to bother about my salary; I learnt afterwards from a friend that in 1930, when I came to the journal, Maynard Keynes remarked that 'Martin seems to be a far-sighted man. He is much more interested in the success of the paper than in his current salary.' This was quite true; in 1930 I would have taken over the *New Statesman and Nation* for half the money.

Clifford Sharp might just have turned the financial corner in the late twenties if he had not run into heavy legal costs. One or two serious libel actions and the remark that no one could 'hope for a fair hearing in a court presided over by Mr. Justice Avory' were naturally expensive.[1] I was myself only just saved on one occasion

1. For a full account of this case, see Edward Hyams, *The New Statesman*, (Longmans, 1963) pp. 102 ff.

from an even graver contempt of court because I was so angry with the Chief Justice in a case where Lord Hewart gave a decision in favour of Oswald Mosley that I wrote a note implying that he was biassed by his own political sympathies. It happened that we had a board meeting that day and just as we were going to press Keynes arrived at the office and persuaded me to cut this paragraph out. I suppose this was just as well, because the comment might have ended my editorship and perhaps the *New Statesman and Nation*. If I had stuck to my guns and refused to apologise in adequately abject terms, I might well have gone to prison—which I have always half thought was an experience that I ought not to have missed. The Lord Chief Justice could not have kept me permanently in prison, even if I had not 'purged my contempt'. In fact, editors can go much farther even with the law in its present condition than most people imagine. You may accuse a judge, as I have done on several occasions, of passing a savage sentence; you can criticise his interpretation of the law and you can safely be rude to him in most ways, as long as you do not imply that his motives are corrupt or biassed.

Libel is an infernal nuisance to editors, because they can so easily commit it unintentionally. It is now true that a mere coincidence of names, mentioned without malice, can be disposed of by a simple explanation, and even in my early days we could afford to ignore a lawyer's letter which was obviously a try-on. One of my first experiences of this kind arose from a puzzle in our competition page, where *Caliban* (whose real name was Hubert Phillips) invented a story of how a certain Dr. Bolus (meaning a horse-pill) was described as behaving in a dishonourable manner. He had three daughters, whose hair was black, brown and yellow, and you had to deduce the name of the engine-driver, or something of that kind. We received a solemn lawyer's letter saying that Dr. Bolus, who, incidentally, had a daughter with yellow hair, was gravely defamed, etc. We could afford to ignore a threat so obviously trumped-up, but such libel actions, not always clearly fraudulent, but perhaps promoted by a shyster lawyer, can be a devastating annoyance to an editor. He may prefer to pay money out of court, rather than spend time and money consulting solicitors, and often counsel.

It should be said that our libel laws have the advantage of preventing journalists from personal defamation, when there is no public interest involved. This, I think, is a good thing; one recalls cases in France where public men have been hounded, sometimes even to suicide, by continuous 'exposures' of their private lives. But the British seem to go too far in the opposite direction. It may be, for instance, that a City scandal, well known to have a basis of truth, cannot be discussed in the Press because it is not capable of proof until investigated. It may even be necessary to persuade an M.P. to raise the matter in the House of Commons, after which it may safely be quoted, since all matters raised in Parliament, if reported, are privileged. As a result of our law, actions arising from deliberate attacks on people who need exposing are less frequent than they should be. Though it is true that a good journalist can commonly find a non-libellous way of saying what he thinks, the general result is that our Press is unnecessarily cagey in cases where it should be particularly frank. Once, in reviewing a volume of Lloyd George's war memoirs, I discussed a passage in which he described how generals in the war had regularly lied to him about casualties at the front. I referred to the 'lies distilled' in General X's department. An action was threatened and I consulted Lloyd George. Was 'lies' too strong a word, and what exactly did 'distilled' mean? Lloyd George was delighted; he was in his element and foresaw a boost to the already huge circulation of his *Memoirs*. I remember him discussing with relish, as a solicitor with much personal experience, whether it would be wise to employ Sir Patrick Hastings as counsel, in which case we should be sure to get Sir William Jowitt against us. Or would it be better the other way round? The action got no further, because when the General heard that Lloyd George was behind me, he was very ready to drop it, and our lawyer, thinking of the possible costs to our insurers, for whom he acted, hastily agreed to make an entirely innocuous apology. Both Lloyd George and I were deeply disappointed.

The more usual type of libel which is liable to keep the editor awake at night is due to a careless writer or to an unintended innuendo. It may well occur in a review when nobody but the

C

reviewer could know the facts. In my early days, Lord Olivier, once a distinguished colonial governor, referred in a long review to a certain judge who had behaved unfairly in a case involving racial relationships. It would not have occurred to any one reading the review that this was not ancient history. But it turned out that the judge, now an old gentleman in retirement, was still alive and able, of course, to produce a formal letter from the Colonial Office praising his work in the colony. He demanded an apology and was obviously in a strong legal position. I was prepared for an immediate apology, but Olivier, always a tough customer, refused to apologise and took refuge in a remote village in Switzerland. Fortunately, I had a secretary who could speak German and I told her to get hold of Olivier on the telephone, however difficult it might be. She traced him from one hotel to another and I recall exactly our conversation. 'No, I will not apologise,' said Olivier. 'But you must be associated,' I said, 'with an apology; otherwise there will be an action. *Are you a very rich man?*' 'Well, if you put it like that,' said Olivier, 'of course . . .' 'I do put it like that,' I said, and I slammed down the telephone. I included him in the apology. In fact, of course, we always took responsibility for libels in the paper, but on this occasion I felt that my bluff was justified.

Then there was the strange case of a short story in which, as we went to press, it occurred to us that it might be founded on fact and recognised in a damaging way by a character who had acted oddly in a district not very far from London. We could not get in touch with the author and, as a measure of precaution, we changed the part of the country in which the incident was said to have occurred from, say, Rutland to Durham. By an extraordinary coincidence, the incident in the story was recognised and had taken place in the very area we had chosen as a disguise. On another occasion, by accident, I committed a really serious libel. A letter was sent to me from a responsible person in which the woman writer alleged that she had been sexually persecuted by a British official in a foreign country. My informant urged me to expose this scandal and, in a *Diary* paragraph, I quoted the allegation, deleting the area in which the incident was supposed to have occurred. But on the same line I 'stetted' another word which had been accidentally crossed out, and the printer assumed that the whole passage, including the tell-tale district, was to remain unchanged. As it happened, this pin-pointed the official, and the lady who had written the letter then blandly admitted that she had invented the entire story in a fit of pique. In this case, an apology to the official would have been much worse than useless, because the reader would have assumed that there was some truth in the allegation and that we were merely making a legally enforced apology. We paid the unfortunate official compensation, and published a letter of apology which contained no names and which he could privately show to anyone who had noticed the libel.

On another occasion, I committed two libel actions in one article, and Lord Monckton, who acted as counsel in the case, said that it was the only example in his long experience in which an editor got himself into serious legal trouble when he was quite blameless and, indeed, because he had taken excessive precautions. The story is certainly an odd one. Special reporters were rare during the war, and I decided to try out an applicant who offered to do special research for me. As I knew nothing of him, I tried him out in a rather delicate job. He performed it most efficiently. When, however, he arrived with an article, alleging that two ladies who both wrote in the Sunday press and whose name began, shall we say, with 'E' were really one and the same person, although their articles in effect contradicted each other, I refused to publish something so improbable. The article was extremely funny and was headed 'The Two "E"s'. My correspondent insisted that what he wrote was true and produced a letter from a private detective agency to support him. I was still unconvinced and sent the correspondent to a well-known libel lawyer to get him out of the way. To my surprise, the lawyer rang me up to say that he had cross-questioned my correspondent, was satisfied that the article was true, and encouraged me to publish it. I did so, and on the following Monday morning received two formidable envelopes, one from each of the two 'E's, stating that she had been outrageously accused of hypocrisy. I sent for the private detective and I recall how my heart sank into my boots when he opened my door. He did not look any too sober and on examination admitted that his charge was based on nothing more substantial than a conversation with an old colleague from Scotland Yard, where he had once been employed. The result, a full apology to both the 'E's, £100 to one, who merely wanted a formal denial, and, if I remember rightly, £750 to the other 'E', who began by asking for £20,000. This is the one occasion in my memory in which a solicitor did not ask a fee for his official advice and certainly the only one in which I can recall getting into trouble by over-verifying my information.

This record may suggest that I was careless about libel, but in the thirty years in which I was editor, I only fought one case in court. I lost it, though the general opinion was that I was in the right. Nor did the paper suffer at all heavily from that case, or from the others I have mentioned, which occurred at a time when the Government was taking all our excess profits, so that, in fact, it was the Chancellor of the Exchequer who met most of the expense. It may be asked whether a newspaper cannot insure itself against libel and whether a weekly, like a daily, ought not to employ a lawyer who would read the proofs before you went to press? The answer to the second question is that the lawyer would be foxed by the same errors that pass your eye, and that he would be compelled to raise queries about almost every critical comment you made. The editor of a paper which consists largely of critical remarks must take the responsibility. As to insurance, we were, of course, insured against libel, but there is always a difficulty here, because as juries are so uncertain and liable to award unreasonable damages—in one recent case, £100,000 —your libel insurers are liable to increase your premium if you run them into too much expense; anyway they make a lower limit beneath which they are not liable and an upper limit over which they will not pay. Moreover, an insurance lawyer must be under some pressure to settle out of court, even in cases where you think you ought to fight. In my experience, however, it has been worth while for the paper to insure against libel, and I am rather proud to say that we always maintained our insurance while I was editor, though I was not mealy-mouthed in my criticisms.

Not many authors are foolish enough to take libel actions because they are enraged by reviewers. The book, after all, has been sent for criticism, and if the review is unfavourable their only recourse is to write an angry letter to the editor. The correspondence that follows may well be amusing to the readers and I never quite know why I used so often to deprive myself of excellent 'copy' by writing soothing letters to the outraged authors, whom I often advised that it was wiser to suffer in silence. For the author, it must be said that he loves his book as a mother does a child; he has carried it under his heart, perhaps for many months or years, and finds it hard to bear when the reviewer, who makes a living by skimming through a dozen books in a week, treats his offspring with contempt.

Occasionally, one may have the reverse experience. I learnt a lot from a conversation I had soon after the war with Commander Kenworthy,[1] in his way intelligent and sincere enough in his desire to improve the lot of his workers. In 1933 he wrote an egotistical book which was critically reviewed in the *N. S. & N.* At a Labour Party gathering before the parliamentary session I saw the Commander, a great battleship of a man, bearing down upon me. There was no escape, and I braced myself for his reproaches. What he actually did was to say with a charming smile: 'My dear fellow, I must thank you warmly for that most discerning review in last week's paper.' I learnt a most important lesson from this. It is of the utmost importance for a politician to grow, or at least appear to grow, the hide of a hippopotamus. All publicity, good or bad, must be regarded as a form of flattery for which he must appear becomingly grateful.

1. Kenworthy, later Lord Strabolgi, had a surprising capacity for making a fool of himself. When he first entered the House of Commons, he made a pompous speech describing the plight of workers and sailors (he represented Hull) who were evicted. He said their 'very Lares and Penes [*sic*] were being torn from them'. Eyres Monsell, on the Front Bench opposite him, wrote on the back of his Order Paper the following:

'A gallant and nautical member, aspiring to classical form,
Said that from workers and sailors their Lares and Penes were torn,
Now all you sailors and workers, remember the two golden rules,
That sailors should stick to the ocean and workers should stick to their tools.'

II

Life on the *N. S. & N.* was always a battle. After all, I had been brought up as a dissenter and I tended to see all problems as moral issues. I was no longer the salad-green idealist who had been disillusioned at Cambridge and had discovered that politics were not simple when I wrote on the *Manchester Guardian*. But I still reacted swiftly and often vehemently when I heard of people being oppressed or cruelly treated, and, if I had been asked what I stood for I should have said that the *N. S. & N.* was primarily fighting against the domination of property, and wanted to expose the absurdity of a society in which there was poverty in the midst of plenty, in which coal-miners were hungry because they could not afford to buy food and other people were cold because they could not afford to buy coal. I was, of course, something of a crusader, and, like most other people, became obsessed with the threat of war, which overshadowed everything else in the thirties.

The 1914 war was the first in modern history to collect no romance or glamour around it. Old soldiers did not glorify their deeds of valour; no children or grandchildren could feel envy when they heard stories about lice, mud, rats and what was commonly called 'bloody murder'. The anti-war books poured out in a steady stream, exposing the class nature of the Army, the futility of spit-and-polish, the betrayal of ideals for which men believed they were fighting and the folly of the peace which, as the current phrase went, sowed dragon's teeth for the next world war. Some ten million men had been killed in the war, in addition to thirty-six million casualties. The first, and in many ways the best, of the anti-war books was C. E. Montague's *Disenchantment*, published as early as 1924, but most of the books which profoundly affected the mind of the British public by reviving unspoken memories of the horror of the trenches appeared between 1926 and 1930. The oath of 'Never Again' which we swore at a thousand meetings was not a Labour aberration nor the soft notion of pacifists and pro-Germans. Almost everyone, Conservatives, Liberals and Labour alike, regarded the

French notion of keeping Germany permanently as a second-class power as absurd, and agreed that the Versailles Treaty must be revised in Germany's favour.

There were throughout basically three attitudes to the problem of peace. There were pacifists who were just opposed to war itself; some of them even believed that, if we disarmed and did nothing to offend anyone, there never need be another war. The conventional Tory and Foreign Office point of view, especially after the emergence of Hitler, was that we should be strong and rearmed so that we might bargain better with the Nazis and, if possible, prevail upon the French to agree to a revision of the treaty without bloodshed. Only a few argued with Churchill that we needed Russia and other allies for an alliance against Hitler. Many were opposed to any friendship with Russia; some rather hoped that Hitler would fight with the Soviet Union and leave the West alone. This was the core of Nazi propaganda. The third view which long united a majority of the public, but not the official world, was based on the concept of the League of Nations. After 1935 the idea of collective security became increasingly a mere slogan. It was originally a sensible organisation set up to prevent war. All the nations at Geneva promised to unite economically and, if necessary, militarily against an aggressor. The advocates of this policy were not naive enough to believe that no revision of the treaty would have to be made, but they held that, if there were a genuine measure of disarmament and a system of peaceful revision grew into a habit, then the League need not stand as a method of maintaining the *status quo* but one for fostering peaceful change.

I believed, in common with a large part of the intelligentsia, that international anarchy was the root cause of war and that the object of policy should be to create a World State or some other form of international government. I thought this long-distance objective was unlikely to be achieved under Capitalism. But which came first? Economic or political change?

Controversy between people who thought that war was primarily due to the economic structure of society and those who argued that it was mainly a political and psychological problem raged through-

out the thirties. It seemed a matter which could be usefully argued
out, and in 1935 I was responsible for arranging a small and long-
forgotten book called *Does Capitalism Cause War?* It had a foreword
by Lord Cecil and the chief combatants were Norman Angell and
H. N. Brailsford. Others who contributed were Harold Laski and
Leonard Woolf, who made a characteristic and, I think, particularly
apt comment. He held that Brailsford was right in thinking that war
was inevitable between Capitalist, Imperialist states, but that he
absurdly underrated the psychological causes of war and that many
of these were 'compatible with a socialist structure of society'. Two
Socialist states could fight each other. This proved indeed a prophetic
remark, though few Socialists in the thirties would have seen its
truth.

An odd survival from the Blitz which I found among my papers
recently is a cutting from a leading article in the *Daily Express* of
16th March 1931. It bears the imprint of Beaverbrook's own
inspiration. Not only had the *N. S. & N.* criticised the *Daily Express*
attack on the League of Nations but it had also been so monstrously
absurd as to advocate the end of national sovereignty, the acceptance
of arbitration by some bunch of foreigners and the beginning of
genuine disarmament! 'A World State?' asked the *Express*, under
the heading, 'They First Make Mad'. Mad or not, that is what we
believed and I still do; man cannot reach a less-perilous eminence, if
indeed he ever can, until national sovereignty has been abolished.
None of us on the *N. S. & N.* believed the 1914 war had been caused
by Germany alone, any more than former wars were the fault of
single nations. We had to get out of the international jungle, which
would still be there, even if Nazi Germany could be appeased or
once again defeated. The next war, when it came, according to
Winston Churchill, was 'an unnecessary war', but in a condition of
anarchy war would have happened, one way or another, before long.
I do not think this is understood even today. People seem to think
that a tough line towards Hitler, when he invaded the Rhineland or
attacked Czechoslovakia two years later, would have prevented the
war. In fact, as we now know, if Hitler had been resolutely opposed
in 1936 he would have withdrawn and waited for a better oppor-

tunity, and the odds are that he would have behaved in the same way in 1938. Hitler's foreign policy was Germany's. Even if he had been overthrown, Germany would have continued to press for revisions of the Versailles Treaty; there would have been the same arms race and, at best, war would have been postponed.

Our foreign correspondents did not agree about the Europe they described, but none of them—like Tories at home—regarded the Nazis as a temporary aberration who could be appeased. The Left Wing analysed Germany as the final example of class-war conflict, so that the Nazis were seen as capitalists and bourgeoisie, who were challenged by the proletariat. Our first German correspondent was for a short time Hugh Carleton Greene, now Director-General of the B.B.C., and after him our regular correspondent in Germany was Betty Wiskemann,[1] who is now regarded as one of the leading authorities on Central Europe. I remember that it was she who persuaded me that the Nazis represented a deep, nationalist force in Germany which appealed to something more primitive than class. The Nordic idea swept away the great majority of the Germans and left only a million or so Communists, pacifists and intellectuals to die in concentration camps. In France, our chief correspondent during the critical years was Alexander Werth, an admirable reporter who later made a great reputation during the war by his reports from Russia, and then returned to us as our correspondent in France. During the thirties our news from Russia came from Louis Fischer, who then loved the Soviet Union and wrote an admirable book on Soviet foreign policy. He wrote some of the best-informed anti-Soviet books afterwards from the U.S.A. It would be interesting to trace the stages which led to the breaking-point for American and British correspondents in Russia. Louis Fischer had already discovered the cruelty and double-dealing of the Russians when I went with him to Spain during the Civil War. Werth's final break with Stalinism was its treatment of musicians and its persecution of intellect. In every case there came a point beyond which honest people with a Western training could not stomach the Stalin regime.

The British eggheads of our generation could not win the battle

1. Elizabeth Wiskemann, *Czechs and Germans* (Macmillan 1938: 2nd ed. 1967).

for a workable League, but we scored some triumphs in a small way. We maintained our liberties when many countries were losing theirs and when war came the *N. S. & N.* played an important part in ending the absurdity of locking up the German refugees, who turned out to be our stoutest allies. In such battles the *N. S. & N.*, of course, was not alone; the *News Chronicle*, under the editorship of Aylmer Vallance and then of Gerald Barry, was broadly with us, though both editors were hampered by the timidity of their directors. The *Manchester Guardian* maintained its reputation for liberal and honest thought, though it was always mindful of the dictum, once repeated to me by one of its editors, 'our job is to make the Manchester business man think twice'. The *N. S. &N.* went a good deal further than that, because a Cambridge don I met the other day told me that his life had been moulded by three forces: 'Hitler, the Spanish War and the *New Statesman*.' One man, later a friend, the son of a British general, enlisted in the Spanish Government Army as a result of reading our columns.

Another friend who became a distinguished journalist has described to me the impact of the *N. S. & N.* on him when he first became a junior reporter at the age of twenty. He was completely puzzled by the events of 1931 and the formation of a National Government and asked his friends and colleagues where he could educate himself. They gave him the names of two established books about money and banking, and told him to read the *N. S. & N.* He became an addict of the paper, not because he necessarily agreed with it, but because it was, in the early 1930s, the only source from which he could understand the current trends of thought, where he could read articles by Clive Bell and Roger Fry on art, by Harry Roberts, unique among doctors in relating medicine to poverty, and by Joad explaining with great clarity the philosophical controversies of the age. In short, he was introduced to the rationalist thinking of Bloomsbury and soon got over the shock of discovering that issues like sex could be frankly discussed in a weekly paper. Nobody else at that time was similarly frank. We seemed to many people the only paper which spoke its mind, even when it was foolish.

Michael Ayrton, for instance, has told me what the *New Statesman*

and Nation meant to him in 1936, when he was an art student. He
was already committed to the Left, believed the Spanish War was
crucial, and was doubtful of the political potency of his liberal and
cautiously left-of-centre elders. He went out to fight in Spain, but
was refused; he was only fifteen at the time. As the Spanish War
went on, he was confused by what seemed the almost 'deliberately
inadequate role' played by the U.S.S.R. in the general fight against
Fascism. He did not at this time, of course, understand the nature of
Stalinism or realise Russia's 'deliberate isolationalism', but as political
animals he and his friends 'felt much the same about the U.S.S.R. as
we felt—being art students—about Picasso. Both, we believed, were
bastions of the *avant-garde*, to be accepted and supported regardless,
little knowing how inconsequential our acceptance and our support
must have seemed to either Power.' What none of them did believe
was what they read in the daily papers, nor what the politicians in
France and England were feeding them with, even when they paid
lip-service to the Republican cause in Spain. They did not believe
them when they preached moderate notions about the evolution of
democratic socialism in Western Europe. Michael writes:

'That was where the *N.S.* came in. We did not believe it was
necessarily accurate, nor did we feel that it was invariably forceful
enough in its advocacy, but *we did believe that it was not actually
lying* and this made it rare indeed. We also believed that you
personally as Editor were far more often right than wrong and
that your opinions were respectable because you applied principles to political judgement which were not conditioned by
either journalistic or political expediencies alone. . . . Personally,
I continued to believe that where you were wrong was much
where I have been wrong, and for not less tragic or less bitter
reasons. Nor do I find, as many of my contemporaries seem subsequently to have found, that these principles were immature, but
rather that you reposed faith in various people and institutions,
and were betrayed by them.'

In 1934, when I had recently acquired some of the more amusing items from the defunct *Weekend Review*, Beverley Nichols wrote to me:

'And may I take this opportunity of wishing you all luck with the paper, now that you've taken on the *Weekend Review*. It must be almost terrifying to think that you are now almost the only spokesman for sanity and decency in England. I think it vitally important that we should all give you the utmost support. If the *New Statesman* were to fail—which is happily unthinkable—I should apply for Finnish nationalisation papers at once.'

Beverley Nichols, I am glad to say, was never driven to the extremity he threatened, and his opinions have since changed. He now writes to me about this youthful letter:

'If I had to sum up my own attitude, I think that I should probably say that when I wrote *Cry Havoc*, it was still possible for an earnest and intelligent young man to imagine that the pen—in some remote but not quite inconceivable circumstances—might prove mightier than the sword. I really did feel that the book might—although it probably wouldn't—play the part of a red flag along the road which we were all taking to destruction. It was a thousand to one chance, but it *was* a chance. Today, no young man, whatever his convictions, could possibly be inspired by such a belief. The power groups have solidified, and if ten million pens were arrayed against them they would make no difference upon the fortifications. That, in my opinion, is the great difference between ourselves when young and those who have succeeded us. We felt that we might do something with words, they are all too bitterly aware that they can't.
'All the same, I imagine that we shall both continue to fight, as long as there is any ink left in the pot.'

Yes, we shall all go on writing down to the last Biro, and I am not sure that the present period in which the pen seems so impotent against the sword is permanent, or that the things we say during a period of upheaval are so unimportant. Words may have an un-expected and lasting effect.

A. J. P. Taylor declared of me that 'No one expressed better the confused emotions of the 1930s—collective security and pacifism, hostility to the German Nazis and hatred of war, all in the same parcel. He was a compendium of the time, or at any rate, of the Left.'[1] If a compendium of the Left means that, like most English socialists, I was also a liberal; if it means that my pacifism gave way with difficulty to the alternative of collective security and that I shared the universal hatred of war with an inconsistent desire to destroy the German Nazis, he is, of course, right. If he means that I wavered in my advocacy of collective security as long as any vestige of it remained to be fought for, he is wrong. The truth is that I did not disguise my conflicts of mind even when our editorial policy was firm; that I deliberately, as a matter of policy, explained in the *Diary* the difficulties I had had in reaching editorial decisions and that I also opened our columns to opinions of all kinds, so that people who dis-agreed with the leading article would somewhere find expressed a rational reply which might be their own.

This display of various minds in the same paper was its strength. The public during the thirties was confused, and all eggheads found the greatest difficulty in making up their minds. We published many articles from people of opposite views, and our correspondence columns were filled with letters from some who would be astonished today if they were reminded of the opinions they then held. The intelligentsia of England read what the paper had to say in the assurance that they would find something they could argue about, even if they hated its guts. Anyway, no one was wholly consistent in the thirties. Winston Churchill wrote constantly in favour of Mussolini and once in praise of Hitler; most of the newspapers favoured appeasement until 1938, and the more intelligent people were, the more difficult they found it to make up their minds.

1. A. J. P. Taylor, *English History, 1914–45* (Oxford University Press, 1965).

III

We were often called 'the bilious weekly' by A. P. Herbert, but, odd though it may seem, it is possible to combine high spirits with a gloomy outlook. Perhaps Maynard Keynes was right in saying that there was no pleasing us—we were equally angry when we thought there was not going to be a war and when we thought that there was. Our anger was always tempered by enjoyment in the battle. And then—we made so many agreeable lapses from good taste! I believed that there was no subject which could not be discussed in those days, including birth-control and abortion, hanging, the rights and wrongs of premarital intercourse, and even whether it was advisable for homosexuals to be sent to prison just because they were homosexuals. It sounds odd today to read a letter from Maynard Keynes writing to me to ask whether I had made any consumer research to find whether my readers approved of us using the words 'cissy [*sic*], bugger and copulation' in the same issue, and I remember that many readers threatened to withdraw their subscriptions when in 1933 I published a most innocent story by Dame Ethel Smyth called 'The Waterfall' in which she described how she first discovered the difference between boys and girls.

Almost everyone who could claim to be a thinker or a writer became a contributor of one sort or another during the next ten years. T. S. Eliot wrote a note declining some assignment; he is the only exception I can remember. I tried in 1932 to persuade Virginia Woolf to write regularly for us. She replied:

'Leonard tells me that you asked him if I would consider writing the World of Books page in the *New Statesman* for a few weeks.

'It is very good of you to suggest it, and I have been thinking it over. But I have come to the conclusion, not for the first time, that it would be a mistake for me to try. I used to write regularly for *The Times Lit. Sup.*; but I was very glad when I could give it up. For one thing I am not an expert journalist—that is, it takes

me three or four mornings to write an article that most people
do in one. Then books one wants to write about don't appear
every week, so that one has to write about boring books or books
out of one's line. And then I feel the worry of being up to time a
great burden. So for these reasons I have decided not to bind
myself to regular journalism again. But I am very grateful to you
for having given me the chance.'

Later, I sent a book to her to review and she replied:

'I have developed such a repugnance to the thought of writing
a review, that I don't think I shall ever write one again. If I ever
feel inclined, of course I will let you know, in case you have a book
you would send me. But as things are, I feel it is wasting your
time to let you send me books—kind though it is of you. Also of
course the 1500 or 2000 word limit, necessary as it is in the *New
Statesman*, is a very great drawback—if one has to say anything
about a book, one wants, I find, more like three or four thousand
words to say it in.

'I am sending back the book today therefore.'

In spite of these letters, she did, in fact, contribute articles on
several occasions. I should certainly not have refused to allow her all
the space she needed.

Even James Joyce wrote for us; I think the *N. S. & N.* was the
only British periodical to which he ever contributed. It came about
in this way. Robert and Sylvia Lynd gave a party one summer night
in 1931; we strolled and talked in their garden in Keats Grove,
Hampstead, by lantern light. Joyce was the guest of the evening. He
was standing in a corner in the deep shadow when I was introduced
to him. I could see nothing except a dark suit and the outline of his
spectacles. He began talking volubly about a singer named Sullivan,
who had been recently banned in England. His words poured out
indignantly. Sullivan was the greatest living singer. People talked of
singing *Otello*. In *Otello* there were so many Gs in alt and so many
lower Cs. This was nothing. Sullivan could sing *Guillaume Tell*,

which needed a far greater range; in that part there were some hundreds of Gs in alt and even more lower Cs. He reeled off figures and suddenly stopped. He'd forgotten how many. He was thoroughly annoyed and there in the blackness he began to feel in his pockets for a piece of paper on which, it seemed, all these musical statistics were written down. His annoyance had something grotesque about it. No one minded in the least how many top Gs there were. Even if the figures were written down in such large handwriting that he could read it, it was far too dark to see anything. But clearly he felt that he had failed in some way; the figures which must have taken hours to work out from the two parts were of great importance to him. He was like a collector who has lost an unusual piece that spoils the set. I suggested that he might write for the *New Statesman and Nation* about Sullivan. Eventually, after some correspondence, he agreed, not to write an article direct for the paper, but to send us a letter to his favourite singer. We got over the difficulty by publishing his article with an editorial note explaining that it was a letter written to Mr. Sullivan after an occasion on which he had been carried through the streets of Marseilles in celebration of his performance of *Guillaume Tell*. The article finally appeared in the *New Statesman and Nation* on 27th February 1932. It is full of enthusiasm, strange expressions, obscure references and private jokes. It ends up: 'Send him canorious, long to lung over us, high top-seasoarious! Guard safe our George!'

Of course, the beauty of a paper is that the unexpected always turns up. One night, for instance, just as I was leaving the office a young barrister named Scholefield Allen (now a M.P.) called on me in some excitement to say that his client, an insurance agent named William Wallace, had just been sentenced to death at the Liverpool Assizes for the murder of his wife, with whom he had apparently lived on the best of terms for eighteen years. The story was so remarkable that I sat down then and there and wrote an article called 'An Alarming Verdict'.

The prosecutor's theory was that Wallace had himself arranged a bogus telephone call and had managed in the course of a quarter of an hour to commit the murder and remove all traces of it, although the actual murderer must have been covered in blood. In summing up, the judge said that as far as he could see 'not a trace remained which would point to anyone as the murderer'. In that case, why did the jury convict? Without doubt because they had been conditioned to believe in Wallace's guilt by the story revealed before the magistrates. The case followed soon after the Rouse verdict, in which it was clear that, whether he was guilty or not, the jury had made up their minds beforehand because Rouse was a disreputable character and the murder exceptionally brutal. The conclusion I then reached was that there should be some limitation on newspaper reports of preliminary hearings in murder cases. F. E. Smith (Lord Birkenhead) once wisely remarked on the difficulty of persuading a jury to see the difference between the gruesome nature of a murder and the guilt of the accused. The publication of full details in the magistrates' courts is still permitted, so that it is hard to get a reasonably unbiassed verdict in the district where a murder has been committed. The murderers in the Moors case were properly convicted, but I am sure that no local jury could have withstood the prejudice against them, even if they had been innocent. Nor do I see why newspapers should object to this prohibition; they have not suffered because they are forbidden to print the details of divorce cases, nor does the public suffer from a limitation which allows counsel on both sides to see that justice is done and the public to know the nature of the case from the judge's summing-up.

In the Wallace case the Court of Criminal Appeal quashed the verdict. This, I think, is unique, for the court will usually only override the lower court on a point of law, or of misdirection by the judge, but in this case it quashed the verdict because there was *no* evidence against the accused. In 1966 I was informed that an elaborate research had been made into the Wallace case, that a new effort would be made to limit reports of murder cases, and that my article had probably had a material effect on the release of Wallace, who died two years after. The man who *did* commit the murder may well be still alive.

Soon after I came to the paper I championed the cause of Mr. Montalk, which I think very few people did, though an appeal from

D

his prison sentence was instituted by Leonard Woolf and others in
Bloomsbury. Montalk had enquired from a printer the cost of
producing an obscene poem for private circulation; the printer
reported him to the authorities. He was prosecuted and sent to prison
for publishing indecent literature, though the only other person who
had read the poem was the printer. This monstrous technical use of
the word 'publication' made me angry, but Montalk was not grateful to his backers. After his release from prison he called on me,
saying he 'had a bone to pick' with me. I replied that I thought I
had done him a good turn by denouncing the injustice of his treatment. He answered:

'No, you called me Geoffrey de Montalk and "Mr. Montalk".
My name is Count Potocki de Montalk.'

I said, 'You care a good deal about titles?'

He replied, 'I care about them more than anything else except
women. You see, I hope to be a king. Not the King of England, for
I would not wish to jump a legitimate claim.'

Whatever the reason, we succeeded in one thing which I had never
imagined when I first took over a small paper with a circulation of
12,000 copies, or, after its amalgamation with the *Nation* and
Weekend Review, some 18,000 copies. Before the end of the war it
sold more than five times that number of copies and was read by
countless people all over the world, it was especially popular with
soldiers who fought none the less bravely because they were its
readers. In fact, it had become, for better or worse, a national
institution. A well-known American critic who wrote in the
National Review in 1944 spoke of our 'tradition of political inepti-
tude' and said we were 'utterly untaught and unteachable by events',
but added:

'But the fact that the *New Statesman* can provide a liberal
education in political fallacies does not seem to have deprived it of
its influence. If you spend the weekend with an educated man,
with a university man, a barrister, a higher Civil Servant, the odds

are you will find the *New Statesman* is the only weekly taken. Your host may affect to laugh at its politics; he may say that he only takes it for its literary articles or its film criticisms; but the point remains that he does take it, and that he and his like have been reading it and its predecessor since the last war. A whole generation of the best-educated people in the country have grown up with its brittle intellectualism as their creed. Now they, in their turn, are teachers and administrators; and they have no thought of anything else to offer.'

Malcolm Muggeridge gave a slightly different account of the *N. S. & N.* in the thirties on the occasion of my twenty-fifth year as editor in 1956. He wrote:

'In any case, the *New Statesman and Nation* is, for all egg-heads, an inevitable addiction. We may try abstinence, take cures, but in the end the old craving asserts itself; we are found, head in hands, with the tell-tale bottle at our elbow.

'Editing the *New Statesman and Nation*, however, through this turbulent, strange, enthralling twenty-five years has required something more than being an able journalist. The fact is that Kingsley himself is an embodiment of the age.

'Its illusions, its restlessness, its quest (which I believe to be an impossible one) for the peace of man which encompasses understanding, all exists in him. He is himself our own fever and pain.

'If he had been more doctrinaire, less prone to grope and feel his way along, he would have been less successful. No one ever knows quite where he stands. I doubt if he does himself. And that, in a curious way, has been his strength. . . .'

He adds that 'the files of the *New Statesman and Nation*' should be useful to future historians, if only because 'they will convey, as nothing else will, the shifts, devices, misguided enthusiasms and loyalties, the wear and tear of minds, which, for good and ill, have been immensely influential in shaping the contemporary world'.

One difficulty about telling this story is that I made myself so much a part of the paper that I can scarcely disentangle my own opinions and conflicts from those of the *New Statesman and Nation*. I ate, drank and slept with the paper. An editor's paper should be his mistress. A very competent attempt at writing its history has already been made,[1] but no history of a newspaper can be satisfactory, because it changes with changing events, which cannot be adequately summarised. It was, I think, my old journalistic enemy, J. L. Garvin, editor of the *Observer*, who remarked that the policies of a paper must change from time to time, but that it is wiser for an editor to proceed in curves rather than right angles.

1. Edward Hyams, *The New Statesman* (Longmans, 1963).

CHAPTER TWO

The Breakdown of Social Democracy

I

BERLIN, August 1931. I had come to Germany to see how the
Weimar Republic was surviving the slump. Fascist and Communist
thugs were every day fighting in the streets. Unemployment was
far worse than in England, where the figure was reaching the
3,000,000 mark. Every week the *New Statesman and Nation* was
shouting to the French to agree to end the reparation farce; only the
Nazis would profit by a further financial collapse. We demanded an
international monetary conference. There was a hope, if the French
were reasonable and the Americans constructive, that Ramsay
MacDonald, who always cut a fine figure at conferences, might
persuade the world to throw off the curse of indebtedness which was
strangling trade and perpetuating the economic blizzard. With me
in Berlin was my friend C. M. Skepper, half-French and equally
efficient in French, German and English. In the Second World War
he first fought for the Chinese and was captured and tortured by the
Japanese. When as an exchange prisoner he came back to England
he told me that he was so angry when he was tortured that he never
even thought of talking. Then he was parachuted into France, where
he was captured and put to death in some horrible way by the Nazis.

Revolution in Germany already looked likely in 1931. Skepper
and I went to call on Breitscheid, the leader of the Social Democrats.
Nobody could have been more rigid in his doctrinaire Marxism, no
one less imaginative or constructive about the desperate plight of
Germany. We came away from the interview sure that, whoever
won in Germany, it would not be the Social Democrats. The Reichs-
banner was fighting bravely enough in the streets, but with the mark
ricochetting down and the mass of the workers unemployed, the
reasoned case for Socialism only sounded irrelevant. In 1931 Communism looked a better bet than Hitler. We could not guess that Red

Berlin would be so easily and swiftly destroyed. We did not know that at the crisis in Prussia the Communists and Socialists would refuse any kind of collaboration and that many Communists would prefer Hitler in the naive belief that a short spell of Fascism would be followed by a Communist reaction.

One day I met Dorothy Woodman, whom I had already come across before in her capacity as secretary of the Union of Democratic Control. This organisation, founded in September 1914 by people like Ramsay MacDonald, Charles Trevelyan, Norman Angell and E. D. Morel, was about to change its character completely under Dorothy's leadership. We became close collaborators in many ventures, which I must describe later. She was never a Communist, but was then closely in touch with Party members; she became a Labour Party candidate in the thirties. She was then not much more than a girl, an enthusiastic newcomer to politics. She had come from an evangelical home where she had never been allowed to read any fairy story, *Alice in Wonderland* or other work of the imagination, but had been kept strictly to the Bible. She had formed so strong a resistance to this regime that she did not know whether Job came after or before St. Paul. She was an intensely musical child and at the age of eleven a famous organist had offered to take her under his regular professional tuition. Her father had refused to allow anything of the sort and I doubt if she ever forgave him. She had played all the hymns three times a week at his Methodist chapel, knew by heart every tune in the hymn book, but remained in complete ignorance of the words. Her greatest pleasure had been with dogs and cats and ponies, and she became a strict vegetarian for the rest of her life when she realised she was expected to eat one of her favourite rabbits. She had run away from home, mainly, I think, because she couldn't stand being prayed over.

When Dorothy left school her headmistress had sent for several of the senior girls and said that now they were going out in the world it was time they knew the facts of life, which she hoped were new to them. She then told them that it might happen to them that men would sometimes become 'nasty' and, if they did, they would 'grow'. Fortunately Nature had provided women with a weapon to meet all such cases; they should 'lift the knee sharply'. Thus equipped for life, Dorothy swears that she long wondered if she would suddenly see men increase their stature to seven feet every time they made a pass at her. At the University of Exeter, where she took an honours degree in geography, she remained a rebel. She also played hockey for the University. After a time as a teacher she was made secretary of the Women's International League—an organisation which contained many distinguished women—led by Jane Adams in the U.S.A. and Kathleen Courtney in England. It was really a branch of the Suffragette movement of the Pethick-Lawrence non-militant type which organised itself in the field of international peace. I think Miss Courtney had found Dorothy altogether too much of a firebrand and allowed her to move on to the U.D.C. with a mixture of relief and regret.

The three of us, Dorothy, Skepper and I, were completely fascinated by the Berlin scene, which has been inimitably described by Christopher Isherwood.[1] Society was plainly disintegrating. It was typified by the art of the period, which I remember as a strange mixture of abstraction, ugliness and obscenity. George Grotz was the Gerald Scarfe of the period. Sex and violence seemed to obliterate everything else. The Friedrichstrasse was lined three abreast with prostitutes; women wearing boots to advertise their 'speciality' stood at every corner. The shop windows displayed books portraying acts of violence and inviting people to the joys of flagellation. I spent one hot, sunny afternoon on the sands of the Wannsee, where highly respectable young people in bathing costumes were hour after

1. 'Again and again I have noticed in boys like Waldemar this rather sinister instinctive acceptance of sadism; they don't have to read one page of Kraft-Ebbing or even know what the word means. I'm sure that Waldemar instinctively feels a relation between the "cruel" ladies in boots who used to ply their trade outside the Kaufhaus des Westens and the young thugs in Nazi uniforms who are out there now pushing the Jews around. When one of the booted ladies recognised a promising customer, she used to grab him, haul him into a cab and whisk him off to be whipped. Don't the S.A. boys do exactly the same thing with their customers— except that the whipping is in fatal earnest? Wasn't the one a kind of psychological dress-rehearsal for the other?' Christopher Isherwood, *Down There on a Visit* (Methuen, 1962).

hour enjoying a game of forfeits. A pile of scarves and jumpers provided a haphazard guide to the next participants and as the leader
called out the names he would also monotonously demand that this
boy and that girl should kiss each other's lips or smack each other's
behinds a prescribed number of times. '*Ein, zwei, drei* . . .' he would
call with military precision, and only pull the boy off if he seemed,
amid screams of laughter, to be more amorous than the forfeit
required.

In Berlin itself there was a remarkable and unashamed display of
homosexuality. Skepper took me to one underground bar where, as
we entered, the barman, by way of welcome, leaned over the counter and kissed me. 'Oh, no,' said Skepper hurriedly. '*He's* not like
that.' In another nightclub all the girls danced together on one floor
and, above, the boys danced with each other, languishing on each
other's shoulders. In one nightclub when Dorothy was with us we
entertained an attractive hostess who told us, after half an hour's
coversation that she was really a man. Dorothy refused to believe
him, but he offered to prove it for a few marks; we were happy to
take him at his word. Of course, not all Germans were homosexual.
I noticed in my hotel room that odd little attentions were being paid
to me, presumably by the chambermaid. My tooth-glass, for instance, one morning contained a rose. When I left a pathetic little note
appeared on the dressing-table saying that the fräulein hoped that I
was not *böse*. I regret to say that I had not even had time to notice
what she looked like.

When in the weekend of 22nd–24th August I heard that the
Labour Party had given place to a National Government, I hurried
back to London. Was this a mild British substitute for Fascism?
I knew, of course, about the Labour Party's financial dilemma and
incompetence to deal with it. Nicholas Davenport had been writing
with some brilliance about it on our City page; G. D. H. Cole and
J. M. Keynes, who were both members of the Government's
Economic Advisory Committee, had been discussing the problem
every week since March. But the notion that the Labour Government would not either solve its problem or resign had never occurred
to me. Yet its dilemma was that of all Social Democrats. At the

election they promised victory over the Capitalists and the gradual introduction of Socialism; in office they found themselves responsible for running an impersonal system which they did not know how to change, short of an unimaginable revolution, they saw no alternative but to obey the Treasury. There was no television in those days; no doubt there were photographs of Swiss and U.S. gnomes calling at Downing Street.

The part played by the *N. S. & N.* in the crisis was unique, because J. M. Keynes used it, to my delight, as a vehicle first for putting forward his own proposals to meet the financial crisis and then to develop the early stages of his famous theory which, A. J. P. Taylor has remarked, gives him 'a good title to be regarded as the greatest benefactor of the human race'. Maynard was the only active director of the *N. S. & N.* Right up to his death in 1946 we met frequently at his Sussex home at Tilton or his house in Gordon Square, and he wrote me many private letters agreeing or disagreeing with my policy. His biographer, Sir Roy Harrod, mentions his intimate connection with the *Nation* and then says that as the years went by he 'fell out of sympathy' with the *N. S. & N.* policy. This does not tell the story. He wrote numerous articles and letters for publication in the *N. S. & N.* Harrod mentions his famous article on the Revenue Tariff, which was published on 7th March 1931. He was exasperated by the inability of the economic advisers of the Government and by the members of the Government themselves to make up their minds. A Revenue Tariff seemed to him the best solution; characteristically, he hoped that his proposed tariff, because it was in the interests of revenue, might meet our financial difficulties without too much outraging the Free Trade prejudices of the Chancellor and the Treasury. Harrod does not mention that he followed up this article with another ten articles attacking the Government, mainly on the score of its deflation policy; or that he first championed Baldwin's isolationism, and then wanted collective action in Spain. It escaped Harrod's notice that Maynard was a conscientious objector against conscription in the First World War[1]

1. This fact was not revealed by Roy Harrod in his *Life of Keynes* but in the *Economic Journal* of March 1960.

and, as our correspondence will show later in this volume, that he
favoured frontier revision of the Sudeten area just before Munich
but wrote an article attacking the Munich settlement on 8th October
1938. Maynard was the ablest man I ever knew, but his judgment
was not as good as his brain. Our differences of temperament are
apparent in a savage, but quite unwounding, letter which he wrote to
me on 23rd April 1933:

'I am sure that it is this endless obsession with grievances which
completely spoils the whole effect of what you are trying to say.
Although I know it would be injustice, I so often lately after reading the paper want to take up my pen and write to you "you seem
to love a grievance and to love nothing else". And it makes it
worse that running under the grievance there is a sort of sub-
current of defeatism, not the note of a crusade which is going to
be victorious, but an undertone of "and I know nothing can or
will be done about it". And towards any constructive effort on the
modest lines which are alone practicable in the present world,
your interest very soon gets tepid. You know that the Indian
White Paper is broadly speaking the utmost progress which can
be made at this stage; yet you are quite ready to inflame, rather
than pacify, Indian grievances against it.

'Well, all this means that you are really by temperament an
agitator and revolutionary! No harm in that. And the more
frankly you put that point of view the better I like what you
write. But when, for my sake or the sake of others, you try to
substitute for this, without yourself feeling that you lose your
sincerity, a moderate and statesman-like demeanour, such as the
best-minded Liberals would approve, it is then that the flavour
which irritates me inevitably creeps in. Alas, it is when you are
trying to be "good" that I feel like this!

'This is all exaggerated, I know, and largely unfair, and do
not, therefore, pay too much attention to it. But these are
the easiest words I can find as a means of conveying from me
to you what I feel. We must talk again as soon as we are both
free. . . .'

People might at first think it surprising, if he felt that I was 'an agitator and revolutionary', that he was so patient and affectionate, put up with me for so long, and paid so much attention to what I said. There was an unorthodox maverick as well as a deeply tolerant aspect of Maynard which Sir Roy Harrod never understood. He took the greatest care not to interfere with me in my capacity as editor; only on one occasion did he threaten to do so and then he said he would resign if he was outvoted on the Board. His disagreements with me were private and they make good reading, because nobody could express disagreement more effectively. But we carried on this constant correspondence and these ceaseless arguments for twenty-five years and I cannot ever remember his losing his temper, or our relations being anything but affectionate.

To return to the period of the amalgamation between the *Nation* and the *New Statesman*, he was always in revolt against the current policy of the Treasury. In the last days of the *Nation*, in a series of delightfully unorthodox articles called 'Economic Possibilities for our Grandchildren', he wrote:

'We are suffering, not from the rheumatics of old age, but from the growing pains of over-rapid changes, from the painfulness of readjustment between one economic period and another. Our problem is that technical efficiency is taking place faster than we can deal with the problem of labour absorption.' And in an article on 'Inflation and Deflation' he asked:

'Why not pull down the whole of South London from Westminster to Greenwich and make a good job of it—housing on that convenient area near to their work a much greater population than at present, in far better buildings with all the conveniences of modern life, yet at the same time providing hundreds of acres of squares and avenues, parks and public spaces, having, when it was finished, something magnicent to the eye, yet useful and convenient to human life as a monument to our age. Would that employ men? Why, of course it would! Is it better that the men should stand idle and miserable, drawing the dole? Of course it is not.'

The idea that the solution of the unemployment problem was to prime the pump and not to damp down activity had been advanced by a progressive group of Liberals, who thought possibly 'Lloyd George could do it', before the 1929 election. The great slump in America in that year was no fault of the Labour Government, nor were its repercussions when the European banks began to fail. Unemployment in England rose from 1,000,000 to 3,000,000. At Labour Party Conferences J. H. Thomas, in charge of the unemployment problem, was a pathetic sight, pretending to have a remedy when he was obviously helpless. One of his confidential civil servants told me that Thomas was found in tears, vainly trying to understand the mountain of documents which his advisers loaded on to his table, designed, according to the Treasury recipe, to show that all the constructive proposals of public works were futile wastes of money. The Treasury never had so rigid and doctrinaire a Chancellor as Labour's nominally Socialist Philip Snowden. Whatever was proposed at the Economic Advisory Committee, Keynes told me, Snowden turned down with the biting and final comment, 'I can imagine no proposal more certain to result in the ruin of this country.'

Keynes's remedy of a limited tariff to raise money quickly was published in the *N. S. & N.* in March 1931, and it led to one of the greatest economic controversies which ever appeared in any newspaper. For about two months, the Liberals and Free Traders raged in our columns. About two thousand people dropped the paper, some writing to say they would never buy it again. But the net result was to increase circulation; there were more young Socialists ready to welcome new ideas than there were out-of-date Liberals who believed with Snowden in the sacred principle of Free Trade.

My economic advisers did not wholly agree with each other. G. D. H. Cole, the Socialist, was inclined to believe that the bankers were engaged in a deliberate plot to destroy a potentially Socialist policy; Keynes was prepared to attribute to them stupidity rather than malice. This was even more damaging. He wrote in August:

'The present signs suggest that the bankers of the world are

bent on suicide. At every stage they have been unwilling to adopt
a sufficiently drastic remedy. And by now matters have been
allowed to go so far that it has become extraordinarily difficult to
find any way out.

'It is a necessary part of the business of a banker to maintain
appearances and to profess a conventional respectability which is
more than human. Lifelong practices of this kind make them the
most romantic and the least realistic of men. It is so much their
stock-in-trade that their position should not be questioned that
they do not even question it themselves until it is too late. Like the
honest citizens they are, they feel a proper indignation at the perils
of the wicked world in which they live—when the perils mature;
but they do not foresee them. A Bankers' Conspiracy! The idea is
absurd. I only wish there were one! So, if they are saved, it will
be, I expect, in their own despite.'

There were others only less outspoken than Keynes in the Conservative as well as the Labour Party—Harold Macmillan and Bob
Boothby, for instance—who opposed deflation. There was one
member of the Labour Party who held similar views to those of
Keynes, and demanded action at once. I met Sir Oswald Mosley at
Labour Party Conferences. He was supposed to be helping J. H.
Thomas with unemployment, but in fact bypassed him by appealing
with a memorandum sent direct to the Cabinet. He seemed the
bright hope of Labour, and had known what it was to face opposition at his own meetings. I cannot resist quoting his own remarks
when, in 1927, a meeting at Cambridge at which he was speaking
was broken up by 'several hundred undergraduates, carrying Union
Jacks and Fascist flags'. In his own words: 'We have lost the good old
British spirit. Instead we have American journalism and black-
shirted buffoons making a cheap imitation of ice-cream sellers.'

He was clever, arrogant, handsome, impatient, rich, endlessly
ambitious and, above all, wilful. His memorandum recommending
bold proposals for ending unemployment was torn to pieces by
Treasury civil servants; with a little alteration and more inside
information it might, my friend Wilfred Eady, then at the Ministry

of Labour, told me, have been made watertight. It was characteristic of Whitehall that it seems never to have occurred to the
bureaucratic experts that instead of finding faults in it they might
have suggested amendments which would have made it unanswerable. Defeated in the Cabinet and then in the House of Commons,
Mosley resigned to form a New Party in which for a time he was
joined by a group including John Strachey, Harold Nicolson, W. J.
Brown and C. E. M. Joad. But the New Party turned into the
British Union of Fascists. None of these associates relished anything
that resembled Mussolini's Fascismo with its army of black-shirted
thugs. One by one they drifted away; Joad to become a pacifist,
W. J. Brown also a famous broadcaster, Nicolson a distinguished
man of letters and Strachey the most persuasive Marxist who has
ever influenced this country's thinking.

When I returned from Germany in August I instinctively sup-
ported the Labour majority which refused to go with MacDonald,
Snowden, Thomas and a few others into the National Government.
I wrote an article supporting Henderson, now leader of the Labour
Party. Keynes wrote to me that this was 'the path of reason'. The
Labour politicians were quarrelling bitterly not only with Mac-
Donald but also among themselves. How far had any of them agreed
to any of the policies of the National Government? Henderson, at
any rate, had never agreed to cuts in the unemployment benefits
which reduced an adult man's dole from 17s. to 12s. 6d. a week and
left a permanently-unemployed man in a half-starving village with
30s. a week on which to keep a wife and three children. It was adding
wanton insult to call such reductions 'equality of sacrifice'; how
could they be compared to ten per cent cuts in the salaries of professional people? I got to know Arthur Henderson at that time; he
was the most honest of Labour leaders, if not the most bright. With
Philip Noel-Baker I organised a lunch where he and Keynes could
meet. The remark on this occasion that I remember was made by
Keynes who, supporting Henderson, turned to him with a laugh
and said, 'I can give you a slogan for the next election. Hitherto, the
pound has been looking the dollar in the face, now it's kicking it in
the arse.'

The 1931 election was the first in which the radio played a part. Nothing could so have increased bitterness at what was felt through the Labour movement to be betrayal as Snowden's 'Bolshevism run mad' speech—perhaps the most influential political speech ever made in England, if we except Winston Churchill's great radio appeals of 1940. Here was an old I.L.P.-er, a Socialist who had preached the coming of human brotherhood and written of 'The Christ which is to be' when Socialism arrived, calling all his colleagues cowards who had run away from the crisis and describing the policies which he had seemed to have spent his life advocating as 'Bolshevism'—a word which in those days called up nothing to most listeners' minds except murder and anarchy.

I never did more than shake hands with Ramsay MacDonald, but I now read the attempts to refurbish him as a great man with some scepticism. I heard him speak; he was eloquent and had a fine Scots accent, though, as Bernard Shaw once remarked, 'having three false registers in his voice did not justify him in regarding himself as permanent Prime Minister'. He was a good chairman and in his rather tricky way had done an important job in building the Labour Party. He had a good record as Foreign Minister, but no more idea than any other M.P.s about economics. Norman Angell remarked to me at the time that if Lloyd George had half an hour's talk about the Gold Standard with Keynes, he would always afterwards have talked as an expert on the subject, while Ramsay MacDonald would have spent the half-hour lecturing Keynes about it. MacDonald had become fascinated with the technique of politics. H. N. Brailsford in *Property or Peace?* describes how, when he was editor of the *New Leader*, he invited MacDonald to lunch to discuss the new economic policy just worked out by the I.L.P.:

'He wasted neither breath nor time upon any consideration of the effects, for good or evil, that might be anticipated from the proposal in the economic field. But with unerring precision he foresaw every retort, every accusation, every *tu quoque*, every move of Parliamentary intrigue with which his opponents would counter any move in this direction—if by some inexplicable lapse of fortune, he should be betrayed into making a move. In a company that happened to start a close discussion of a difficult economic subject, he would sit silent and bored. Shifting the subject to day-to-day Party politics, he would grow animated and talkative and would explain the movements of the game in intricate detail. He, Mr. Y, said in the House that A was B. His opponent, Mr. Z, looking for a trap, took him to mean in his inner thoughts that A was C, and therefore declared, with much emphasis, that A was D. Mr. Y, in his turn, knowing that Mr. A was lying, took him to mean that A was E. He therefore expanded his original proposition and announced that A was both B and F. Mr. Z, again suspicious, asserted . . . but here the record must end, for the company, lost in the intricacies of the narrative, gave up. . . .'

One is irresistibly reminded of the battle between those two great politicians, Lord Coodle and Sir Thomas Doodle, in Dickens' *Bleak House*.

MacDonald would have lasted better if his wife had lived. As it was, he grew out of touch with his party. He appreciated good pictures and music, enjoyed a cultured life and became increasingly allergic to the 'horny-handed sons of toil' who were always bothering him with talk about Socialism. Stalin is said to have made the same complaint about Sir Stafford Cripps when he was Ambassador in Moscow. It was only in his last period, when MacDonald had become a figurehead, that his mental deterioration became obvious to the public and made him an object of ridicule. But this is not the whole of MacDonald, and we await a biography based on documents and his private papers.

The first reaction of the Labour Party remnant now in opposition was that it had got rid of its worst non-Socialists, and for a long time the pretence was maintained that a new, strong and united party would succeed the old one. In fact, the Party was riven by bitter dissensions. At the end of 1930, before the Government collapse, an organisation called the *S.S.I.P.* (the Society for Socialist Inquiry and Propaganda) had been founded as a ginger group by G. D. H.

and Margaret Cole; it was joined by Ernest Bevin and a number of
prominent Socialists from the Guild Socialist movement. In 1932 an
amalgamation was attempted with dissident members of the I.L.P.,
and the Socialist League, which became Stafford Cripps's organisation, was created. Unhappily, Bevin's deep hostility to Intellectuals
was reinforced when E. F. Wise from the I.L.P. was chosen as
chairman instead of himself.

The fact that Bevin was himself an Intellectual, though he would
not admit it, only increased his contempt for those who carried the
label. He saw in them the type he most despised—the man who talks
in generalities without experience and criticises without inside
knowledge; who proposes action without responsibility for the
consequences. I recall his characteristic retort to Sir Charles Trevelyan, who was Minister of Education in the Labour Government,
a baronet, landowner, and Lord Lieutenant for Northumberland.
Sir Charles, an admirer of Russia and a Left-Wing Socialist, suggested
that the workers should strike in protest against the foreign policy of
Chamberlain. 'You want a strike?' said Bevin. 'O.K. I am to call out
600,000 dockers; will you call out the Lord Lieutenants?'

The key to Bevin's political mind was his belief in loyalty. He was
out to smash any group which threatened the unity and strength of
any organisation which he led. He built his trade union at the expense
of many bitter fights with the Communists and was said to regard
the Soviet Union 'as a breakaway union from the Transport and
General Workers'. He was a past master at the art of winning his
own way in a mass meeting. He liked to wait until his opponents
were thoroughly excited and, with a louder voice than theirs, provoke them until they were tired and the uproar died down. Then he
would settle down to massacre them, bringing to his aid every
bullying device of ridicule and abuse. From these battles he stored up
a stack of hatreds.

Before he was himself a Minister and was accustomed to be called
by his first name by Foreign Office officials he had fine ideas about
the world that could be created at the end of the war. I have heard
him perorate splendidly about mankind's economic future, a future
in which passports could be forgotten and nations co-operate. I find

E

I was full of hope about the transformation of British foreign policy when he was first made Minister. I wrote:

> He struggled to put the pettiness of national rivalries into the framework of human welfare, and in his concluding remarks he let the argument lead him to those inescapable conclusions which, in the mouths of others, he was apt to dismiss as the unreal abstractions of the Intellectual. In fact, of course, he is himself an Intellectual; he is interested, that is, in ideas and wants to understand where he is going. He knows that as things are, we are going straight to perdition, and he has the commonsense and courage to state the obvious truths that practical men are usually too timid to utter.

That was before he became immersed in the politics of the Cold War. He made a remarkable speech in the House of Commons about world government and said that no international problem was soluble except through a Parliament of Man. To M.P.s who congratulated him afterwards he contented himself with a single comment on his own speech. 'It was 'istoric,' he said, and so, I think, it might have been.

I met him frequently over a period of thirty years and, though we were friendly enough, he seldom missed an opportunity of jibing at me as an 'Intellectual' who would 'stab him in the back' at the first opportunity. Sir Stafford Cripps was his chief *bête noire* and though the Socialist League included people like Attlee and Tawney, he treated it as an enemy of the Labour Party. He was the most difficult man I ever met in controversy. If you attempted to make an argumentative point he would at once turn on you with a personal denunciation which had nothing to do with the subject. At times he was a bulldozer rather than a colleague.

At Labour Conferences Bevin denounced Stafford Cripps as a revolutionary, whereas he was, in fact, a much too doctrinaire and academic Christian Communist. He was above all a Churchman and his arguments were theoretical and Christian; Socialism was the same thing as Christianity. He seemed at times to have a great capacity for leadership; his mental and moral stature seemed to make him far preferable to all competitors. But Stafford was a lone wolf, too conscious of his superiority to those around him and completely incapable of making intimate contacts with the rank and file. Eventually he was turned out of the Party, with Aneurin Bevan and G. R. Strauss, for attempting to create a 'united front' with a memorandum which he personally circulated without permission from the executive. Churchill sent him as Ambassador to Moscow and in the most dangerous period of the war in 1942 made him a member of the Cabinet. It seemed likely that when he returned to the Party after the war he might become reconciled to Bevin. One day I was talking to Ernest Bevin in the smoking room of the House of Commons. Amid a milling crowd of M.P.s and journalists Bevin roared in a voice which hushed all other conversation, 'Stafford Cripps now says he wants to rejoin the Labour Party. That's all very nice when things are smooth, but will he stick it when the winds begin to blow and there are stormy days ahead? I don't believe it for a minute, not he.'

Herbert Morrison was more tactful. I saw a good deal of him in the thirties and thought him the best available leader for the Labour Party. I supported his candidature against Attlee and Greenwood in 1936. He had far more drive than anyone else in the Party except Bevin. They were both of them, in their way, political bosses, though Morrison built his leadership on a kind of democratic cajolery which was very different from Bevin's autocratic bullying. They hated each other's guts, partly, I think, because Bevin assumed that, as the London Labour Party's paymaster, Morrison must do what Bevin told him. Their fight was the struggle between the political boss and the trade union boss in its crudest form.

Morrison usually made the final speech for the Executive at the Labour Party Conferences. It was he who was responsible for outlawing Left-Wing groups in the Party, but he had been a conscientious objector himself in the First World War, and declared that pacifists were the one minority he would never 'steam-roller'. He was always very complimentary to the *N. S. & N.*, but annoyed with me because I thought in terms of converting people to Socialism by argument and did not care whether in the short run my criticisms were damaging to the Party. In private he would talk very frankly. It was not until the end of his life that he became soured; he believed that Attlee deliberately deprived him of the leadership. I have a note of a conversation with him in 1936 which may bear quotation:

Diary—14th January 1936

Fabian At Home for Fabian M.P.s. Walked home with Morrison in snowstorm. He had been reading the Webbs' *Soviet Communism* and was clearly deeply impressed. Lucky devils, the Bolsheviks—no election coming on, as he had, to upset his hold, perhaps. Talked with him about danger of half-Socialism, as in Germany, control of Capitalism which is not Socialism. Defends London Passenger Transport Board as best in the circumstances that anyone could have got, but agreed that dangerous to apply this to industry. But how far is he really prepared to fight?

Talks very much as genuine proletarian in private. Felt strongly about deputation of titled and comfortable people who had never seen a slum and claimed to agitate against the Hackney Marshes proposed scheme. They had objected on the grounds that if a bit goes, all goes. He had half-deliberately got angry and told them this was the only way of clearing the slums. He could get no other ground, and would willingly go elsewhere if they could find some. He felt like hanging them on a lamppost. They were a mixture of genuine people who minded about open spaces and people who were trying to make capital out of his difficulties in pulling down slums.

I am interested in Morrison. He's said to have hesitated and been willing to go with MacDonald in 1931. He certainly talks Lib-Labishly in public, but often goes further than he says—an unusual quality, as Tawney has remarked. Not afraid, and might, tackled wrongly, really fight. Cockney attitude, very decent and able and growing fast. But too much impressed with big business men.

II

I must return to my experience of the Labour Party after the split of 1931. It was not only the Labour leaders who failed; the inadequacies of Social Democracy were revealed. There was a great gap between the picture of the Socialist future which M.P.s prophesied on the hustings and the realities they found at Westminster. At a street corner of a smoky town in Lancashire or Scotland it was easy for a man who had fought his way to the top by sheer hard work to see himself building the New Jerusalem in Parliament. The vision quickly faded at Westminster, where he became an accepted member of an excellent club, and was courteously received by those he had been denouncing as 'grinders of the faces of the poor'. Lacking a philosophy which would steer him past the intelligent reasons for doing nothing advanced by the Civil Service, and perhaps avoiding the dangers of the 'aristocratic embrace', he too easily became just one of a herd of M.P.s, whose unity, after all, was essential for his party's success.

I think particularly of the fate of the Clydeside group, who came to London full of revolutionary fervour. I cannot make my point better than by quoting an extract from an article which I called 'Letter from an Old to a Young Tory'. It appeared in 1935,[1] but it describes from the Conservative point of view how the 'aristocratic embrace' worked in the thirties:

> Then he [Kirkwood] was elected with the other Clydesiders to the House of Commons, and came to Westminster, declaring, as he tells us, that they would soon 'change all that'. He knew all about what the *New Statesman and Nation* calls 'the aristocratic embrace' and determined from the beginning to show the big nobs that he was not to be put down or bamboozled. He started off by calling Baldwin 'Uriah Heep' and then felt thoroughly ashamed of himself when Baldwin very gently asked him afterwards if that was how he really appeared to him. He hurled every

1. *New Statesman and Nation*, 16th November 1935.

abusive epithet that Parliament allows (and probably some that it
does not) on Neville Chamberlain. He says that he meant to hurt
Chamberlain, but Chamberlain came up to him afterwards and
said that he was afraid he must have said something to hurt
Kirkwood. And then Davie gave notice that he was going to make
a bitter attack on Ll.G., who promptly wrote him a note apologising for not being able to be in his place in the house when Mr.
Kirkwood made his speech! Kirkwood, whose notion was that
one knock deserved another, was flattened out by all this courtesy.
And now he writes an autobiography with a nice introduction by
his old friend, Mr. Churchill, and another by George Lansbury
(to show that he is still a Socialist and a hundred per cent Labour
man), and a concluding chapter in which he says how much
better things are for the poor than they used to be when he was a
boy, and described with proper pride a long conversation he had
with the Prince of Wales at Lady Astor's.

That is how it is done in this country, and a jolly sight better
way it is than all those concentration camps and beatings-up that
we hear of on the Continent. There is an old taunt that the House
of Commons is the best club in England. So it is, and it is a
compliment. We could never get on if we did not stick to the
rules of the game; there must be some give-and-take and courtesy
in private, whatever we say in public. If you've called a man an
agitator and sedition-monger in the House and he's called you a
bloodsucker and battener-on-the-poor, you must have a drink
with him afterwards or you might begin to believe what you've
said. Actually, you both find out that you are not bad fellows and
it's all forgotten. The personal touch is the salvation of this
country and the safeguard against Socialism.

Of course, not all the Clydesiders were so easily managed as David
Kirkwood. Geordie Buchanan remained a tough and well-informed
champion of working-class rights. James Maxton, one of the best
orators who ever lectured a deaf House of Commons, refused to dine
and wine with the rich. He was proud that no one could buy him.
He had once been a Tory when Walter Elliot, a fellow-member of

the University of Glasgow was a Fabian. Unlike most rhetoricians, Maxton had a fine, rich humour and would jest in the House of Commons about himself and the size of his own party—which he calculated to amount to two. Occasionally he would tell a story about his experience when he was imprisoned during the war in Calton Gaol, Edinburgh. At exercise one morning an old lag whispered to him, 'What are you in for, mate?' 'Sedition,' muttered Maxton out of the corner of his mouth. 'Ugh,' said his fellow-prisoner indignantly, 'why didn't you marry the girl?' But Maxton's humour was not usually of the anecdotal kind. He surprised and delighted with a sudden whimsical phrase. It saved the most sophisticated from the bathos into which an orator so easily falls when he has led his audience to the mountain-tops. I was responsible for a profile of him published in the *N. S. & N.*:[1]

> In the House he has been making good speeches for eleven years. It is sad to think that probably not one of them has deflected a single vote from one lobby to the other. Members used to fill the House to hear him. Now if they are at dinner, they need not bother. They will have another opportunity soon. They have taken his measure and know how to deal with him.
>
> The ruling class in this country have various ways of dealing with revolutionaries. Where it cannot buy them its usual method is flattery. But Maxton has refused the 'aristocratic embrace'—he makes a rule of never dining with rich men—so they have found another way. They have made a House of Commons character of him. He is their raven-headed pirate, a Captain Hook, who waves a menacing finger but who, everyone knows, is really the most lovable of good fellows. They treat him as an institution and an entertainment; they like to show him off to foreigners as a proof that England can produce orators, too. It is a point of honour among them to 'appreciate' Maxton's burning sincerity. Are they not tolerant? Does anyone doubt that they 'understand the working-class point of view'? His presence in the House, they will tell

1. *New Statesman and Nation*, 2nd December 1933.

you, 'raises politics to a higher plane'. Of course 'he is hopelessly impractical' but 'how sincere, what an idealist'.

So it comes about that a set speech by Maxton in the House of Commons is like the first night of a play. There is the hush, the emotional tension. No one ever attempts an answer to his dramatic, vehement and unanswerable indictment. If what he has said is true, most of his listeners would be better dead. They pay just about as much attention as they do to the pointed jests of a Shaw play. They troop out, saying 'Very fine, very fine', and it is raining, and they catch their taxis and get down again to the serious business of life which they have enjoyed forgetting under the orator's spell.

The failure of the Labour Party is not, of course, wholly explained by the Tory cleverness in buying-off, side-tracking and cajoling Labour M.P.s. They came to Westminster without realising how difficult and complex their problem was. They did not realise that politics is a question not so much of being right as of exercising power. R. H. Tawney put the matter well when he wrote that Capitalism was a system which hung together and that Capitalists, if pressed, would fight together. 'You can peel an onion,' he wrote, 'skin by skin, but you can't peel a live tiger paw by paw.'

The Labour movement did not understand the relation of power to politics, and this was the principal reason for the hold that Marxism obtained amongst the intelligentsia in the thirties. Even if the Labour Government were to win a majority, could it overcome the opposition of the Press, the machinery of Whitehall, the Law Courts and police and all the rest of the paraphernalia of established force and propaganda? The Red Letter scare of 1924, the Post Office Savings swindle of 1931 and a dozen other instances of the use of the Press were there as examples. The immense influence of John Strachey on the young minds of the thirties was not due only to the ability and argumentative force of his Communist book *The Coming Struggle for Power*. It appealed because it read like a true interpretation of the period. He once told me that his English Marxism was not regarded as orthodox by the Communist Party, of which he was never actually a member. But he did submit the manuscript for the approval of Palme Dutt, the high priest of Communist orthodoxy. Dutt returned it with the remark that it was not really a Communist book at all, but a roughly Marxian analysis which would serve a useful purpose in Britain in the thirties. It convinced thousands of young people, particularly undergraduates, of the general truth of the 'economic interpretation of history', whereby Feudalism had given way to Capitalism, Capitalism to Imperialism and Fascism, which in turn would give way to a social revolution and the dictatorship of the proletariat. In the same way Harold Laski, whose influence was even greater than Strachey's, wrote book after book urging that though in England the ruling class has often given way to demands from the proletariat, it remained doubtful whether it would peacefully yield to the serious challenge of a Socialist government. These questions may seem academic in the England of today, but they had force and immediate impact in the thirties. After all, Marxian prophecy had been fulfilled in Italy in 1922 and proved only too terribly accurate in anticipating Hitlerism in 1933. In Britain we were faced by many of the conditions of Fascism, the breakdown of the party system, 3,000,000 unemployed and a vociferous and violent, if small, Fascist party. The success of the Left Book Club, which Victor Gollancz at first expected to attract some few thousands of members, but which was actually supported by some 50,000, was due to the belief in wide circles of British life that we should all have to fight to retain our liberties and maybe to establish Socialism in this country.

III

Some such account of the thinking of the intelligentsia in England in the thirties is essential if I am to explain my own state of mind and the growth of the *New Statesman and Nation*. I was, of course, open to many other influences and as editor of a paper which catered for a wide variety of opinion, I did not join any of the numerous Left-

Wing organisations whose doings I duly recorded in the paper.
There were many counteracting influences which prevented me
falling into the easy fallacies of orthodox Marxism. I was influenced
by it, but never a convert. The most important contact I had with
very different modes of thought was in the Tuesday lunches of the
R.S.G. or Romney Street Group. It had grown out of a club of
journalists, Civil Servants and politicians of different parties which
had been originally founded by Peter Thorp, once a famous name in
Punch. It attracted people like Arthur Greenwood and other public-
spirited people who had once hoped that such a private gathering
might have a permeating effect on political life, and carry through
reforms which party politics would sidestep.

In my day the conspiratorial atmosphere of the R.S.G. had been
maintained; we met in a cellar in Dean's Yard, Westminster, where
a homely body cooked an omelette for each arrival, which he
washed down with beer. Later we moved to more comfortable sur-
roundings in the P.E.P. offices in Queen Anne Street. The company
included Tom Jones, who had been Private Secretary to successive
Prime Ministers—Lloyd George, MacDonald and Baldwin. He
wrote something about the R.S.G. in a book[1] which incidentally
gives a unique insight into the minds of the appeasers and what
became known as the 'Cliveden Set'. J. J. Mallon, the continuously
amusing Warden of Toynbee Hall, was usually there, sometimes
also Salvador da Madariaga, the Spaniard who had made a great
reputation at the League and was to make an even greater as an
author. Regular attendants included C. K. Munro, a civil servant
in the Labour Ministry and a pacifist playwright, St. John Catchpole,
creator of the Y.H.A., acted as devoted secretary. Others were John
Hilton, who taught future generations how to broadcast about common things to common people, W. G. Eady, one of the wisest and
most experienced of Civil Servants and Edward Thompson, the
novelist and expert on India. Hubert Henderson, the late editor of
the *Nation* and by this time a member of the Cabinet Economic
Committee and a Fellow of All Soul's, came regularly; he could

1. Thomas Jones, *A Diary with Letters, 1931-50* (Oxford University Press,
1954).

never resist an obstinate Scottish argument with anyone prepared to take him on. Tom Jones never failed with memorable stories about the corridors of power. In the mid-thirties he was writing Baldwin's speeches into which he introduced, to everybody's surprise, quotations from R. H. Tawney and other Socialists. Visitors from overseas were occasionally admitted and they would often have hammer-and-tongs arguments with Walter Elliot, then Minister of Agriculture. He came regularly to our luncheons and was never discreet. Tom Jones was the anonymous author of a profile of Walter Elliot which I published in the *New Statesman and Nation* in November, 1933:

> 'It is not true to say that every statesman has to maintain his popularity by pretending to be rude, ignorant, sentimental, super-stitious and stupid. Cabinet Ministers are of all sorts and conditions, from the superlatively clever to the superlatively dull, and they are kept together, Morley said, by a dough of mediocrity. Elliott is on the side of the clever. That would be a drawback only if he had to succeed Lloyd George. Under a National Government, it is a positive and immense asset. He has vitality, volubility and vision. His talk, like Browning's, is "copious, emphatic, brisk". But he does not impart information and bore you, like Amery, or improve you, like Ormsby-Gore or Eustace Percy. He has too much humility to be a pedagogue or a pedant. It keeps bubbling through. The effect of his conversation is like that of changing a pound note before a machine on the Underground. A button is pressed, and out come tumbling silver and copper coin in confusion. You gather them up in faith, and hope they add up all right.'

We were all interested, one way and another, in Soviet Russia. With an army of permanent unemployed at home and no prospect of a government with a constructive policy, we could not ignore the claims of the Soviet Union to have cured unemployment and to have a national plan of development. We were too experienced to take notice of the endless stream of vituperation about Russia poured out in the Tory press. We wanted to know what was really happening in the Soviet Union; it might be bad, probably was, but worth understanding. In July 1932 a Fabian group visited Russia; it included many distinguished people, amongst them Hugh Dalton, who recalls in his memoirs:[1]

'There was no unemployment in the Soviet Union. That was the biggest claim of all that Russian planners could make, in the early thirties, to visitors in the Capitalist West, from Britain or the United States or Germany, those lands of despairing dole queues. Here was no "industrial depression", no inescapable "trade cycle", no limp surrender to "the law of supply and demand". Here was an unceasing industrial upsurge, based on a planned Socialist economy. They had an agricultural problem, we knew, in the Soviet Union, but so had we in the Capitalist West, where primary producers had been ruined by the industrial slump.

'We knew that in Soviet Russia there was no political freedom. But there never had been under the Russian Czars and, perhaps some of us thought, we had over-valued this in the West, relatively to other freedoms.'

This was exactly my own state of mind when in the same year I went to see the Soviet experiment at work. The fact that Communism could not be a British solution did not prevent the exciting question whether the Soviet system might not be the hope of the future. None of us suffered from the illusions of John Strachey, who wrote a letter in the *New Statesman and Nation* in September 1931 arguing that Communism could be quickly and effectively adopted here, as everywhere else. Confronted with the fact that Britain depended on exports and would starve in a revolution, he blandly asserted that if we became Communists the Soviet Union, then itself starving, would provide for our necessities.

The party with which I went to the U.S.S.R. in 1932 included David Low, already Britain's leading cartoonist. We visited Leningrad, Moscow, Nizhni-Novgorod, Rostov, Kharkov, Kiev and the

1. Hugh Dalton, *The Fateful Years* (Muller, 1957), Vol. 2.

Russia: 'What! Cabbage again?'

Dnieper Dam. We went down the Volga by boat and through the
Ukraine. He shared my detestation of the humbug talked about
Russia, and my hopes as well as my fears for its future. He had come
on to the board of the *New Statesman and Nation* when Arnold
Bennett died in 1931, and I had also introduced him to the R.S.G.
luncheon club. We used to return from this on Tuesdays in vehement argument, which was good both for my coming leading
article and for his next cartoon. One reason, I think, why we became
intimate friends was that I never took any notice of the Australasian
chip on his shoulder. He seemed always on the look-out lest someone should play him for a sucker. He felt safer if he began by contra-
dicting any observation made by a member of the British ruling
class; after a little conversation he was the most reasonable of men.
After a rather up-and-down childhood in New Zealand, he succeeded
in making his way on to a leading paper in Sydney, where he established a world reputation by cartoons of Hughes, the Australian
Premier, which were as savage as anything by Daumier. When the
Star was looking for a cartoonist Arnold Bennett suggested Low,
and he was brought here to scarify the British public. We became
firm allies, found ourselves at one in our hatred of Fascism and our
doubts about the Labour Party and were equally curious about the
Soviet Union.

After our visit we produced a book called *Low's Russian Sketch-
book*, which contained some of Low's most brilliant satirical drawings. They also included many laughs at the professional anti-
Communist, who interpreted every delay before meals—and they
seemed interminable—every mechanical failure—and they seemed
irreparable—as a proof that Communism was breaking down. Low
ragged the Soviet Union, but he approved of my more serious text
and told me years afterwards that he never regretted anything that I
had written or he had drawn in this book. There was throughout an
ironic twist in my account of Soviet development, but the net effect
was certainly too favourable. I did not imagine that their treatment
of crime was as perfect as their theory or think for a minute they had
found a good substitute for democracy. I did not overlook their
poverty or justify the excesses of the G.P.U., but in everything I

suggested that their failures and excesses would be overcome in the not-too-distant future. They claimed at least to be trying to raise the miserable standards of poverty, though they were certainly ham-handed about it. I did not fully appreciate the tragedy of the kulaks, but I noted that the fields which should have been golden with corn were in fact so many acres of weeds, and I quarrelled with Mrs. Webb on my return by saying that I feared at least a million would die of hunger. I listened to Communist theory, assumed that in time it would work out in practice and saw the basic truth that we were watching the efforts of a fanatical and clumsy élite to revolutionise and modernise a vast, superstitious and conservative peasantry. Our Soviet guide would say with pride, as we looked at one more new and extremely inefficient factory, one more crèche where women workers could leave their children, one more Park of Culture and Rest, one more prison with open doors, 'Come back in ten years' time and you will see how all this new machinery will have made Russia the most powerful and prosperous state in the world.' I never ceased to complain of their autocratic methods, but I was inclined to believe that Russia would become more liberal and I assumed it would solve its economic problems and become a great nation. Here I was not wrong, except in timing. I mistakenly assumed that the problem of the land would be quickly solved and that the problem of peaceful co-existence could be solved before the world war.

Our book was banned in the Soviet Union, not only, I was later told, because Low made fun of its failures, but because I had not pretended that a future Utopia was already open before my eyes. I am often reminded of this book and the subsequent history of the Soviet Union when I read rival accounts of China in the 1960s.

Though I never thought Communism a solution for the West, I wondered whether there might not be other countries, particularly in Eastern Europe, where the Soviet remedy for unemployment and the class struggle might be relevant. In 1934 I went with a group of journalists to Hungary and was introduced at a spectacular party to the dictator, Admiral Horthy, who welcomed us in the uniform of the non-existent Austrian Navy. We stood round in a formal circle and he addressed each of us in turn as if he were royalty. The party was a very grand affair, with halberdiers in leopard-skins, and I was introduced to the Prime Minister, Gömbös, who told me that his greatest problem was the growth of the middle class. I was flabbergasted by this, since Hungary in those days was purely feudal and had no middle class in our sense. I think he meant that the younger sons of the aristocracy constantly demanded jobs in the Civil Service, perhaps because of the dearth of Court sinecures and bureaucratic appointments as in the days of the Austro-Hungarian Empire. He may also have had in mind the increasing numbers of educated, cultivated young Jewish people who by virtue of an excellent education were becoming, as doctors and other professional people, an important element in Hungarian life. They have since been prominent as economists, scientists, musicians and artists in every part of Europe and America. But the regime was purely feudal, an aristocracy with an overgrown bureaucracy, no economic policy, a starving proletariat and a dictator sitting on the top. The country was landlocked and much of it was hungry. The ruling class was itself hard put to keep up appearances. I remember a village which was not more prosperous than any you would find in the Soviet Union, and I visited the huge flat area outside Budapest where some thousands of dispossessed people lived in shacks built of old bits of wood, corrugated iron and newspaper, without water, sanitation or any visible means of livelihood. They lived largely upon the tips given to them by the idle aristocracy when they opened the doors of their motorcars, and they searched the sewers for oddments of food and clothing. No one talked about this kind of poverty, but I did not think it would have been any the worse if the Communists took over.

In midsummer 1936 Low and I spent a short holiday in Copenhagen and Stockholm. It was grand fun watching the Scandinavians enjoying a Walpurgis Night with bonfires and effigies of the traditional witch, broomstick and all, stuck up like Guy Fawkes and sent up to heaven with fireworks. Everyone in Sweden was discussing the danger of Nazi Germany, and Beaverbrook rang up Low before we started to warn him not to get kidnapped. Nothing had actually happened to him except that the Swedish press accused him of mak-

On holiday in Sweden

ing fun of Stockholm architecture. What impressed me was that
here at last was an apparently rational society where people simply
could not believe that if two persons committed adultery they could
not obtain a divorce (still true at that time in England), where they
had apparently solved the problem that had defeated us by reducing
unemployment from 200,000 to 30,000 and had, in effect, already
adopted the Keynesian policy of curing 'poverty in the midst of
plenty' by an expansionist instead of a deflationary economy.

The issues that were to dominate political life until the war were
already presented to me in 1931; events had compelled me to face
them. I was no longer the hesitant Liberal pacifist who had discussed
everything at Cambridge, had not been compelled to think things
out at the London School of Economics and had been prevented
from taking decisions as a leader-writer on the *Manchester Guardian*.
I now had to make up my own mind about the problem of peace

F

3 Rodborough Road,
Golders Green N.W. 11

Oct 14 1934.

Dear Kingsley -

We were discussing your having one of the Russian drawings when we got side-tracked on to that very unsatisfactory talk about war and peace.

Would you tell me which one you would like?

Or, better still, mention three or 4 because some of them have gone.

Yours ever

Low

No charge for this work of art.

When Sanguinary duty's to be done—to be done
An International Policeman's life is not a happy one —— or hardly one.

and I discovered that it was impossible to play a part in political life as an absolute pacifist; Fascism was already advancing in Europe and we had to run the risk of war if we wanted to stop its advance. I now doubted whether the Labour Party, as we knew it, would solve the problem of unemployment and social misery and equally sure that Communism was impossible and undesirable in the West. We had to have a new kind of Labour Party. In the meantime we had to prevent England from suffering the same disasters as Italy and Germany. My enemy was the Fascist state of mind, and my job was to make not necessarily Labour Party voters, but Socialists and Internationalists. That meant, broadly, trying to mobilise a group of resolute individuals who would support Socialism at home and abroad, who would work for world government and the reformed society which Capitalism automatically opposed. Mainly this meant criticism and sometimes denunciation of the existing rulers of England. In these objects I found the intelligentsia of England delighted to co-operate.

CHAPTER THREE

The Webbs

I

I NEVER agreed with the Webbs. My Liberal heritage disliked their view of the State and I argued continuously with Beatrice Webb when, as I thought, she was quite silly about the Soviet Union. There was something richly comical about them; partly it was the result of Mrs. Webb using a royal We to prevent you falling into the error of disagreeing with herself or Sidney. I had met them off and on, especially during the period when I was at the London School of Economics, of which they were the founders, and naturally got to know them better as editor of the *New Statesman*, which they had also started as a a Fabian organ in 1913. I grew much attached to them; as time went on I found them less comic and more sympathetic.

Like almost all the other intellectuals of the thirties they ceased to believe in the possible survival of Capitalist Democracy when the Labour Government fell in 1931. As early as 1923 they had written *The Decay of Capitalist Civilisation*, a short book which said many of the things that were generally believed by Socialists in the next twenty years. They analysed 'poverty in the midst of plenty' and ended with a remarkable chapter on Imperialism as the most important cause of war. Until 1914 they had never considered the connection between profit-making as a basis of society and the imperial friction that often led to war. A few days before the war of 1914 Liberals and Socialists agreed in regarding Tsarism as the most dangerous and reactionary force in the world. Graham Wallas brought them a manifesto demanding that Britain should keep out of the war, which they thought we were dragged into by an agreement with Moscow. They refused to sign, saying, 'We are not experts in foreign policy and do not know whether we ought to enter the war or not.' On August 2nd Graham Wallas brought them a new manifesto, demanding Britain's participation in the war on behalf of Belgium. They replied, 'We are not experts on foreign affairs and do not know whether we ought to take part in the war or not.'

This sublime detachment was characteristic of the Webbs. They were totally disillusioned about the Labour Party and its leaders and decided to leave politics to younger people. They would not join Bernard Shaw in attacking British democracy; on the contrary, they thought *The Apple Cart* and its denigration of the British Parliament irresponsible. They would continue their enormous and disinterested labours. Webb accepted a peerage, and they retired to Passfield Corner to study the Soviet Union. Mrs. Webb insisted that she had changed her name once for Sidney and wouldn't do it a second time. She was delighted to get him all to herself. She had always been doubtful whether it was wise for him to go into Parliament and become a Minister. He was essentially a Civil Servant, who wrote memoranda for other people, not a man of action. She liked him better as an *éminence grise* than as a public figure, and the intrigues and over-simplification demanded by party warfare morally disgusted her. Many years before she had written in her *Diary*:

'One sometimes wonders whether all this manipulating activity is worth while: whether one would not do almost as much by cutting the whole business of human intercourse and devoting oneself to thinking and writing out one's own thoughts. It would certainly be far pleasanter, because a far less complicated life, with fewer liabilities for contraventions against personal dignity, veracity and kindliness. It is so easy to maintain these qualities in a vacuum! In rubbing up against others, one's vanity, one's self-will and any strain of spite get uncovered and revealed in all their ugliness to oneself, one's friends and one's opponents. But someone has to do this practical work. . . . If one frankly realises one's own moral incapacity during spells of activity, it makes one more careful not to admit unworthy desires and thoughts in the times of withdrawal from the world—and the whole level of one's mental life is raised and supported by the wholesome fear of the eternal fall of the man of action.'

Now, at last, they could be genuinely disinterested. Though they thought Shaw's attacks on British democracy mere idle caricaturing, they were immensely impressed by his description of the Soviet Union on his return from Moscow with Lord Lothian and the Astors. Perhaps, after all, they were living to see their dream of the Soviet state translated into reality. 'We are not interested,' they would say, 'in British politics. Russian methods and problems are too dissimilar to ours.' But what if the Russian experiment would work? Beatrice said, 'Old people are usually absorbed in something, usually themselves; we prefer to be absorbed in the Soviet Union.' They visited the Soviet Union, and with the help of translators read innumerable documents and books. They interrogated visitors to Russia, of any nationality, who could be induced to make the journey to Passfield Corner. The result was two large volumes, which are monuments of industry, honesty and disinterested labour. They are also about the most unrealistic books ever produced by able people.

This concentration of interest did not mean that the Webbs lost the desire to keep contact with British politics. They worked to-gether, and intensively, all the week; they liked people to go down on Saturday afternoons for a weekend of sustained conversation. They regarded people like me, I think, as useful channels of informa-tion and an excuse for discussion. I became a regular pilgrim to Passfield Corner. The truth was that the Webbs, especially Beatrice, fascinated me. She had been once deeply and romantically attached to Joseph Chamberlain. They rejected each other because he demanded that his wife should subordinate herself in all things to him.[1] In rejecting Chamberlain she renounced personal happiness and quite consciously and deliberately decided to marry the man with whom she thought she could do the best constructive work. She wrote about Sidney with the most uncompromising and un-flattering frankness before they were married. She didn't much like

1. The story of Beatrice Webb's attachment and disappointment is to be found in her published *Diaries, 1924-1932* (Longmans, 1952), edited by Margaret Cole, and in *Beatrice Webb: a Life* by Kit Muggeridge and Ruth Adam (Secker and Warburg, 1967).

his 'Jewish nose', the shakiness of his Hs, his 'inexhaustible self-complacency' and 'his tadpole body'. Undoubtedly, however, she grew fond of him, in a rather motherly, domineering way. She decided, as a piece of calculation, that together they could perform 'a considerable life's work'. But this did not prevent them from reading poetry together in Epping Forest, or her from growing worried if Sidney went away without a warm vest in his suitcase.

It is a mistake to believe that the Webbs' basic idea was State Socialism. It was in fact nothing less than the application of scientific thinking to politics. About this I had many arguments with Beatrice. Like Bernard Shaw, she totally lacked the strain of dissenting morality which is so strong an element in the British character and especially in the Labour Party. They seemed to me absurdly to over-simplify all the psychological factors and to forget what government is for. They were interested in the economic and political structure of society; they were disinterestedly, and I would even say passionately, desirous of social improvement and greater human happiness. Their watchwords—and they are very good ones —were 'measurement and publicity'. That is to say, they wanted to substitute quantitative for qualitative arguments, to find a solution and to subject it to criticism instead of gassing about justice and liberty. To avoid the danger of tyranny they agreed that there must be freedom of criticism and 'public accountability' for all State action. But they were never really interested in liberty—that is to say, they did not recognise the intractable complexity of individuals. People must be placed in categories for the purposes of government, and if they did not fit, so much the worse. How could authority deal with you if you were not a married man, with a quota of children, or perhaps an unmarried charwoman with a couple of babies you ought not to have had? They acknowledged, theoretically, that there were people, like artists, for instance, who didn't fit. But what they did not appreciate was the element of the artist in each individual. Shaw never fitted anywhere; Mrs. Webb put him into a special category of 'sprites'. The function of government must be performed by detached people, who were above human weaknesses and moved by a desire for public service, unencumbered by slogans of morality. Shaw regarded the Webbs, in their old age, as the nearest human equivalent to the Ancients in the last act of *Back to Methuselah*. The tendency to fall in love, to seek adventure and useless artistic achievement were childish nuisances that were got out of the way as early as possible. Perhaps I can best summarise by recalling a conversation with Lowes Dickinson, philosopher, poet and anarchist by nature. He told me that he had decided not to be a member of the Fabian Society because he had heard Mrs. Webb say that 'marriage is the waste-paper-basket of the emotions'. To people like Lowes Dickinson love, intensifying through life, was the supreme object of living, and the test of good government was the opportunity it gave for love to achieve its most creative potentialities.

Once it was understood that the Webbs' basic desire was to turn the pragmatic art of ruling into an impersonal science, it is easy to understand their enthusiasm for the Soviet Union. They admitted that Russia suffered from 'the disease of orthodoxy'; they agreed that there were many growing-pains in the Soviet Union; that the Communist Party, which they rightly saw was the energising force holding together the vast scheme of producers' and consumers' organisations, was often autocratic and unnecessarily intolerant. They were prepared to admit defects. But the whole system was a model application of State Socialism; in Russia only was there an assured hope for the future of the world and the birth of a new civilisation of abundant vitality and promise. They declared that in Russia the Socialist world was being built by realists. They agreed with Bernard Shaw that two- or multiple-party government had become an absurdity. Mrs. Webb was particularly interested in the conception of a new ruling aristocracy, always provided there was popular participation. She could not admit that the popular ingredient had totally disappeared under Stalin. The idea of the ruling *élite* fascinated her all through her life; after her discovery of the Soviet Union it took a more mature and realistic form than that conceived by H. G. Wells, for instance, in *The Research Magnificent*. She was contemptuous of anything like mysticism in politics, and in particular of people who could not face the need of discipline in a country like Russia. She wrote to me when her nephew Malcolm Mugger-idge first wrote about Russia: 'Have you seen Muggeridge's hysteri-cal tirade about the U.S.S.R. and the journalists and tourists—Fabian and otherwise—*A Winter in Moscow*? He has an incurable impulse to libel persons he meets.' In January 1938 the theme was the same. She wrote:

'I have been reading the autobiographies of Somerset Maugham, Priestley and Aldous Huxley—an odd absence of any vision of a new social order, national or internat[ional]—but a return to mysticism in the two last, and, in the case of S.M., a pessimistic materialism or agnosticism, with the idolisation of loving kind-ness—without any indication that knowledge and its application are needed as well as good intentions whether in the treatment of disease or the organisation of a public Health Service.

'I thought y[ou]r review of Eugene Lyons' book excellent. He, like Malcolm Muggeridge and Aldous Huxley, suffers from the neurotic joy in libelling persons and institutions; they ought all [of] them to join the R.C. Church and confess and be absolved every few months—to rid themselves of hatred of everyone else, as a way of manifesting their own superiority to men as they see them. It is strange this delight in debunking everything and every-body.

'About *Our Partnership*. I have settled not to publish any part of [it] during my lifetime. I am tired of publicity and don't want to hurt anyone's feelings even by leaving them out of my picture. Also there is my own family to consider—170 of them!

'Do come and see us some weekend or week day in March?'

Mrs. Webb decided that the necessary mechanism for carrying through social change is a disciplined, poor and devoted body such as the Jesuits were in the days of Loyola, and such as Commu-nists were in the days of Lenin. In such arguments one always recalled that the Webbs, and Mrs. Webb in particular, themselves belonged to a governing class. Shaw writes somewhere, contrast-ing the journalists and ideologists and talkers with the 'governing

people' who know the methods and the compromises that have
to be used to rule. In her early diaries Beatrice analysed the minds
of this class with an intensity that would have surprised the politicians if they had known the scrutiny to which they were subject. She
studies her father, outlines his good qualities, lists occasions on which
he refused money-making where it involved dishonourable conduct.
But she notices that in his business deals he was ruthless to competitors, and actuated by a desire to make money without any consideration of the public interest. She remarks: 'As life unfolded itself, I
became aware that I belonged to a class of persons who habitually
gave orders, but who seldom, if ever, executed the orders of other
people.' And later she writes:

> 'Deep down in the unconscious herd instinct of the British
> governing class, there *was* a test of fitness for membership of this
> most gigantic of all social clubs, but a test which was seldom
> recognised by those who applied it, still less by those to whom it
> was applied—*the possession of some form of power over other people*.
> The most obvious form of power, and the most easily measurable,
> was the power of wealth. Hence any family of outstanding riches,
> if its members were not actually mentally deficient or legally dis-
> reputable, could hope to rise to the top, marry its daughters to
> Cabinet Ministers and noblemen, and even become in time itself
> enobled.'

The British ruling class she thought inefficient and irresponsible.
Socialism she saw as the application of science and public spirit to
social organisation; Capitalism as the survival of an emotional and
selfish attitude in matters which are inevitably in their effects public,
and which should be efficiently organised as public services. A
society founded on private enterprise the Webbs regarded as
anarchy; and to make more out of society than one put into it was
quite literally theft. The job of the intelligent and self-respecting
was to build an efficient, incorruptible and non-acquisitive society.
To do so they must be blameless in their private lives as well as
realistic in tactics. Here there was some difference between Beatrice

and Sidney. Professor Hobhouse, who was always a Liberal, once described Sidney to me as Machiavellian. Mrs. Webb had another phrase for it; she said that Sidney 'had a reversed conscience'. She was always concerned about the choice of means and deeply troubled when they seemed to her immoral. Sidney and Beatrice were, however, completely together in believing that their task was first to analyse society, and then so marshal and publicise the facts and the policy arising from them that argument and opinion would eventually defeat the vested interests in anarchy.

The Webbs were never moved by individual examples of blundering, hardship or cruelty. They did not, for instance, deny that the O.G.P.U. made mistakes, but individual and national liberty had never been important items in their creed. They were interested in carrying out the changes which, alone, they believed would result in a good life for the masses. Mrs. Webb would get very cross when I suggested that the Communist Party might be too much concerned with power and forget it was justified only if it brought happiness. She wrote angrily defending Stalin in 1932. Obviously the statistics of the dead in the vast peasant tragedy of the Ukraine were grossly exaggerated for purposes of propaganda, and she defended the Soviet Government during the great purges of 1937 in the Introduction to a new edition of *Soviet Communism*. She used to argue, quite correctly, I think, that, after a revolution, it is never possible to grant full liberty to those who have been defeated. She cited the treatment of Catholics in this country in the seventeenth century. A hundred and fifty years passed before they received full civic rights. I tried, I'm afraid vainly, to persuade her that even granted the parallel was relevant it did not absolve democrats from the duty of criticism. To me it has always seemed obvious that Protestant England was justified in the seventeenth century in excluding from governing positions Catholics who were frequently allies of an enemy power, and certainly disloyal to the newly established Protestant Succession. But I could never see that this justified the excesses of the Restoration, and I think it would have been a good thing for England if critics had been encouraged.

II

The pilgrimage to Passfield Corner was sometimes exhausting. The Webbs had been working intensively all the week, and their immense fund of argument and conversation was bottled up inside them. You arrived for tea on Saturday. Mrs. Webb met one very graciously at the door. Sidney gave you a rather perfunctory hand-shake. You were taken upstairs and your part of the house, including your bathroom, very firmly indicated. You went down to tea where there were probably other guests. Serious talk began at once. The condition of the world and of the Labour and Socialist movement in particular, and immediate topics of the day, were systematically dealt with. One could almost hear Mrs. Webb putting a mental tick after each item, when it had been discussed and nothing more of importance was likely to be said on the subject. The long, meaty conversation would continue at night by the fire. At 10.30 you went to bed. At half past eight next morning you would be having break-fast, and Mrs. Webb, who had already been up for several hours and done a lot of work, would be standing arms akimbo between you and the window, lecturing you—as I remember on one occasion—on the defects of the Douglas credit system. You were released for an hour after breakfast, but you started promptly at eleven on the walk over the heather and through the lanes of Hampshire. Mrs. Webb would usually remark that 'the English climate is the best in the world, because it is never too hot or too cold to work or to walk'. Since the Webbs did both tirelessly, and had no desire to ski or sunbathe, there was no point in arguing, you put on your rain-coat and followed along.

There was always the strange and to me incomprehensible incident with Sandy, the terrier in Nicholson's portrait of the Webbs. Just before the walk started, he began to bark, as dogs do when a walk is in prospect. Mrs. Webb knelt and hit the ground violently with a walking stick, while she shouted loudly and repeatedly, 'Sandy! Sandy!' Sidney stood silently by watching. Perhaps, though she did not know it, she was really working off her feelings about Sidney;

was she vicariously hitting him with her stick? Certainly her suppressed love of power was revealed in this extraordinary, regular ritual. She, and maybe the dog, found in it some mysterious emotional satisfaction. In the end Sandy made a final and tragic rebellion. I suppose he reached the end of his patience. Anyway he bit Mrs. Webb and had to be destroyed.

At lunch there would be some distinguished visitor, for years almost invariably an authority on Russia. He would be scientifically cross-examined, and the information he provided would be used to elaborate or correct some passage in *Soviet Communism*. Russia would have been the main topic of talk the night before; it would have overflowed during the morning walk, and would still be pursued during tea, when a taxi would arrive to take one home, so full of mental food that even the strongest digestion was somewhat exhausted.

The endless argument about Russia, however, was not all, or even the most memorable, part of one's visit. After supper on Saturday night, it was possible, if one was dexterous, to switch the conversation into another gear. The car steered by capable hands along the road towards scientific Socialism could be put into reverse, and, with pleasing jolts of memory, carry one back along amusing by-roads peopled with interesting characters, like the young Lloyd George, Haldane, and Winston Churchill, whom the Webbs had entertained during the early years of Fabian permeation and thought nothing of. Mrs. Webb, with her skirts turned back over her knees, and her fine hands extended over the fire, as you see them in Nicholson's picture, would allow herself to relax, and talk about her family, and the early days of their marriage, and to reveal passages from her unpublished diaries. The dog Sandy sat now quiescent by the hearth, and Sidney, looking absurdly like a cockatoo, perched on a chair with his tiny feet scarcely reaching the ground and a high feather of hair standing up on his huge head, would break in now or then to correct or embroider an anecdote from a still more accurate memory.

The contrast between these two never ceased to fascinate me. One needed no very great discernment to know that they were deeply fond of one another. Many have poked fun at their 'love among the

blue books'. Mrs. Webb has told us indeed of early matrimonial
disagreements about the administration of the Poor Law in the early
seventeenth century and suchlike, and of how they 'ended in kisses'
with Mrs. Webb sitting on Sidney's knee. How, people ask, does
this fit with a courtship in Epping Forest reading Wordsworth, who
was Sidney's favourite poet? Beatrice confesses she could read no
poetry. The fact is that those early kisses, and the spirit of their courtship among the blue books, somehow or other survived through
fifty years of married life. Their love was happy and commonplace
and human. When they overwhelmed one by their dual personality,
each beginning and interrupting with a pontifical 'We think . . .', it
was because they had genuinely thought out each problem together,
and come to a joint decision which was the result of the truest
marriage of two minds that has ever been achieved.

And yet two minds were never less alike. Sidney was really the
man of pure reason. He once told me he had 'no inside'; he had never
had a headache, never an attack of physical or spiritual indigestion.
His mind was stored with accurate and valuable information, neatly
arranged and strung together on a single strong thread. He read and
digested books at a superhuman rate: it was said he could read and
remember 200 pages an hour, and a story is told of his reading the
whole of Chambers' *Encyclopaedia of English Literature* in the train
between London and Edinburgh. He seemed to remember everything that was useful to his purpose and to know nothing that was
not. After his death a correspondent wrote to describe a walk with
Sidney Webb in the garden of Passfield Corner. He halted at the end
of a row of fine sweet peas, and said, 'Those are very pretty; I don't
know whether they are the sort we eat, do you?' His notions of
literature and art were rudimentary in the extreme. The story too
was told that the Webbs were once given tickets for a Wagner opera.
Webb was asked if he enjoyed it. 'Oh yes,' he said, 'we had a most
enjoyable evening. We happened to be sitting just behind Herbert
Samuel. I was able to have a most useful conversation with him in the
interval about the importance to industry of sickness in pregnancy.'

It would be a complete mistake to imagine from such incidents
that Webb was inhuman, a man of blue books and statistics. He was,

on the contrary, full of accurate and unusual information. He was never patronising, never superior, always kindly and particularly helpful and encouraging to the young. He possessed to a higher degree than anyone I have ever met the unusual quality of disinterested reasonableness. Because he was single-minded and infinitely benevolent, I would have preferred to go to him in a difficulty rather than to Beatrice, who was a complex mixture of class superiority, intellectual impatience and puritanical morals. When we summarise Sidney's life, we see the closest parallel in the life of Jeremy Bentham. Like Bentham he studied English law and institutions and social customs, judging them always by the criterion of their utility to society, and in every case suggested, with astounding fertility, the reasonable alternatives which a wise legislature could substitute. From this intellectual cornucopia everyone was free to pilfer. From him, as from Jeremy Bentham, it may be truly said that all the world borrowed and left him rich.

Beatrice Webb was as complex as Sidney was simple. She was endlessly troubled by emotional conflicts and sought a personal religion as well as an impersonal solution for the world's problems. She was intensely interested in people and human character; she would like, she tells us, to have been a novelist, and regretted, when some of the younger generation, her eight sisters' children or grandchildren, proved ultra-modern, that she had not had the opportunity earlier of seriously studying the new science of psychology. She was, in point of fact, thoroughly Victorian in her attitude both to sex and to the younger generation. She was immensely interested in her innumerable grand-nephews and nieces—I say innumerable because she tried to keep up with the proliferation of their families and took a pride in thinking, even after the 150 mark was passed, that none had been missed—and she tried hard to be tolerant and understanding about their personal problems. When Malcolm Muggeridge, husband of one of her nieces, read a clever play he had written, which gloated, in the manner of the twenties, over the sexual peculiarities of our society, Mrs. Webb was very much shocked, not, of course, as she explained, for herself, but because others, less used to frank speech, were also among the audience.

The problem of sex became mingled with the problem of Soviet development. She had been, I recall, perplexed by the sexual freedom at first encouraged in the Soviet Union, and was fond of emphasising that puritanical discipline which the early Bolshevik Party imposed on itself. She was relieved when a new abortion law was passed, explaining that in imposing severe penalties the Soviet Government was actuated not so much by a desire to increase the population as by its discovery of the social evils that resulted from excessive sexual freedom.

Quite early in our acquaintance I learnt that Mrs. Webb was more interested in religion than in any other topic. Her *Diaries* reveal how large a part prayer played in her life. Her formula was that 'the two big forces for good in the world were the scientific method applied to the processes of life, and the use of prayer in directing the purpose of life'. She read a great deal of philosophy, and found temporary satisfaction in a variety of thinkers, including General Smuts, whose Holism seemed to her valuable. But I doubt if any of these philosophers satisfied her for long. What she knew was that prayer was of practical value to her. She records on many occasions that it was 'the habit of prayer which enabled me to survive and to emerge relatively sound in body and sane in mind'. Prayer was not to her a petition, but a consecration of purpose and a purifying of motive. She believed, I think rightly, that in discarding contemplative prayer as one of the superstitions of religion, her rationalist friends had lost an important technique of the good life. What is perhaps more surprising is that adolescent struggles, which she recalls in *My Apprenticeship*, continued into her middle years. In girlhoood, she constantly records her regret for wasting time at parties and in flirtations and in showing herself off in pretty frocks among clever people. These temptations still continued twenty years later, when in her diary she excuses the brilliant dinner-parties which she gave or attended by saying, only too truly, 'Our social adventures always have a purpose.'

She didn't for a moment lose her interest in public affairs, and in 1941 wrote to me saying:

'We are living in terrible times and I doubt whether this war

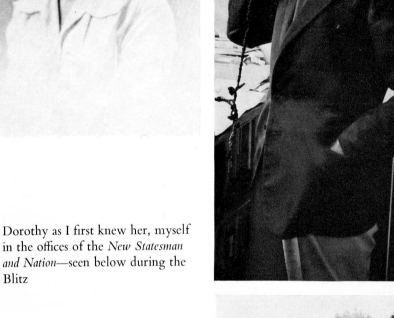

Dorothy as I first knew her, myself in the offices of the *New Statesman and Nation*—seen below during the Blitz

Dick Crossman comes to tea. The cottage: assisting with the thatching, and the sitting-room annexe I built myself—John Strachey just visible on the step

will be ended for another two years especially if we carry out the policy of Vansittart of calling all the Germans "butcher birds" and add to that abuse, lack of friendliness to the U.S.S.R. If we fail to get the wholehearted participation of the U.S.S.R. in the peace conference, however much we may be able to beat Germany and even occupy her territory, we cannot prevent her re-arming if the U.S.S.R. remains merely a detached neutral. It is strange that our statesmen do not see that eventually, and that our government goes on refusing to recognise the incorporation of the three Balkan States within the U.S.S.R. Without that recognition and the liberation of the gold and the ships we shall not get the participation of the U.S.S.R. in the peace conference.'

In 1943 I went down to see her with Raymond Mortimer. Her letter inviting us may be worth reproducing:

'Dear Mr. Kingsley Martin,
    'We should very much like to see you and Mr. Raymond Mortimer: the most convenient time for [us] is 4 o'c tea. There is a train from W'loo arr. 4.2 and leaving every half hour—back at 6.15 and 6.43 and getting to W'loo ab[out] 8 o'c and we cd. send to meet you—it wd be after the issue of the *N.S.*
    'We are very glad that you are back in London—the readers of the *N.S.* have missed y[ou]r comments on current events—tho' y[ou]r articles on the U.S.A. have been interesting. We are, of course, cheered by the success of the Soviet armed forces in pressing the Nazi hordes out of their territory—I wish we cd help them more vigorously. The Maiskys were here on Wednesday: they are confident of victory before the end of the year—but still doubtful of whether or not our government means to have a second front so as to end this devastating war by occupying Germany early in 1944. What do you think of the Beveridge Report? I enclose my review of it in the *C.N.*—the official organ of the C.C. Movement.

    'About entries in my diary concerning G.B.S.—I am afraid

G

they are not quotable—we have been contenders in a common cause for over 50 yrs—but our close friendship makes publication during my lifetime undesirable. The Shaws are having a hard time of it as Charlotte is a hopeless invalid and suffers severely from old age and rationing and living at Ayot St. Lawrence with its cold and damp climate. He has been writing a book *What's What to the Politics?*[1] [*sic*] but has had to finish it because his printers told him that there was no more paper. Sidney is well and happy but I am rather a wreck suffering from a swollen foot and leg and sleepless nights. However, we can talk about the present state of affairs when we meet. I thought W. J. Brown M.P.'s *I Meet America*—very enlightening. These Diary records of journalists are the great successes of today and have superseded the novel? I wonder whether Raymond Mortimer thinks so?

'Ever,
'Beatrice Webb.'

Wearing a lace cap, emaciated but with an aquiline beauty, she looked, as Raymond said, like a most venerable and formidable abbess. The love of power, which she had never openly exercised, was unmistakable. The manœuvrings of politicians, the outwitting of dull people on Royal Commissions, the attractive glitter of social occasions, exhilarating for the moment and regretted afterwards, the waste and distraction of entertainment, and moral problems and enforced Machiavellianism of political achievement—all these interferences with personal dignity, veracity and kindness, were over long ago. Sidney did not need to pray because he had no chance desires to overcome. Lacking all vanity, and enjoying all the pleasures of life simply and in moderation, asceticism tempted him no more than excess. Mrs. Webb once hazarded the view that he too 'believed', but I never could detect that he had any religious views; the subject bored him, since there were so few established facts on which to form a hypothesis. The concentrated life of research and public service had demanded, it is clear, great sacrifices of Beatrice Webb, but none of Sidney. They had set out together, as they would

1. This appears to be what she actually wrote.

tell one, with great advantages: £1,000 a year of unearned income, unusual experience and knowledge, and a remarkable coincidence of purpose. They had accomplished 'the considerable work' which they had set themselves to do fifty years before. They were not dissatisfied. Even when Sidney had his first stroke, and could no-longer remember consecutively or talk easily, I had no impression that he felt frustrated or unhappy. His life's work was done; he re-read Victorian novels. Beatrice also gave one the impression of conscious success; she had never been sympathetic with failure, and liked to remember what the Webb partnership had achieved and to speculate about the future. But there was always an under-current, a restless dissatisfaction, about her. She said that their chief mistake had been 'to reject the Marxian theory of the decay of Capitalism'. But I think what really perplexed her was a growing doubt whether any reorganisation of society which she and Sidney had envisaged or Soviet Russia tried to carry into effect would satisfy the needs of human beings if, as seemed possible, most of them were, like herself, complex, religious and emotional, and not, like Sidney, simple and rational.

CHAPTER FOUR

Shaw and Wells

IN common with the Webbs and most other leaders of thought in the thirties, H. G. Wells and Bernard Shaw both took it for granted that Social Democracy was pretty well played out. Both of them assumed after the 1931 collapse that Capitalism was doomed and that Socialism must soon take its place. Neither of them thought this could be achieved by the gradual and painless stages which orthodox Labour took for granted. Both of them shared the common excitement about the progress of the Soviet Union, which was the one country which claimed to have achieved full employment and to be deliberately planning a Socialist economy. They disagreed about every other aspect of the U.S.S.R. G.B.S., immensely flattered by his reception in Russia, used the Society of Sensible People as a foil for British democracy, much as Voltaire once pretended that everything was fine in China in contrast to eighteenth-century France. Wells, on the other hand, was sure that violent revolution was evil and unnecessary and, as time went on, hated the doctrines and intolerance of Marxism every year more intensely.

Soon after the First World War, Wells had visited Russia and had a long conversation with Lenin, with whom he was greatly impressed. Unlike Bertrand Russell, who visited the Soviet Union in the same period, he concluded that Lenin was necessary if Russia was to emerge from chaos; what other force was there but Communism to save Russia from anarchy? In 1934, he paid a second visit to the Soviet Union. He came back in a thoroughly bad temper. All his good advice had been neglected, Stalin had shot scientists and technicians and Wells had been subjected to the usual round of crèches and workers' rest-homes. But he had had a thoroughly satisfactory interview with Stalin, which he gave me for publication. I asked G.B.S. if he would like to comment; he did so in a manner that was certain to infuriate H.G. He represented Stalin as being kindly and polite to H.G., while H.G. did not listen to a word Stalin said, and assumed that he could put Stalin right about revolution. The truth was that Wells, then in his Clissold mood of thinking that business men might be brought to see the light, had made the case for what we have since learnt to call the 'managerial revolution'. Stalin smilingly insisted that the class war had to be won and the dictatorship of the proletariat take the place of Capitalism. Many other people took part in the debate in the *N. S. & N.* Keynes, who supported Wells, wrote in a memorable passage:

'The capitalist has lost the source of his inner strength—his self-assurance, his self-confidence, his untamable will, his belief in his own beauty and unquestionable value to society. He is a forlorn object, heaven knows—at best, apathetic well-meaning Clissold. Lord Revelstoke the First, Lord Rothschild the First, Lord Goschen the First, Sir Lothian Bell, Sir Ernest Cassel, the private bankers, the ship-owning families, the merchant princes, the world embracing contractors, the self-made barons of Birmingham, Manchester, Liverpool and Glasgow—where are they now? There are no such objects on the earth. Their office-boys (on salaries) rule in their mausoleums.'

This correspondence turned into a splendid dialogue about Socialism and I thought that the interview, with the correspondence, should be made into a pamphlet. I rang up Wells, who said, 'Of course it must be a pamphlet. Shaw has behaved like a cad and ought to be exposed.' I then rang up Shaw, who said, 'Certainly not. I have a great respect for my old friend, H.G. He's made a perfect ass of himself and I wouldn't want it put on permanent record.' A comic period followed. Shaw still insisted that the pamphlet ought not to be published and wrote to me:

'Dear K.M.,
'I still think the interview quite disappointing; it's like a conversation between Louis Napoleon and Lord Melbourne in 1840; not a word of it belongs to 1934. A cover by Low—or better still, a set of illustrations—might give the book some value; but

you would have to pay him at least £100. I leave the decision with
Wells and Keynes: if they want to exhibit themselves at their
worst, I will give way. Mrs. Shaw is writing to H.G. to that
effect, making it clear that I am against.

                                                                    'G.B.S.'

Whereupon Wells replied:

'The Shaws want the pamphlet suppressed but I want it
published. I hope you have it set up and under way. G.B.S. made
a rotten attack on me and he ought to take his dose like a man.'

We were just going to press when H.G. sent a final letter. He had
discovered an old article by Shaw in the *Daily Herald*; Shaw's views
about Stalin and revolution had then been very much the same as
those of Wells ten years later. I sent it to the printer for the *N.S.*, but
Wells insisted that it must also go into the pamphlet. It so happened
that Shaw was having one of his rare illnesses at the time and I explained to H.G. that I could not include it in the pamphlet unless
G.B.S. had had a chance of seeing it and replying to it. Wells became
extremely cross and silly. G.B.S. was ill, was he? Well, he had dia-
betes and rheumatism and goodness knows what else, and he didn't
run away from controversy. I must remember what a greater pub-
lisher than I had said, 'Publish and be damned'. Next morning his
secretary rang me up to say that if his new letter was not included in
the pamphlet H.G. would not consent to the pamphlet appearing at
all. I rang Shaw's number and Mrs. Shaw replied. G.B.S., she said,
was ill and it was too bad to have Wells' letter in the paper because
when G.B.S. woke up—and she was afraid I might have awakened
him by telephoning—he would want to write a reply and he wasn't
really well enough. I rang off, much abashed. Half an hour later she
rang me up again in the happiest of moods. G.B.S. was sitting up in
bed writing a reply to Wells. He was delighted and said that H.G.'s
letter had given him a chance finally to wipe the floor with him.
Would I like to fetch the letter myself? So I went round and found
G.B.S., looking like Father Christmas, in bed with a very pink face

and very white whiskers. (He had originally, as H.G. remarked, had very red hair and a very white face.) He was very pleased with himself and asked me to read the letter there and then. He had added a footnote to his reply. In an earlier letter he had referred to Wells 'trotting into the Kremlin'. Wells had replied:

'Shaw can have all the glory of saying that I "trotted" into the Kremlin while, by implication, he and Lady Astor, with the utmost grace, strode, swam, stalked, danced, slid, skated, or loped in, and conversed in some superior imperial fashion of which no record survives.'

Shaw replied in his footnote:

'I cannot withdraw the word "trotted" as descriptive of Wells' entry into the Kremlin. A man's mood is always reflected in his locomotion. Wells did not strut; that would have been vulgar; and Wells is not vulgar. He did not stalk or prance for he is not tall enough for such paces. He did not merely walk; he is too important for that. Having eliminated all possible alternatives, I conclude that he trotted. If not, what *did* he do?'

Later it was suggested to me that Wells would be hurt by this reference to his height. Shaw was tall and handsome, Wells was tubby. Adler would have seen in this the basic reason for Wells' irritability. I rang Mrs. Shaw and said I was sure that G.B.S. would not wish to tread on so sensitive a corn. He enjoyed teasing Wells, but wouldn't want to hurt him. She agreed and went to consult G.B.S. I remember her voice on the phone now: 'He thinks we are rather silly but he has made an amendment to please us and the sentence should now read *"he did not stalk nor prance in the Shavian manner".*'

In these comic rows Shaw usually scored because to him it was all a fine game of wits, while Wells was always deeply and personally involved. Shaw was vain but his vanity was what we are accustomed to call 'female vanity'. He was vain of his superb appearance, of his perfect enunciation, his bearing and his wit; in fact, he was vain about being G.B.S., but he didn't care what anybody said about his work, and his judgment, which was often bad, was not affected by criticism. Wells, on the other hand, couldn't let anything pass. So G.B.S. could be sure of a 'rise' when he teased H.G. But there was one occasion when it was Wells that did the scoring. Shaw arrived at lunch (I think I owe this story to Sir Harold Nicolson), complaining in his lordly way that it was really very difficult; he couldn't get any privacy. Children came to him for his autograph when he was taking his morning stroll in the park. Wells piped up, 'Well, Shaw, if you don't like publicity why don't you cut off your beard?'

I once told H. G. Wells and, after reflection, he agreed with my analysis, that at least two people struggled inside him, Herbert and George. Bert reacted; George dreamed. Bert was often cross, but, because he was a man of genius, he worked off his irritation in splendid stories about the frustrations of innumerable other Herberts who were bullied and patronised as he had been in Bladesover —the big house he describes in *Tono Bungay*. He never forgave his feudal superiors at Up Park, whom he regarded as really inferior to himself. Wells hated all the bombasined upper servants. You remember how little Bealby kicked the butler's shins and had all the flunkies tearing their velvet breeches on the brambles as they ran after him. Kipps and Mr. Polly are similar protests, magnificently transformed into great novels, against his treatment as a draper's assistant. His mother had an astonishing determination to turn him into a nice respectable shopkeeper, who might eventually become his own master, though of course not bankrupt like Mr. Polly. He escaped at last to an impoverished life as a student when he learnt some science for a year under Thomas Huxley, who remained his greatest hero. But he never forgave society for depriving him of the education which the upper classes were able to buy. He remained bitter about public schools and universities all his life. The contrast here with Shaw, who was also not academically educated, tells one a lot about both of them. Shaw, instead of reacting, explained his own superiority to ordinary mortals on the ground that he was educated in music and not mis-educated in dead knowledge. Wells' direct reaction was always liable to come through. Even late in life an amusing book like *Apropos of Dolores* was an undisguised explosion of irritation against an identifiable person who had long exasperated him, and so, notoriously, was his slap back in the *New Machiavelli*, which was not fair to the Webbs or Graham Wallas and other identifiable people such as Professor MacTaggart.

When George took over from Bert, books like *Kipps* and *Mr. Polly* were born. Here experience has passed through the magic process, the alchemy which turns revolt into art. George Ponderevo is Pip in *Great Expectations*, despised but striving for Estella, or David Copperfield barking his shins against the rungs of the social ladder. *Kipps* and *Mr. Polly* are in origin stories, not only about Wells himself, when he was for two unhappy periods a draper's assistant, 'living in' as the system of shop slavery used to be called, yearning for a dream life of adventure, for the companionship of gorgeous women, seen in daily life only too well protected by immaculate males in unattainable evening dress, but they had been transformed into universalised figures, Dickensian in their individuality and permanence. And then Bert was sure to turn up again. He couldn't stand criticism. He could be unbelievably touchy and tetchy.

Not long after I came to the *New Statesman* I found waiting for me on my desk a quite absurd correspondence between H.G. and Leonard Woolf. Wells had taken exception to a phrase in a review of his *Health, Wealth and Happiness* and demanded an apology. Leonard himself tells the story in the third volume of his autobiography. He is mistaken in saying that I received a telegram from H.G. asking him not to publish it. In fact I went to see him and begged him, as one of the world's greatest thinkers, to forget such a petty grievance. He began by saying that Bloomsbury was trying to undermine his reputation among the young. 'But surely,' I said, 'you are the creator of masterpieces, one of the immortals. Have you time to spend replying to every review and criticism you don't like?'

And then, quite suddenly, George took over from Bert. He was telling me that no one ought to spend his meagre span of life bickering with critics. We were standing together on a hill-top, looking back far into remote ages when men lizard-like oozed from the primeval slime, and looking ahead into the future when the younger generation, upright and emancipated, with heads erect were marching towards the dawn, no longer afraid of gods or priests or devils. The New World was not so far off. . . .

On another occasion during the war I found myself at lunch with H.G. and expressed my pleasure at seeing him after a long interval. It happened that that very week we published a savage review of H.G.'s latest novel—one of a number of pot boilers that he wrote at that time. On Monday morning I found a card from H.G. which began: 'So you really had that stinker up your sleeve when you greeted me so warmly last Tuesday', and ended by saying that I was a cad. A copy of my reply turned up the other day amongst some papers. I wrote:

                                                                26th January 1942

'My dear H.G.,

With your note in front of me it takes some effort to recall that you are not really the vain and abusive little man that its petulance would suggest. I know that you are not, because I have known you behave like this before and on one occasion persuaded you not to damage your great reputation by publishing a silly correspondence in which you had lost your temper, while on another occasion I even persuaded you to withdraw some nasty remarks. I know well that by some inner compulsion you must work off your anger when anyone is in the least critical of you, but being a scientist and therefore interested in facts, you will realise after a minute's thought that on this occasion you have been more than usually hot-tempered.

When I saw you on Wednesday, I was friendly because I felt friendly to H.G., whom I have always admired and to whom I owe a great deal of my mental furniture. I knew nothing of your new book which I've unfortunately not had the chance of seeing yet; I did not know to whom it had been sent for review or whether a review had been written. It was not in my mind. Why should it be? I did not actually see the review until it was in page proof after I had seen you.

But that is not the point. The important question is how you can think that if I had seen the review or known that we were printing an unfavourable review of your book, I would somehow have behaved differently. Do you mean to suggest that because a reviewer had written something unfavourable to you that I should therefore cut you when I met you? Or that I should be in tears or blushing from shame? Or what *do* you suggest? Or can it be that you imagine that when I saw that an unfavourable notice of your book had reached the paper I ought to have said 'My old friend H. G. Wells, will not like this review, and therefore I cannot print this reviewer's honest opinion of his book.' If I had done that, I should therefore have blushed when I saw you. We have some remaining standards of integrity to uphold. One of these is that if we send a book to a reviewer who is generally regarded as competent, and he gives his honest opinion of the book, and if it is not libellous or for some other reason definitely unpublishable, we print it over his signature as his honest opinion. What would you say, supposing you had written a review and then the Editor explained that he could not print your criticism because he was a friend of the author or did not like to hurt his feelings?

No, no, You have nothing to forgive. But if you consider the matter, I know you will regret using such words and return to your usual eupeptic and genial, understanding self.

Yours,

To this H.G. replied with another card beginning: 'Now you are pretending you don't edit your own paper!' Some weeks after, at a party, I recall, at the Chinese Embassy, H.G. came up to me, shyly putting his hand out with a comic gesture, shamefaced, mutely asking to be friendly again.

Wells was always touchy about reviews. Here is his comment on the correspondence following our review of his book, now I fear forgotten, *Bulpington of Blup*—a novel which, as his autobiography shows, he specially valued. It was reviewed by Harold Laski, and Francis Birrell followed up with a letter that clearly got deeply under H.G.'s skin, so that he wrote:

'7th February 1933

'Sir,

'I am so sorry to see that my *Bulpington of Blup* has touched Mr. Francis Birrell in a raw place and still sorrier to realise that beneath the fair friendliness of our many meetings he had been hiding so much scorn and contempt for me. Apparently he has not realised that the *Bulpington of Blup* is a novel and not a statement of opinion and that I had not the remotest intention of making Theodore a "type-aesthete" or the Buxteds "type-scientists". And anyhow Mr. Birrell's citation of his own admirable classical education is a trifle irrelevant. He has every reason to know that there were young scientific workers among the conscientious objectors. Theodore had neither a classical nor a scientific education; that issue doesn't arise; he had a sloppy ill-trained mind and his reveries ran away with him. That is the theme of the book, the way in which a human mind slides away from disagreeable realisations.

'Whether I am the sort of shyster who is "inevitably found on the side of the big battalions" it is not for me to say. I haven't felt like that and I am distressed to find that that is Mr. Birrell's matured opinion of me. In 1914 I thought it was England that was up against the big battalions. I doubt if *Boon* (1914) with its reflection on Mr. Osborn and the "Wild Asses of the Devil" or *Mr. Britling* (1916) can really be cited as the work of a bloodthirsty Jingo. Nobody has ever read *Joan & Peter* but that too is a wartime book with a reasonable attitude towards the war. Mr. Birrell sneers at my "unparalleled services to the State as a war propagandist". I suppose he refers to my time at Crewe House which ended in a breach with Northcliffe. There is a sufficient record of my work there to show that I did my utmost to help on the movement to extract a statement of War Aims from the

Foreign Office and to commit this country to a not yet Wilson-
ized League of Nations. That I thought would bring the war to an
end. What heroic measures Mr. Birrell was taking to end the war
are lost in the obscurity of the past. No doubt he was displaying
enormous energy and courage in some field unknown to me.

'During and after the war I have put in a good lot of hard work
upon the problem of world peace. I think Mr. Birrell's manifest
belief that anyone who is not an ex-conscientious objector should
be warned off this field is an extravagant one. I have the friendliest
feeling for him and—what is it?—his friends the other "aesthetes"
but I have not nearly sufficient confidence in their power and
vigour and I am far too anxious to work on the road to world
peace myself, to let them monopolise the business.

'Nevertheless I am prepared to hear in all humility from Mr.
Birrell just what he and the aesthetes generally are doing to make
another great war impossible.

'Very sincerely yours,

H. G. Wells.'

After this the correspondence branched out, getting more acri-
monious, into the general question of pacifism, but coming sharply
back to personalities, with complaints by H.G. that the aesthetes
were ganging up against him.

This anxiety about what reviewers would say remained. I find
a letter from him dated 26th December 1939:

'My dear Kingsley Martin,

'I have a new book coming out on January 1st. the *New World
Order*. Will you for once save a bit of my work from the hands of
that philosophical defective, Joad? Book after book of mine he
fumbles, misrepresents and mauls. Just for once give me a holiday
from him.

Yours ever,
H.G.

All this side of Wells was comparatively trivial and unimportant.

I owed more of my ideas about the world to him than anybody except Shaw. Maynard Keynes wrote that they were our two schoolmasters, Wells was the stinks master, while Shaw taught divinity. This was true of my generation. Wells venerated science as the key to the future, Shaw treated facts in a most cavalier manner, relying, as he said himself, on pure divination. Wells had made his reputation by scientific fantasies which he told me in later years he had never taken seriously, but he had believed that the twentieth century would be magnificently transformed by science and described the future in his *Modern Utopia*. He warned us, however, in 1909 that 'Everything crawls forward but the science of war; *that* rushes on.' Modern war would be an insanity of destruction and economically ruinous, and after war had actually happened in 1914 he said, 'I let my imagination play about it, but in the bottom of my heart I could not feel and believe that it would ever be let happen.' So it was that 1914 hit him with all the force of a hideous surprise and, after discussing in *Mr. Britling Sees It Through* the decent citizen's state of dismay at being plunged into war with Germany, he yielded to popular clamour and decided that 'Every sword that is drawn against Germany is now a sword for peace.' He presented Northcliffe's propaganda organisation with the best of gifts in describing the conflict as 'The war to end war'. Afterwards, disillusioned by a purely nationalist peace, he bitterly attacked the League of Nations, 'this little corner of Balfourian jobs and gentility—what could that lead to?' He tried first, in the *Outline of History*, as the first of a trilogy to educate mankind. People did not realise the story of human progress and the splendid future that awaited them. They refused to realise it and the job must be done by an *élite*. His Philosopher Kings in the *Modern Utopia* were called 'Samurai' after the bloody ruling order of old Japan, and he developed the same idea in a whole series of books, ending with his doctrine of the 'Open Conspiracy' which was to emerge as an increasing number of people realised that their old ideas of Capitalism and sex and social conformity were out-of-date and that they could lead mankind to a splendid destiny.

I believe, in the long run, the crusade on which Wells had most influence was the emancipation of women. It may well be that *Ann Veronica* is his most important book. It hastened the notion of the 'equal mate', the splendid girl striding fearlessly side by side with her man and sharing all his interests and adventures. It sounded fine, especially as the adventures included free sex relations and we had not then discovered the difficulties that arise when both partners are free to experiment and both try to do a job and have a family at the same time. Wells shocked his own generation by his own sexual freedom and one could fill a book with the stories which were rife in my day about Wells' love affairs. It was obvious, in my view, that he was deeply and always in love with his wife, Catherine Wells, about whom he writes with much affection in his autobiography. He published after her death the novel she had written and his preface makes clear that he felt that he had not adequately appreciated her. But I find myself having more respect for the amorous H.G., who was always genuinely falling in love, getting into scrapes and had children by more than one woman, than for the austerity of G.B.S., who, in order to satisfy his instinctive asceticism, invented the theory that one could store up one's sexual energy as a camel does its food and afterwards turn it into drama or poetry.

The best and usually least printable stories about Wells' private life are mainly about his relations with Odette Keun, who shared his home near Grasse. She had the utmost contempt for convention and enjoyed using words that were not publicly current in the thirties. H.G. told me how on one occasion when Sir Wilfred Grenfell and his wife were visiting the South of France he suggested to Odette Keun that she might enjoy writing a book about Labrador, where communications had been developed by Sir Wilfred. Odette desired to return for a time to a more adventurous life and she welcomed the idea of a book about Labrador. H.G. warned her that the Grenfells were strict Nonconformists and that she must take particular care not to shock them. When they arrived at tea their fellow-visitors included a Mr. Casanova, and H.G., by way of mild persiflage in introducing him, said, 'This is the last living descendent of the great Casanova.' 'Casanova?' said Lady Grenfell. 'What did he do?' The pause which followed was filled by Odette saying the simple word

'Fuck'. 'The word,' said H.G., 'lay on the tea-table like a turd.'
Odette never visited Labrador.

No such stories are told about the life of G.B.S. There was a
period when he experimented with sex; his published letters perhaps
explain why he was apt comically to refer to his 'gallantry' when he
means 'love affair'.

Once I talked to Jung about Shaw. I referred to his remarkable
detachment, his disinterested approach, his capacity for being personally above the battle, his universal benevolence and complete lack
of rancour. I spoke of these qualities as proof of Shaw's superiority
to ordinary mortals. Jung's response at first surprised me. Perhaps
Shaw had never been deeply in love? That was my view; he had
told us about his early love affairs; he was much attached to his wife
with whom he had lived on terms of good companionship; he had
had grand but remote passions for Mrs. Pat Campbell and Ellen
Terry. I doubt if he had ever lost himself in love. And when we
come to his real philosophy in, say, the last part of *Back to Methuselah*,
we find him scoffing at love just as he did at art and the other
aesthetic and emotional experiences which are the highest goods to
so many men and women. He treated them as so many infantile
diseases out of which you ought to have grown up when you have
left your teens. To Jung all this was proof, not that Shaw was a sage,
superior to the rest of us, but that he was still a child, a Peter Pan who
managed to evade real experience.

If Jung was right, this explains Shaw's limitations. He produced
such triumphs of the intellect as the Hell scene in *Man and Superman*.
He had occasional moments of poetry; the kingfisher scene in *St.
Joan* is an example. But for the most part one must recognise that
Shaw's supremacy lay in his power as a debater. J. B. Priestley once
remarked that he was, perhaps, the very best dialectician who has
ever written in the English language. As he had a superb sense of
theatre, the debates became plays. People do him an injustice who
say that he could not create characters and that he merely used them
as mouthpieces for his ideas. He created many original and memor-

Maynard Keynes and (below) Sidney
and Beatrice Webb with Sandie, by
Sir William Nicholson

Friends: Harry Roberts by Flora Twort, myself with a boa constrictor,
H. N. Brailsford, and Joad and I at summer school

able characters. But he did not run the risk of passion. He preferred debate in which no one won, though every one scored. He wrote dramas of ideas and it was his unique gift that the ideas became alive and wrestled and sweated in disembodied conflicts. I can think of no literary exercise so difficult, or so instructive, as to take the last act of *Major Barbara* and to attempt to find an alternative ending. Almost any other dramatist would have been content with a neater and perhaps dramatically more satisfying solution of the personal situation, but Shaw had become so absorbed in the intensely difficult problem of power and its relations to ideas that he leaves his players and his audience to continue the wrangle without any neat dramatic solution.

Desmond MacCarthy, whom I tried to persuade to write a new appreciation of Shaw in old age, noticed a real deterioration in Shaw himself. The Shaw who had praised Mussolini and justified Hitler grew increasingly irresponsible in suggesting that people who were a nuisance should be killed. This strain in Shaw, and his characeritsic inconsistency when he dropped back suddenly into individualism, after maintaining the State's right to liquidate anyone it disapproved of, had been growing steadily stronger from *Major Barbara* onwards. He ceased to have a genuine humanism such as he had shown in the splendid preface to *John Bull's Other Island*. In general, re-reading Shaw, MacCarthy said he could find nothing but 'a chaos of clear ideas'.

W. H. Rivers (the psychologist and anthropologist who is the hero of Siegfried Sassoon's *Sherston's Progress*) once told me about a long voyage with Bernard Shaw. They were on a cargo ship which, if I remember rightly, took a month or more from the West Indies to Britain. They spent many hours every day talking about what people used to call 'fundamentals'. Rivers described these conversations as the greatest treat of his life. They arrived in the Thames about Christmas time. A pilot boat came out with reporters on board. The effect on Shaw, Rivers said, was exactly as if G.B.S. had suddenly found himself on a stage with the curtain up, the audience waiting, and only just time to throw on a cloak and a comedian's mask. Why had Shaw been away at Christmas time? 'Oh,' he told

H

the newspaper men, notebooks in hand, 'as an Irishman and a Christian, I disapprove of your pagan festivals and I have to keep out of England at such a time, to avoid over-eating and watching other people get disgustingly drunk in order to keep up a festival which was out of date in the days of Mithras. . . .' And much more to the same effect. The reporters went off satisfied with a newspaper story; Shaw had once again proved himself the wisecracker that the public expected him to be. This public image of Shaw, this *persona*, had really nothing to do with the G.B.S. whom I knew off and on during a period of thirty years.

There are very few public persons who can afford to be natural and sincere in their relation to the public. No one can explain to the Press quickly, truthfully and seriously, just what he thinks about religion, the future of civilisation and the pros and cons of devaluing the pound sterling. But that is just what you are expected to do if you are a public man, and you must speak with the knowledge that the public will form an opinion of the sort of man you are from your unrehearsed comments and the manner with which you deliver them. You will be ticked off in the popular imagination as a funny man or a good sound patriot or a long-haired aesthete or put into some other unreal and simple category. For this reason most public persons must be in some degree actors; indeed, unless you have an actor's temperament and get some pleasure from seeing yourself dramatised and built up as a fictitious personality, you will find the whole business of becoming a public figure completely intolerable.

This contrast between the public and the private personality explains why people so frequently complain of the mistake they have made of meeting in private life the great men whose whimsical, wise or witty utterances have so delighted them from a distance. For the great man himself the process is highly dangerous. Take a person like Ramsay MacDonald; he became so fascinated with the public figure he cut, so identified with this posturing, booming and excessively handsome creature, that he ceased to have time to culti-vate the lively and studious young Scotsman who had once cherished disinterested ideals of serving the Labour movement. He became all *persona* and less and less a person.

It was because G.B.S. understood this danger so early in life that he played such a delightful game with the Press and the public. It was easy for him, of course, because his natural exuberance and overflowing flagon of fun enabled him to make a quick popular success of the famous comedian and irresponsible jester whom the public knew as Bernard Shaw. He could act this part without effort and remain intact with his real personality untouched by temptation. The technique was precisely suited to his capacities and his temperament: there are not many people to whom I would recommend it. His numerous imitators in the field of popular clowning soon bored the reporters and were so strained by the effort to maintain their *persona* that they never did anything else. But the effect with Shaw was to build a personality which the public knew while he studied economics, devoured Blue Books, thought about philosophy and allowed his soul, as he once said, to 'consort with the great immortal dead'.

I have, of course, overstated the case. Shaw himself knew that he had not always kept the jester under control. His persiflage turned into nonsense in old age. In a moment of self-revelation he said he had never been able to achieve the heights which he should have reached because, when he was approaching them, the clown inside him would 'trip him up in a most dreadful way'. Certainly there were times when this G.B.S. mountebank obscured the serious purpose of Bernard Shaw. He understood early the weakness of democracy; he was naturally impatient with the shallow humbug of much political talk. There was so much in it to laugh at, and so much to expose, that he even allowed himself to praise Mussolini and Hitler and to excuse all the darker deeds of Stalin. In 1948 he sent me a letter describing Russia as a democracy in which Stalin would be pushed out of power in ten minutes if he offended the majority of the Communist Party. He enclosed a card that read: 'Put the attached in the fire if it is senile drivel. I can't be sure of myself at 91¾.' I did.

The first argument I ever had with Shaw was in 1929 when I was an anonymous leader-writer on the *Manchester Guardian*. Professor Salvemini wrote attacking Shaw for making light of the destruction

of liberty in Italy. I wrote leaders supporting the attack and Shaw
wrote long letters of reply which evaded the point. I had not then
been long on the paper and C. P. Scott, who had not yet learnt that
I was politically dangerous, flattered me by his praise of my articles.
Later Mrs. Shaw told me how much she was distressed by the pain
G.B.S. had given to old friends who knew at first hand what
Fascist cruelty was. Mrs. Webb, who had not then fallen in love
with totalitarianism, has a revealing passage in her *Diaries*. She wrote,
deploring Shaw's picture of Mussolini as a superman:

> 'His argument seems to be that either the haves or the have-nots
> must seize power and *compel* all to come under the Fascist or the
> Communist plough. It is a crude and flippant attempt at recon-
> struction, bred of conceit, impatience and ignorance. The result
> would be to reinforce tyranny. What is new and deplorable is the
> absence of any kind of sympathetic appreciation of the agony the
> best and wise Italians are going through, any appreciation of the
> mental degradation implied in the suppression of all liberty of act,
> of thought and of speech.'

Wells hit upon the truth when he said:

> 'The worst element in his [Shaw's] mental make-up is the queer
> readiness to succumb to the poses of excessive virility. His soul
> goes down before successful force. He exalted the makers of
> enormous guns in *Man and Superman*; he has rejoiced in the worst
> claptrap of the Napoleonic legend; now he is striking attitudes of
> adoration towards the poor, vain, doomed biped who is making
> Rome horrible and ridiculous to all the world. When it comes to
> the torture of intelligent men, to vile outrages on old women, to
> the strangulation of all sane criticism, and an orgy of claptrap
> more dreadful than its attendant cruelties, this vituperative anti-
> vivisectionist becomes an applauding spectator.'

I recall, not many years before the last war, when he was slanging
and banging at Parliamentary Democracy, I went to see him to ask

what he really thought ought to be done about Parliament. In public he was saying that 'the only person who had the right idea about the House of Commons was Guy Fawkes'. In private he was ready with a sensible scheme to speed up the passage of legislation and to improve the quality of M.P.s without the interminable and dangerous delays entailed by out-of-date procedure in the Commons and obstruction in the Lords. This much publicised anti-democratic phase, which did so much harm to Shaw's reputation as he grew older, would have been avoided if he had been willing, as he was in all his earlier plays, to chasten the clown and prevent the actor running away with the part. In his great days the actor talked to the Press, but the thinker had the upper hand in the earlier plays and prefaces.

Shaw believed that Britain should keep out of the war against Hitler just as he had believed that we ought not to get involved in 1914. He hated all the time-dishonoured phrases about fighting for freedom, democracy and the rest of it. He was very anxious to keep me from getting 'sentimental'. He urged:

'Fire with all your guns, for the Imperialists may again trap you into their war disguised as revolted humanitarians; the old trick. The concentration camps and their leather whips—(one stroke=1 lash) are the Germans' business not ours, just as our cat (ten strokes=90 lashes plus 10 years' penal) is ours and not the Germans. Don't let Belisha, Eden and Co., get you sentimental whatever you do. There is still half a chance of a negotiation before we are landed in a war in which the odds may be against us.'

Shaw had never had many close friends. Lady Astor was certainly one of the few. The Webbs, of course, with whom he had worked for sixty years, were in a category by themselves. He never missed an opportunity of writing or speaking about their unique gifts and the extraordinary character of their partnership.

When Beatrice died in 1943 he wrote to me that he could not write her obituary:

'I knew her too well and saw her too closely at home to get her into a distant perspective as a great woman. If I wrote about her intimately I should write gaily; and that would not have the funeral solemnity proper to the present occasion. Her ashes should go to Westminster Abbey, which is now much too masculine.'

In November 1947 Sidney died and I did an obituary broadcast the same night. The letter I received the next day from Shaw is of considerable historical interest:

14th October 1947

'Dear Kingsley Martin,

'I heard your broadcast. It could not have been improved on at such short notice. *The Times* and *Herald* this morning promise a good press.

'Webb was not the founder of the Fabian Society. It was founded by a Rosminian philosopher named Davidson, and was excessively unfabian, dreaming of money and the substitution of passbooks, or constitutional Anarchism and all sort of nonsense in each others' lodgings.

'It split into a political section led by Hubert Bland, calling itself the Fabian Society, and a Fellowship of the New Life with Perfectionist views. The Fabian section had one working man member named Phillips: and it managed to get out a tract entitled "Why are the Many Poor?".

'This tract came my way. I, being a new convertist Marxist looking for a political shop saw that the title Fabian, obviously educated, was an inspiration. I joined it and found it a handful of hopeless amateurs needing above all things Webb, whom I had picked out as a political genius, and on whom I had forced my very uncongenial acquaintance, I being all artist and an incorrigible actor, and he the simplest soul and ablest youth in the world.

'The one thing that he could not do was to dramatise the situation and dramatise himself. I did all that for him. I wrote the early Fabian tracts and made the speeches at the street corners and on the platform.

'I inflict all this upon you because it shows that our work was a genuine partnership to which we were both indispensable. When, years later Beatrice came in as a third partner, I was abhorrent to her as an unclassifiable person: but with extraordinary good sense she accepted me as Webb's most loyal friend, classifying me as a sprite. But by that time, Fabianism was established and the trick done. Its founders had become eminent in their various ways. Our friendship remained; but we no longer needed one another; and the firm became Sidney-Beatrice with Shaw as a more or less unsleeping partner.

'Now if I were to cut into the obituaries with this correction, I would seem to be putting in a claim for a share in Webb's fame. So I shall hold my tongue.

'I have already said all I have to say publicly about the Webbs in the article I wrote for Beatrice as a preface to her last volume. I have also written a similar preface for the forthcoming memoir of Olivier, who was Webb's fellow clerk—resident at the Colonial Office, and followed him into the F.S. as its secretary. He, too, was a genius, but of a kind quite different from Webb's. He was an autocrat; and had he not been a man of good will, would have been the greatest scoundrel alive; for he had no conscience. He was himself alone.

'I have had to hammer this out in a crushing hurry; you must make what you can of it. My typing is atrocious; the day is too dark for old eyes.

G.B.S.'

After the war I saw much more of G.B.S. in his home at Ayot St. Lawrence with the second-rate statuettes about the place. His wife had died and he lived the life of a recluse, with very few friends I think, going to see him. Lady Astor was a frequent visitor. I tried to get him to recall ancient controversies. I had already received an interesting refusal to my suggestion that he should republish his

correspondence with Tolstoy. He wrote that it had been published
several times and quoted in scraps:

> 'I don't think it is worth reviving. As well as I remember it
> arose out of my play *Man and Superman*, which throws it back
> forty years. What it came to was that Tolstoy remonstrated with
> me for the levity with which I handled religion. I shocked him so
> much by maintaining that God's attributes must include a sense of
> humour that he dropped the correspondence. I also tried to make
> him understand that his contention that the old Leir drama which
> he considered superior to Shakespeare's play was so enormously
> inferior artistically that the comparison was ridiculous and that no
> one whose native language was not English could understand how
> this had made his dislike of the appalling pessimism of Shakes-
> peare's outlook and his preference of a happy ending business
> mere waste of time.'

Shaw was more interested about a scheme of his for a 'Bernard
Shaw Law' which would enable him to leave his property for public
purposes without tax. De Valera, he said, had done this for him in
Ireland, where he had consequently been able satisfactorily to dispose
of his wife's property. Wouldn't the Labour Party, which he had served
so long, give him his law as a reward? He wouldn't want any lesser
honour than a dukedom and that, he said, he couldn't afford. I asked
him for details of the Act of Parliament he wanted. He wrote back:

20th July 1946

'Dear K.M.,

'What I wanted and got in Eire was the Voluntary Civic
Improvement Fund, which makes the municipalisation of
property as easy as posting a letter and cannot be stolen by the
landlords by using it for the relief of the rates. I have demanded
the extension of this to England instead of a title. The Chancellor
is very civil, but thinks that the existing local government acts
provide for gifts to municipalities. No doubt they do, but not
within public knowledge simply and easily. De Valera put it

through the Dail for me in thirty minutes instead of in the English thirty years.

'Another stunt is the Coupled Vote. Votes for Women keeps them out of parliament as I told the Suffragets it would; 40–600 instead of 50–50. I contend that the correct political unit is not a man *or* a woman but a woman *and* a man. No single vote to be valid, only coupled votes. A bicycle made for two, in short. All elected bodies would be bisexual 50–50. This, like the V.C.I. Fund is my own invention, and much more of a staggerer. I propose it formally in my preface to my latest and probably last play: *In Good King Charles' Golden Days*.

'I don't think there is anything else to be said that you do not know better than I. My memory is rapidly ceasing to operate. I can't remember the Chancellor's name. Is it Hawkins? No: Dalton: your letter reminds me.

'Never mind about the Wells obituary. Let it go as the contribution of a profiteering shareholder. And don't bother to send your article to me: I give you *carte blanche*.

G.B.S.'

In the same year he was much bothered by well-meant efforts to celebrate his ninetieth birthday. We arrived, I remember, in the midst of a thunderstorm, and were shown into the overcrowded sitting-room with its strange jumble of good and bad statuettes, and his latest ugly gold Oscar on the mantelpiece. We waited, looking out over the garden to the spinney and fields beyond. When the rain passed over, Shaw came from his hut hidden in the trees and walked slowly with a stick to a place where the grass was terraced. We felt like eavesdroppers as we saw him break into a little run to get up the impetus to mount the grass steps on to the higher level. In a few minutes he was with us talking nineteen to the dozen about the people who pestered him with kindness, especially friends from Dublin who wanted to come over to give him a presentation. 'I wrote and told them,' he said, 'that I knew very well why they wanted to come and see me. It would be a jollification for them. But it would be the death of me and I told them not to come.'

The last time I saw G.B.S. was in March 1950. He was intensely interested in a series of articles on the Drama which were appearing in the *New Statesman*. Terence Rattigan had started the ball rolling with an attack on the Drama of Ideas which he blamed Shaw for popularising. G.B.S. had written to say that when the other dramatists had done their worst, he would come in if necessary and 'wipe the floor with the lot of them'. When Dorothy and I saw him, he had a strong word of praise for Ben Levy's contribution and was enthusiastic about James Bridie's. But he had obviously made up his mind to contribute himself, and a few weeks later, at the age of ninety-four he did actually write a concluding article for the series which had more vitality and vigour than any that preceded it. He talked a lot on that occasion about playwriting as an intellectual job. He said that he had never in his life worried about critics; he had always known what he wanted to do and, as he had been a critic himself, he knew the conditions under which critics worked and the unimportance of what they said. His advantage over other playwrights was the analytic capacity which he had developed in hard study of other subjects. James Bridie wrote to me about Shaw's article: 'Who would have thought that the old man would have so much blood in him? And what a lot of half-baked louts he makes us all look.'

G.B.S. had maintained his freshness of mind and the heartiness of intellectual appetite, and even something of the high spirits which were to a large extent the secret of his happiness and success, but he had at last grown old. He had become so accustomed, he said, to the expectation of death that it no longer entered into his thoughts. 'They tell me,' he said, 'that I am still young. I look into the mirror and I see that they lie.' He died a few months later.

Perhaps my most vivid memory of him was on a visit after the war when he told us how music had always meant much to him ever since he learnt to sing grand opera in his teens, and how he had always sung to his wife before she went to bed. He added: 'When my wife was alive, she always made me go to bed at ten o'clock for the good of my health. Since she died, I stay up till midnight or even after and I have never been better in my life.' No. He had never been better in his life than he was at ninety! He walked out with us to the car in the road and found in it our marmalade cat which he called 'Pussykins' and with whom he conversed as he always did with cats and other animals, finding, as he said, that they apparently enjoyed the conversation as much as he did, even though they might not fully grasp its content. And then as I turned the car round, I heard a surprising sound. I stopped to see Shaw standing in the middle of the lane and singing, at the top of his bell-like voice, an aria from Verdi. He turned round and said: 'My voice is no penny whistle now!' That it had never been. It was a voice that exposed shams, cleared the way, that liberated us from bad conventions and confused ideas. To me his death was very much as if I had been living in a room with the window open and suddenly found it shut. The room had become much darker and a lot stuffier.

Unlike G.B.S., who was in excellent health until the end, Wells died slowly, too conscious of his symptoms and with plenty of time to brood. But that is not the main reason why my memory of his last days is sad. By temperament he was an optimist. No one ever tried harder and he was never discouraged; he never gave up. The failure of mankind in the Second World War he felt as his personal failure. Shaw and Wells provide the best possible illustration of the saying that 'life is a comedy to those who think and a tragedy to those who feel'. This does not mean that Shaw was not serious. That was a popular fallacy which resulted from Shaw's playboy mask. In his early days, when he was poor and unmarried, he worked with a quite extraordinary and self-sacrificing zeal, sitting through endless boring committee meetings, making himself an expert on local government, speaking at street corners. All his life he spent all his wit against superstition and stupidity. Once, when he was young, he said that he was 'a born artist to his finger-tips' but, because the world was the way it was, he had to make himself into a second-class economist. He worked hard for his cause. But he was never more than semi-detached. H.G., on the other hand, was deeply and emotionally involved.

Wells was by nature a humorist, a Dickensian, while Shaw was a wit, a Voltairean. Until the First World War—the change was sharply marked with *Mr. Britling*—he had usually believed that progress towards Socialism and the World State was inevitable. He was a modern Condorcet, restating the philosophy of democracy, universal education and international brotherhood in terms of an age which demanded Socialist planning based on the accumulated achievement of science. Like Shaw, he was a Protestant who demanded that man should permit no official or priest to stand between him and the search for truth. But, while Shaw pushed this belief to the point of reviling scientists—especially doctors—who claimed to be authorities or experts, H.G. believed that the scientists were really discovering truth and knew the way to make men happy. Wells could not abide actors, spellbinders and people who were smart about facts. He had sat at the feet of the great Thomas Huxley who remained his hero. He tested later scientists by their readiness to follow the master in the disinterested search for knowledge. His own job in life he saw as the application to social issues of the scientific method he had learned in South Kensington. He regarded all else as escapism. He did not forgive Shaw for his frivolous attitude to science. What did the man mean by saying that his own scientific method was pure 'divination'?

In 1927 Wells wrote a studied attack on Shaw in an article about Pavlov. Shaw, the 'expressive' man, had called Pavlov, the scientist, a 'scoundrel'. Sentimental, in Wells' view, about vivisection, he had never been serious about anything.

'What has Shaw added to our arsenal of ideas, to our store of knowledge, to the illumination of the world?' Shaw had made free use of his phrase about 'the life force', but 'what meaning he attaches to these magic words is unknown. He expounds the word Will on the lines of various nineteenth-century German thinkers, he seems to be suggesting at times, that man can do anything by merely willing it, that whether that is possible on any dietary or only upon vegetarian nourishment, and whether it can be done without apparatus, is never clear. He has an aversion from sex and children which may be either Butler or temperamental, and he seems to want mankind to try laying parthogenetic eggs, and coming out of them fully whiskered. I doubt if there will ever be this will to the egg on the part of mankind. . . . His ideas are a jackdaw's horse, picked up anyhow and piled together anyhow. . . .'

In his *Experiment in Autobiography* there is a revealing passage about himself and Shaw. 'We found ourselves antagonistic on a number of issues and though we were not quite enough in the same field nor near enough in age to be rivals, there was from my side at any rate, a certain emulation between us.' He found himself differing from Shaw fundamentally for the same reasons that led to his famous quarrel with Henry James. James wanted him to concentrate on perfecting the artistic form of his novels. He declared he was a journalist with an intensely serious and urgent job to do:

'I have tried to set out my own formal and informal education in a previous chapter. Shaw had had no such sustained and constructive mental training as I had been through but, on the other hand, he had been saturated from his youth up in the good music, brilliant conversation, and the appreciative treatment of life. Extreme physical sensibility had forced him to adopt an austere teetotal and vegetarian way of living and early circumstances, of which Ireland was not the least, had inclined him to rebellion and social protests: but otherwise he was as distinctly over against me and on the aesthetic side of life as Henry James. He thinks one can "put things over" on Fact and I do not. He philanders with her. I have no delusions about the natural goodness and wisdom of human beings and at bottom I am grimly and desperately educational. But Shaw's conception of education is to let dear old Nature rip. He has got no further in that respect than Rousseau. Then I know, fundamentally, the heartless impartiality of natural causation, but Shaw makes Evolution something brighter and softer, by endowing it with an ultimately benevolent Life Force, acquired, quite uncritically I feel, from his friend and adviser

Samuel Butler. We have been fighting this battle with each other all our lives.'

One of the most interesting of his books, *The Shape of Things to Come*, appeared in 1933, the year in which Hitler came to power in Germany. He made the next war begin in Poland, as it did, but in 1937, and he foresaw a long series of sporadic wars which would reduce us to the primitive standards of tribal life: he sketched a wonderful world which would follow after a group of world airmen had created an orderly regime in which controversy would be between those who thought it was enough to have conquered the earth and those who wished to occupy the stars. He put the choice—
'If we are no more than animals—we must snatch at our scraps of happiness and live and suffer and pass, mattering no more as all the other animals do or have done.' His own faith he summarised like this:

> 'The truth remains that today nothing stands in the way to the attainment of universal freedom and abundance but mental tangles, egocentric preoccupations, obsessions, misconceived phrases, bad habits of thought, subconscious fears and dreads and plain dishonesty in people's minds—and especially in the minds of those in key positions. That universal freedom and abundance dangles within reach of us and is not achieved, and we, who are Citizens of the Future, wander about this present scene like passengers on a ship overdue, in plain sight of a port which only some disorder in the chart-room prevents us from entering. Though most of the people in the world in key positions are more or less accessible to me, I lack the solvent power to bring them into unison. I can talk to them and even unsettle them but I cannot compel their brains to see.'

It was not, I think, until near the end that he saw this statement of faith as inadequate—not untrue, but lacking in something essential. I remember his talking to me about Aldous Huxley, whom he regarded as the degenerate descendant of a noble grandfather. He spoke with bitterness of *Brave New World*; it was blasphemy against the religion of science. It suggested that knowledge might be the path, not to the modern Utopia, but to a new kind of servile Hell. Aldous Huxley was escaping to the United States, was he? Well— he spat it out with memorable contempt—'that is his quality'. But at the end, looking back on his life, finding much pleasure in dis- regarding Hitler's bombs, and taking, he tells us, an occasional old man's walk to the Savile Club—in this twilight period he found, not that he had lost his faith, but that it was somehow inadequate. He wrote a little mysteriously of the 'smile of approval'. Surely there must be something that was worth while in itself, irrespective of results? What if the bombs—and this was before Hiroshima—did really wipe out civilisation, or even if it proved that man, unable to cope with his new knowledge, destroyed *Homo sapiens* altogether? Would anything then be left of his life's work or of the human drama itself?

Truth and goodness H.G. had always seen as handmaidens. The Rationalists believed that enlightened men would also be good. Because the third member of the Trinity, Beauty, seemed to serve no biological function, the believer in progress was apt to pass it by. But if science is taking us to Hell and not to the Golden Age, then Beauty may, after all, be of supreme value? Scientific materialism has seen evolution as a chain of events, the wheels of cause and effect inexorably grinding out a future in which man's apparently free will can at most play a strictly limited part. But is it not possible that more important than the hypothetical Utopia at which he aims, are the sparks that fly off the wheels as they turn?

It was some such thought as this that led Wells to speak of 'the strange necessity' of Beauty. In his early novels he had noted in *Kipps* and *Mr. Polly* a craving for beauty which mechanical civilisa- tion frustrated. He had spat at the aesthetes and in his sociology made no more of this passion for beauty than a love of adventure which, of course, had its place as a factor in man's survival and progress. But now, he asked himself, whether for all your efforts to improve society, you can ever do better than perhaps slightly in- crease some people's happiness and add to their stature by giving them a vision of a world in which there is less frustration and an opportunity for appreciating the beauty of the sparks as they pass by. I think that was what he meant when, in *The Happy Turning*, he spoke of the importance of the state of mind which is unimportant to survival, but which brings with it, he says, as nothing else can, 'a smile of approval'.

CHAPTER FIVE

The Cottage

W HEN I returned to London from Manchester in 1930 I first lived
in a flat in Ormonde Terrace, Primrose Hill, opposite the Zoo. I
used to enjoy trying to sort out the roaring of lions, the howling of
monkeys and the shrieking of hyaenas. I regularly took parties of
children to the Zoo on Sunday mornings when Fellows had the
place to themselves. I made special friends amongst the animals;
there was a kinkajou who used to come out of his cage and walk me
about, carefully leaving a knot in his tail over one of my fingers.
When he wanted to return he turned round and climbed up his tail,
hand over hand. My favourite playmates were snakes. Boa constric-
tors, if not too large, make admirable pets. I remember one wrapping
himself round my braces, to the embarrassment of the keeper, who
thought he would have to take my trousers off to disentangle him.
I have always liked snakes; I made friends with one later at a circus
in the West of England and again at an extraordinary animal show
put on by the *Daily Mirror* at the Café Royal. There is a popular
delusion that snakes are cold and slimy like worms; in fact they are
like dry, warm silk.

On two occasions I went to the Zoo with Jack Driberg, the
brother of Tom, the M.P., who had had a personal following of
lions in East Africa and wrote for the *N. S. & N.* a series of articles
—later published as a book—about his favourite among them. On
these occasions I was allowed behind the barrier and put my hand
through the bars to feel and pummel Abdullah, the very companionable African lion. This was not really dangerous, but it makes you
feel brave to pull a lion's mane. Jack was an eccentric, powerful,
black-bearded man who had hunted lions with spears as a blood-
brother of wild tribes on the Sudanese-Ethiopian frontier. He was the
only man I ever knew who invented and prevented an unnecessary
war. As an official, he was ordered from Khartoum to carry out a
punitive expedition against some tribe whose offence he understood

I

and whom he knew he could pacify without bloodshed. He protested against his orders and explained that the whole quarrel could be
settled at a palaver. His suggestion was refused. He thereupon settled
the dispute amicably and wrote to Khartoum saying that so many
villages had been destroyed, so many natives killed and so forth.
Unfortunately, some young white 'bloods' who had wanted to take
part in the show discovered the fake and Jack was sacked from the
Colonial Service. A few M.P.s in the 1929 Parliament tried to get
him reinstated, but as Sir John Maffey, later Lord Rugby, Permanent
Under-Secretary of the Colonial Office, explained to me, it was
really impossible to reinstate an official who had so flagrantly dis-
obeyed orders and made a fool of his superiors even though he was
entirely in the right. Jack eventually got a job as a lecturer in anthro-
pology in Cambridge and was killed during the war on some Secret
Service mission in the Middle East. He was never happy, I think, as
a university don; he hated civilisation and his heart was always with
his tribal friends in Africa.

Early in the thirties, I found an escape in Essex. It was an old,
tumble-down pub. The village of Little Easton is about two miles
from Dunmow, then one of the quietest market towns in England.
No one was then talking about a landing-place for jet aeroplanes.
The cottage cost me £425 and a rather larger sum to be made
habitable by an old friend, an out-of-work builder. I did not expect
it to be much more than habitable because my notion of a country
cottage then was not a place where you lived in any kind of comfort,
but a retreat where you drew your own water, cut your own fire-
wood and enjoyed the sort of inconveniences that were not yours
in London. I had the house made rainproof, and although we had at
first to pump our own water from our own well, I soon got on to
the main. After a time, electricity took place of oil lamps, but the
brick floors remained. The bricks were often broken, so that they
wandered about in irregular patterns, difficult to scrub. Village
women, with whom we were on excellent terms, used to help. One
of them, when the bombs began to fall, told us in much excitement
that the 'Emperor of Chelmsford'—she meant the mayor—had been
killed. It was, you see, still a primitive village, though only forty

miles from London. An old man of ninety or so, who sat in the garden opposite, had never been any further distance than Dunmow and it was a great joke at the pub, where I used to play shove half-penny, that when he attended a funeral of an old crony, somebody asked 'And how old be you, George?' and when he said he was ninety, his questioner remarked 'Seems scarcely worth going home, does it?'

It was a picture-postcard of a cottage. It had fine, thick thatch which had to be repaired occasionally, once even in wartime. There were not many thatchers available. Only Bill Parsons round our way could do it. He was over seventy and had to be persuaded to take on the job. He looked as if he had been made of leather; he had a humorous way of screwing up his nose to let you know he was going to make a joke or pull your leg. He looked at you very slyly out of the corner of his eyes when money was under discussion. Once the bargain was struck, he thought of nothing except making the thatch do him credit. He listened to passers-by in the hope of hearing them say 'That's a fine bit of thatching. It must be Bill Parson's work. There, my lad, if you want to learn a skilled job, you go and watch Bill Parsons.' He was worth looking at. He wore knee-breeches of the old-fashioned kind with a fob in front and a pair of leather kneepads strapped round his legs when he was on the job. A red handkerchief was tied in front of his neck, with the ends taken off left and right and twisted round his braces on each side, brought to the middle again, knotted together finally somewhere over his solar plexus. He talked a choice Essex dialect.

You found him first thing in the morning, sitting on a little wooden bench cutting sprindles from hazel-rods. He used a heavy chopping-knife, first carefully splitting the rod from top to bottom, then paring it until he had left a thin white length of rod that he could turn with a single cunning twist of the wrist into a prong that, hammered down, served to keep the straw in place. Then, when he had his sprindles prepared, he turned over the straw that was waiting for use. 'Funny,' he said, 'you have to throw the straw about with a fork to get it straight. I only want the best, but you can't get straw like you used to.' 'Really,' I asked. 'Why not?' 'I don't know,' he replied, 'unless it's all these artificial manures they use now. The straw used to be big, thick stuff, not these odd little bits that break off short.' Then he threw water over the selected straw and piled it up on a special contraption for carrying the bundle of yelms up the ladder. This was a chain and a piece of wood; he could adjust the chain so that the straw was tight against the piece of wood. He climbed up the ladder and laid the bundle in place, getting it so tight that birds and rats and rain were for many years excluded. I went up the ladder to watch him at this point. 'Do you think you could do one just like it?' he asked, his face screwed up in a derisory grin that was all good humour and simple vanity. I shook my head, as well I might, as I saw him sitting astride the roof, knocking in the sprindles with his wooden mallet. 'A rare mess you'd make of it,' he assured me, pressing down the last yelm, 'mind you don't fall; I always say it's what you're used to. I don't take any more notice of working up here than you would walking on the ground.' He finished off the job with a big sharp knife which cut eyebrows over each window in a straight line with never a quaver in it all the way from the last ear to the top of the overhanging edge where the hollyhocks pushed their heads up into the straw above them.

The most enjoyable day to me was when Mr. Bridges, the builder, came over to do a repair job to the lean-to at the end of the cottage which had to be adjusted with Bill Parsons' thatching. All day, as they worked, the back-chat went on. Bridges had a small team of workers; he liked to go round with a carpenter, a mason, and an odd-job boy, and together the four of them would stick at the job till it was finished. 'Where do you want this pole to go, Parsons?' called Bridges, putting it deliberately in the wrong place so that we might all have a laugh at the unsuspecting Parsons. Parsons looked cautiously at the pole and then at us. 'No,' he said, 'there ain't room there for the gable to sit proper. Mine's a skilled job, you know.' He added, turning to me, 'They always have to ask me,' he said. And then he told a story of how a gentleman nearby watched him splitting sprindles. ' "That's a skilled job," he said to me. "Yes," I says. "Not like old bricklaying that anyone can do after trying a time or two." ' And the laugh was against Bridges. Uncovering the plaster, Bridges, who had a long experience of old houses, told me he would soon be able to tell me how old my cottage was. Yes, triumphantly he produced some curved bits of ancient bark, holding the laths in place. 'Osier peelings,' he said. 'The house must be four hundred years old and may be eight hundred, so they tell me. Why's that? Because they used the bark of osiers to tie the laths together before they had nails, and long after they had nails, too, if nails were expensive or difficult to get in the district. Probably six hundred years ago, it means, in this district.'

I had no particular interest in antiquities, though I admit it was rather fun to show people that in the old bar they had a hole in the door to let out the smoke and to persuade people to sit down on a primitive settle which was unexpectedly comfortable. A near neighbour was Pink Crittall, of metal-window fame. He gave me the doors and windows for a modern sitting-room which opened on to the garden. This was where we mostly lived.

The garden itself came out of a fairy story. In front of the house I planted a big hedge of Poulsen roses, whose scarlet shells stopped people gaping in the road. I planted a walnut-tree, which by now must dominate the village street. Leading up to the gate was a thick hedge of lavender and the back garden had a stream running through it which I diverted into a pool. It was usually smothered in yellow musk. You went down to it by a small brick path leading from a hollow wall in which all the alpines flourished, when we remembered to weed it. I cut down and stubbed out eight trees in my early energetic days, but left behind apples, particularly Bramleys and Coxs, delicious pears and a plum tree which always carried as much fruit as a tree can. The greengages were more spasmodic. The cottage garden flowers fought for space and at the back of the garden was a cornfield and below that a sluggish river on which water-lilies grew. If you crossed the bridge you were soon deep in bluebell woods, from which I transplanted wild anemones which you cannot often persuade to grow in gardens. There were giant kingcups, too, nearby, some of which I transplanted. The birds loved the garden; all the three kinds of woodpeckers, tree-creepers and fly-catchers kept one entertained.

The boss of the garden was not I, but Mr. Park, whose conversation provided me with many paragraphs for my London *Diary*. He had all the usual prejudices of a village gardener and much of the untaught wisdom that is usually attributed to peasants. He came to me originally because the lady he was working for wanted to use a chemical fertiliser. 'Very well,' said Mr. Park, putting away his spade in the toolshed, 'then you can look after the garden yourself.' During the war I, too, tactlessly suggested getting an artificial manure when it was hard to obtain the real stuff. He said, 'If you bring it into the garden, I'll throw it out. Poisoning the earth, that's all it is.' I used to dream of getting a bag of fertiliser and surreptitiously digging a little of it into the cabbage patch which he had made in the field next to mine. Would the fertilised cabbages do better than the others? But I never had the courage, for I was sure Mr. Park would find out.

Mr. Park, of course, hated birds and thought people like Lady Astor who wanted to protect them 'should never be allowed to have anything to do with government'. He was always saying that someone or other should be suppressed. If the clergy went Catholic they could have the Church to themselves. The Government ought to save fuel during the war by forbidding all electric light bulbs of more than twenty-five watts. The best light was a paraffin lamp. More than half the people who had to wear spectacles, said Mr. Park, had ruined their eyes by electric light. I asked him if this regulation would not necessitate a lot more of the bureaucrats and inspectors whom he so much detested. Shouldn't we be always filling up forms? When I picked up the *Daily* ——, I found exactly the same confusion. The Government was to order this or that and yet we were to have no bureaucrats. The confusion in Mr. Park's mind was exactly the same in Lord Blank's.

There is this to be said for lumbago—you are not the only one that's had it. Edging along like an aged, decrepit crab, you excite as much pity as ridicule. When I had it, Mr. Park, as usual, had his own remedy to offer. 'Oil of juniper is the best thing, six drops on a lump of sugar—if the Government will give you a lump. Lumbago is almost always kidneys and there's nothing like oil of juniper for kidneys. I had a lot of it in my time. If you're a private soldier they call it "pain in the back", when you're an N.C.O. you can have lumbago, in civvies you suffer from fibrositis, but an officer goes down with myalgia.'

Mr. Park took a poor view of sunshine in late October. He said, with positive indignation, that the frost had not been enough so far to kill any pests, and when I said that summer weather in autumn was nice, he said with emphasis, 'No, it's time to begin the winter now.' On one occasion, I remember, Mr. Park talked as if Essex was the Gobi Desert, protected by the Himalayas. He didn't think it would rain: 'Even when it rains elsewhere, it generally by-passes this village. There are only three ways a thunderstorm ever gets here. It can come up the Ongar valley . . .' and he outlined two alternative routes by which the storm could make its way through the mountain fastnesses of Essex. When the weather was appalling he said, 'It's seasonable, properly speaking. When I was a boy, we always had it regular as clockwork. The weather would break up near the end of February and we had three weeks, mostly sunshine. Then it would change suddenly and blow hard from the north-east. We called it the blackthorn winter. You would get a couple of inches of snow in an afternoon that would last until 28th March and the sun would come out and the snow would all be gone. That happened as regular as clockwork.' I learnt never to argue with Mr. Park.

He was very dogmatic about the moon. 'You saw that full moon last night?' he would inquire. 'Well, you know the old saying:

> "A Saturday moon and a Saturday change,
> Never comes out but that it rains." '

'Does that apply to any change of the moon?' I asked. 'Yes,' he said. 'That's the old saying and it's generally always right that if the moon changes on Saturday, that means rain.' When, on another Saturday, I wondered if it might be fine he answered at once, 'You know the old saying that the sun always comes out on Saturday.' 'Now, really,' I said, 'is Saturday never wet?' He seemed to hesitate a bit. 'Saturday's the old-fashioned Sabbath, isn't it? Anyway, I've always noticed, even when it's foggy or raining cats and dogs on a Saturday, the clouds will blow off just enough to let you see the sun some time in the day.' And on yet another occasion he said, 'You can always tell whether it will rain or not by the wind on Quarter Day. It doesn't shift much in the three months afterwards.' 'Well,' I replied, 'this beats St. Swithin's. Do you mean the wind always stays for the next three months where it happened to be on Lady Day, at Midsummer, Michaelmas and Christmas?' 'Ye-es,' said Mr. Park, 'from that direction or thereabouts.'

Mr. Park didn't hold much with science, but he was a wizard with bees, and would dig their stings out of his face with a pocket knife, saying they never stung him at all. He believed implicitly in the theory that you must 'tell the bees' if anyone died in the house. Should you fail to do this, all the bees would disappear in a few days and 'No one would see them go'. You had to take the key of the house and tap on each hive. Then the queen would come out and hover round for a minute and go back into the hive. If you said nothing, you would lose all your bees, as had happened to a friend of Mr. Park's when the master of the house had died. I pressed him for evidence. 'It's been proved times without number,' he said. 'What happens if you tell the bees that somebody's dead when it's not true? Were the bees deceived?' 'No,' he said, 'you could not deceive them like that.' He had not tried himself, but knew a man who had. Anyway, there was no doubt about it, 'It has been proved, times without number.' This is a good example of a widespread superstition. But Mr. Park had ingenious theories all of his own. 'It's everywhere alike,' he said, 'the scientists ought to leave off destroying everything with their inventions and do something useful. Look at this wind. It's mostly always due to allowing the windmills to decay. It stands to reason that the wind is now quite out of hand. What the scientists ought to be doing is to restart the windmills and build a great many more.'

Talking to Mr. Park, I had to remember that it is unwise ever to contradict assured experience. According to the story, the aged and

formidable Duke of Wellington once told the Mess that during the
Peninsular War his servant had opened a bottle of port and a rat had
jumped out. The awestruck silence was broken by a young officer,
more valiant than discreet. 'It must,' he murmured, 'have been a
very large bottle.' 'No,' said the Duke, 'it was a damned small
bottle.' 'Then,' said the trembling officer, 'no doubt it was a very
small rat?' 'It was a damned large rat,' roared the Duke, and I suppose the point has never been cleared up. Well, Mr. Park bore a
strong family resemblance to the Duke of Wellington and I was not
even annoyed when, forking over a bed, he said, 'What's the use of
scratching about the ground like an old hen?' But the conversation I
remember best was when he assured me that the petals of white
lupins, unlike others, always fall from the bottom as the others open.
When he illustrated this unrecorded fact by pointing to a white
lupin which was shedding its petals, I did not dare to risk any comparison with other coloured lupins at the same moment. But one
day I called his attention to an unusually fine white lupin in which
all the blossoms were perfect. Mr. Park replied that the lupin was
not white. 'But Mr. Park,' I said, 'why not?' 'Because,' he said, 'the
petals of white lupins always fall as they open.'

Where I had most disagreed with Mr. Park, whom I grew to love
dearly, was in his detestation of cats. Dorothy and I supplied the
village and surrounding neighbourhood with a particularly fine
strain of marmalade. A few of them could have been called smoky
because their grandmother was not always faithful to the orange
tom who lived opposite. On the whole, the strain was very pure and
it originated when a Chinese friend, named Hsiao Ch'en, who lived
in Hampstead, had to change his lodgings to an address where he
was unable to keep a cat to which he was much attached. We kept it
for him; he paid many visits to the cottage to see the original Smoky,
who had innumerable offspring. I grew much more attached to cats
than I had been to a Labrador dog which was mine earlier in life.
Their independence, combined with affection, I find more to my
taste than a dog's fawning obedience. As the litters went on, I found
increasing difficulty in finding homes for them, but it is a satisfaction
to me to know now that many descendants of the first Smoky sur-

vive. One cat we called Smudge became so intimately attached to
Dorothy that it travelled up and down to London by train clinging
close to her arm however crowded and alarming the journey was.
I remember the astonishment of fellow-travellers when the object
that they had taken for a fur wrap shifted its position. The finest of all
Smoky's offspring, who bore the honourable name of Winkles,
was I think something of a genius. At least, he accomplished various
feats which I have never known another cat to do. If you threw paper
balls over a three-foot dry wall that ran round part of the garden he
would leap over the wall exactly like a horse at a steeple-chase, bring
back the ball like a retriever and place it at your feet, waiting for
another throw. Unfortunately, Winkles, the first of several so
named, died suddenly of anaemia, which the vets, in those days at
any rate, said was an incurable disease in cats. I think nothing was so
important in finally driving us from Little Easton as the increase of
lorries dashing along our village street and leaving the dead bodies
of our three cats by the wayside.

One of them who died tragically deserves special commemora-
tion. I wrote an account of its career in the *Diary*:

Here is a true story. It might be called 'What's in a Name?' It
begins when we received as a present a small yellow kitten which
we believed to be female. It had a pretty little face, like a flower,
and we christened it accordingly. It settled down on the best of
terms with Smudge, playing happily with each batch of her
kittens. After some months it displayed incontrovertible signs of
being male. When it began to make clumsy advances to Smudge
(a tabby-cum-tortoise-shell with a white front) we had great hopes
of a basket of mixed orange and tortoiseshell kittens. Smudge was
tolerant of these adolescent attentions, but continued every two
months to produce a litter of tabbies, which were only too obviously the offspring of the undistinguished tom across the road.
We assumed that time would solve the problem, but it did not.
Young marmalade seemed willing to continue to dance attend-
ance without ever getting down to business. Unlike other young
toms, he never wandered, but devoted himself to Smudge and her

kitten with touching solicitude. Curled up in the same chair or on the same blanket, both washed the kitten and each other indiscriminately and continuously. The trio, mother, kitten and male nurse attendant lying in a single ball of harmony, offered an object lesson of selfless devotion.

This week a loathsome accident occurred. Smudge was killed by a passing motor-bus. The kitten was fortunately just old enough to lap and eat. The yellow tom looks after it as if he were its mother. With a maternal paw he holds it down and washes it from nose to tail, from top to bottom. Never one to venture abroad, he seems willing to cuddle the kitten and sing to it for as many of the twenty-four hours as it will stay still. I can see no male characteristics in this cat. He seems to be without lust, greed, jealousy or ambition. He is content to act as foster-father to the offspring of his first and only love—by another tom.

Re-reading this story, I see that I forgot the point. We acted in all innocence, believing the kitten to be female. We had no idea that we were doing it an irreparable injury, that we were putting ideas into its head, when we christened it Pansy.

I imagine that the reason why H. G. Wells lived in Little Easton was that the railway service was so meagre and that it was, in fact, in the twenties and thirties astonishingly remote, though so close to London. In *Mr. Britling sees it Through* the village is called Matching Easy. He had left Easton Glebe before I got there, but I learnt to know it well when my friends Paul and Mary Dixey lived there. It was almost unchanged since the days when Wells and his friends played hockey on the lawn almost within sight of our house. The great park, on the edge of which it stood, fell every week more deeply into decay because, I suppose, Daisy, Countess of Warwick, who lived there had failed to make all the money she wanted even by blackmailing (if one may use the word) the Royal Family. She had been in her day a famous beauty, the mistress of Edward VII, and villagers loved to show you the special summerhouse where she entertained Edward and to describe how she met him driving a four-in-hand at the specially constructed station a mile or so away.

I remember her as a gracious but not very intelligent old lady. She was a Socialist of a sort; the sort, as a friend put it, who is 'all heart, like a summer cabbage'.

One curious result of having a Socialist countess at Easton Lodge was that Socialist doctrine was heard in all the neighbouring pulpits. They were in her gift and sometimes she chose very unexpected parsons. One of them lived in a tiny village which could not supply him with a regular congregation. He kept a fiddle in his pulpit and when the congregation was small, which was usual, he would himself conduct the hymns. Occasionally a large party of Socialist youth would turn up and on these occasions he would ask Dorothy, though an unbeliever, to play the organ. Dorothy, as I have explained, knew the tune of every hymn in the Hymnal and she could always improvise an accompaniment. She had not the slightest idea of the Order of Service, so the vicar would cut out the relevant pages of the service book and paste them on to cards so that she could begin playing in the right place.

Having very few parish duties to perform, this musical vicar took up tobacco-growing. He insisted that British tobacco was as good or even better than any other, published pamphlets on the subject and was a very active propagandist amongst English pipe-smokers. His advocacy of British tobacco was, I fear, not much more successful in making converts than his Socialist sermons.

Far the most famous of Lady Warwick's appointments was that of Father Conrad Noel, who was vicar of the superb church at Thaxted. He preached with the authority of a Roman Catholic priest and taught a special brand of revolutionary Christianity which justified the use of force as well as much ritual and incense. He wrote books about Christ, whom he pictured as a man of violence, and I would from time to time go over to Thaxted and argue with him. In the chancel of his church there fluttered a number of beautifully designed heraldic flags which had more significance for him than for other people. In any case they were a compromise which he accepted after a long fight. The Ecclesiastical Court had forbidden him to decorate his church with the Red Flag of Communism or the Sinn Fein flag of Irish freedom. He survived triumphantly much local obloquy and many riots organised in his church by Cambridge under-graduates. In my day he drew large crowds of admirers; many of whom certainly disapproved of his Trotskyist views, but liked him personally. His High Church service appealed, I remember particu-larly to certain members of the Foreign Office. Undoubtedly some of the attraction of his services was aesthetic and I doubt if many people took seriously his political views. The whole performance was wonderfully Chestertonian with banners calling upon you to sing lustily, flowers in every corner of the church and splendid hangings which gave the whole church the atmosphere of a medieval festival. All Thaxted was a bit like that—a great place for weaving, antique furniture and folk-dancing in the village street.

Lady Warwick had become more interested in animals than in human beings. She kept monkeys in large cages near the house and would tell us what a nuisance it was to be compelled to go out in her nightdress on to the balcony to stop the monkeys if they insisted on fighting when she wanted to sleep. She would allow nothing to be killed, neither rats nor rabbits, and I have sat in her grand, if shabby, drawing-room and seen mice running up the curtains. The park was a paradise for rabbits and popular with the village labourers, who at that time received thirty shillings a week and enjoyed a rabbit stew for Sunday dinner. Swarms of rats ate up much of the corn in her granaries. Mr. Cranmer-Byng, the editor of the *Light of Asia* series of books, a near neighbour and good friend, told me more than once how he and Edward, Prince of Wales, enjoyed the sport of rat-killing in the barn. Once when they both were hot and excited and had just reached their three-hundredth victim, they were suddenly interrupted by the enraged Countess. Edward and Cranmer-Byng, abashed and stammering excuses, retreated to change for dinner.

We had interesting neighbours. They lived as neighbours should, within easy distance, but not so near that they were always dropping in. Harold Laski and John Strachey were both available for argu-ment, Michael Denison and Dulcie Gray and that excellent short-story writer A. E. Coppard were in the next village; so were the painter John Armstrong, the poet John Pudney and the journalist

and broadcaster, Lionel Hale. After the Spanish War Tom Wintringham came to live near us and during the Second World War
he was at last allowed to teach young soldiers guerrilla tactics at
Osterley Park. We astonished the neighbourhood with the people
who came to stay. The large cars of the Chinese and various other
Embassies looked odd in the village street, and when Paul Robeson,
at the height of his popularity, came into the pub for a drink he
started every tongue wagging. Paul's personality had had no parallel
in this country. Even the inhabitants of Little Easton knew him by
sight. He stands several inches over six foot in his socks and is one of
the strongest men I have ever met. Utterly devoted to his art and to
the cause of revolution, he was not then a Communist. He would
sing Negro spirituals and revolutionary songs and go on singing
them magnificently hour after hour to vast audiences which worshipped him and which were never tired of his voice. Personally, I
found his mind perpetually interesting. He was deeply thoughtful
about politics and about the prospects of down-trodden people
throughout the world. He was delighted at the discovery of a
natural similarity in primitive folk-music in every continent.

Two occasions I remember particularly. Once we discussed
pacifism. He could not understand my feeling about war; why
should I hesitate about physically fighting for causes in which I
believed? Suddenly he stopped and said, 'Oh, I see now. It must be a
matter not of reason but of feeling. You don't want to kill ordinary
people like yourself just as I would not know what to do if I suddenly
found myself called upon to fight Negroes.'

The other occasion was when he illustrated to me how he had
become one of America's leading footballers at college. He stood in
a corner of the room, all seventeen stone of him, with eyes bulging
from his head and an expression of the utmost ferocity on his face.
'I used to practise,' he said to me, while I was trying not to look
scared in the opposite corner of the room, 'I used to practise tackling
the other fellow at about this distance away. In one jump I would be
on them, like this. See, I used to lay them out completely.' He explained that he was naturally lazy and difficult to rouse. Then one
of the other men on his own side would give a sly kick on the shin

to enrage him. 'Of course, he's yellow, you know.' They would make sure that he heard them talking about him. That would make him mad and after that he could not remember just how many university players he had crippled in a single season.

The villagers couldn't believe that war would come to them. They looked at me anxiously. Nobody would drop bombs, surely, on a little village like this? And then the evacuation began and in that wonderful autumn weather the children arrived, each with gas-mask, bewildered, orderly, wondering where they had got to and where they would live. As it turned out, not many bombs were un-loaded on Little Easton. There were the odd few, just enough to stop the Home Guard repeating too often that 'All was quiet on the Easton front'. Mr. Park came out strong. Our vegetable patch was doubled and for quite a lot of the year we could almost live on our potatoes and greens and raspberries and apples. We usually managed to get enough petrol to drive only to Bishop's Stortford Station, ten miles away, carrying great bundles of vegetable produce with us. One year, all the greengage trees in the village carried a record crop; they hung in great bunches on the trees, ripe and luscious. A greengrocer said that he would pay fourpence a pound and rashly I told my neighbours that I could get a good price for them in London. I saved up the petrol and they all worked hard filling sacks of them and piled them into my car. They were too ripe. When I got to town, we unloaded them on to the pavement outside the greengrocer's, who looked at them with contempt. They had become so much jam. How we got rid of them I don't remember, except that we took the less squashed bags to a hospital. I returned to the village, and, lest my neighbours should think I was cheating them, paid then a pound or two. But some looked at me askance and perhaps never trusted me again.

There was the usual jealousy and backbiting, quarrels and petty rivalries in our village, but there was one occasion when unanimity was complete. The war was over and someone fetched an old piano from the pub smoking room and played us the familiar tunes which set everyone dancing. With what extraordinary vivacity did these respectable, often middle-aged or elderly women lift up their long skirts and dance 'Knees up, Mother Brown'! But it was not that which surprised me. The song that went over best, with much giggling from some and open laughter from others, was 'Roll me over, in the clover, roll me over, lay me down and do it again'.

After the war we began to elect our own parish councillors. Hitherto, five Very Important People, including the local chief farmer and landowner, probably someone from the manor and three others of unimpeachably correct status in the village selected themselves for the council and were accepted by a show of hands in the school hall. For the first time in 1949 the election was by ballot. Several village workers decided they would like a change. They did not see why our village should not even appear in plans for sewage development. When water and electricity passed through the main street of a village, why should it only be laid on to a few houses where people could afford to pay? They even talked about a club room and other amenities for the local youth. They asked me, as a kind of new broom, to challenge the five eminent citizens. No Socialist had ever before been on the council. I was severely told by the big-wigs that it was really very shocking to 'introduce politics into local government'. Conservatism, you see, was not party politics; Labour was. I gave a personal pledge that when the village council consisted entirely of anti-Conservatives, no party politics should ever again be allowed to enter into village life.

The incident had a curious sequel. I explained in the village hall that the ballot was secret and there was no reason why people should not vote against their employers if they wanted. As expected, the five landowners and gentry were elected; I got eighty votes, which, considering the feudal character of Little Easton, was considered a good proportion. It was two-fifths of the possible votes. I was glad that I was not elected because it would have been a confounded nuisance to make a monthly pilgrimage in order to speak up on behalf of William Hodge, whom I might think had a better claim to Ivy Cottage than some Londoner like me. The result of this highly important election was announced on the day when a visiting cricket team was playing on the village green, and it happened that one of the visitors was a journalist who worked for Lord Beaverbrook. To my astonishment, a paragraph appeared in the *Daily Express* saying that though Kingsley Martin, editor of the *New Statesman*, might possibly persuade some gullible people to listen to what he had to say in his paper, those who knew him well rated him at his true worthlessness. Though he had called into play all the resources of modern electioneering, he had been unable to persuade more than eighty people to vote for him. The paragraph did not mention that the total electorate of Little Easton was about two hundred. It appeared almost unchanged I think five times in one or other of the Beaverbrook newspapers. It was kept in cold storage and slipped in to fill an unbespoken space. After all, the *New Statesman* always said something that gave excuse for attack. Years afterwards, Christiansen, who had recently retired from editing the *Express*, asked me if I knew why Beaverbrook had given orders that this paragraph should be frequently inserted. I told him how one night during the war, when Beaverbrook was excluded from office, he had invited me to a suite in the Savoy and lectured me about the way in which Stafford Cripps and Ernest Bevin had managed to get him pushed out, to the great detriment of the war effort. After due consideration, I had written a *Diary* paragraph saying that though Beaverbrook had been invaluable in 1940, I thought it of great importance that he should not again be a member of the Cabinet. 'Ah,' said Christiansen, 'that would certainly be enough to explain those paragraphs.'

On the whole, the village had changed very little during the war. But inevitably our lane, which had led deliciously on to such lovely places as Bardfield and Finchingfield, began to be crowded. It became a busy route through from the new town of Harlow. I am not complaining of the new town; on the contrary I wish that there were more like it, but it had the effect of crowding the roads and all the approaches to it. Also, as I have said, our village became lethal to cats. The village itself changed more in a few months than it had done in several hundred years. Dirty paper and cigarette cartons blew all over our garden; new houses began to spring up, and we could no longer use the footpath to the woods. We held on for ten years

K

after the war until one sunny November day, staying at Rodmell near Lewes in Sussex, we suddenly bought an oddly shaped cottage on the top of the Downs. In 1932 I had published a strong paragraph written by Leonard Woolf denouncing the vandal who had been wicked enough to build a house so high on the Downs. All I can say in extenuation is that trees have grown up round it, that we have made a garden where none was before and that we selfishly enjoy one of the best views in England.

CHAPTER SIX

Three Remarkable Friends

THREE of my closest friends were most remarkable men. Indeed, you might call them strange if you did not find that almost every-body is strange when you get to know them well. The three men I am speaking of must have met frequently; they were all men of mark and one of them became a household name. But the more I knew them, the stranger they seemed, and in the case of at least two of them, the fonder of them I became. I must discuss them in a separate chapter because I have more to say about them than could be included in the passing narrative.

I doubt if any of the three much liked the others. Noel Brailsford, my closest journalistic companion, was so shy that I sometimes think I was his only intimate male friend. Anyway, he was not close to Cyril Joad, famous on the 'Brains Trust' and my companion in innumerable games of chess, and also a constant contributor to the paper. I always enjoyed Cyril's companionship, though I can't say I much respected him. The third, Harry Roberts, I admired and loved more than any other man. He would have scouted Joad as self-seek-ing and superficial.

Noel Brailsford had been editor of the *New Leader*, which had more to do with creating serious Socialists under his editorship than any other influence of the twenties. He was thrown out by a narrow-minded I.L.P. directorate, who thought the paper too highbrow and disliked, for instance, the admirable woodcuts of his friend, Clare Leighton. I think one reason why we became so intimate was that I simply took him for granted, admiring his integrity, his knowledge, experience and brilliant literary gift and, until late in our relations, never bothering about his domestic difficulties or psychological problems. His shyness—a word which needs analysis, but anyway denotes his intense personal reserve—was partly the result of his upbringing. His father, a Wesleyan preacher in different Scottish towns, had, perhaps because he was jealous of his son, only allowed

Noel to take up a scholarship at Glasgow University on condition
that he wore clothes which cut him off from the common herd. He
was to go to college in a specially designed brown broadcloth suit,
with knee-breeches and an Eton collar; he was made to swear not to
shave in days when adolescent boys did not wear beards. Noel
revolted against this preposterous ruling after some six weeks and
had a bitter row with his father when he repudiated his promise not
to shave. Nor did he ever forgive his mother, who sided with her
husband when her son was struggling for independence. It is some
measure of the depth of his anger and humiliation that, though he
visited his mother regularly until her death in her one hundredth
year, he never got to know his sister, who devoted her life to caring
for their mother. She is an exceptionally able woman, now in her
nineties, who has written several historical books, including the best
existing study of the Wesleys.[1] When, in his late seventies, he
developed a serious heart condition and lived in his sister's home, I
one day called on him and had a quarter of an hour's conversation
with his sister before going into his room. I remarked that he had
never told me before what an interesting sister he had. He looked
surprised, having never until that time taken much notice of her
existence. Owing to this casual remark of mine, he began to talk to
her, and in the last three years of his life showed her all the chapters
of the book he was writing and lived with her on the closest and
happiest of terms. She had worshipped him all her life. He waited
until she was seventy-seven and he was eighty-two before they
achieved any companionship.

In the nineties at Glasgow University he was one of a group of
friends, including John Buchan; the whole group seems to have been
in love, more or less fervently, with a capricious and unreliable
beauty. Noel was the most persistent and carried her off, mainly, it
seems, because she wished to escape her admirers and go to Crete
with Noel, where he acted as correspondent for the *Manchester
Guardian*. C. P. Scott had been much impressed with Noel's first
book, *The Broom of the War God*, in which he described his own
experiences in the Greek war of 1897. Noel once told me that she

1. Mabel Brailsford, *Two Brothers*.

treated him with something like contempt. How far this explains the strangeness of his relations with women later I do not know, but he was happy in his friendship with Clare Leighton, and the last part of his life, when he was otherwise lonely and disconsolate, was enlivened by his marriage to the daughter of a German doctor. He tended to treat women with an old-world courtesy, which I thought hid an embarrassed disdain for most of them. This did not prevent his becoming a leader in the Women's Suffrage movement, and he told me how one day he was assured by Lloyd George that the Government was about to make an important concession in a public speech he was making next day. Noel attended the meeting in some excitement; Lloyd George said exactly the opposite to what he had promised. When Noel remonstrated, Ll.G. said, 'Oh, I was watching the audience and saw they would not approve, and so, of course, I had to change the nature of my speech.'

Noel had worked for the *Manchester Guardian*, the *Daily Chronicle* and the *Nation* in many parts of the world. I doubt if he ever made more than £1,000 in a year, except in one lecture tour in the United States. He had had an adventurous life and could tell the most revealing stories about King Boris of Bulgaria and of his experiences in the Balkans, where he had served on a mission to enquire into the atrocities which all the belligerents, no doubt truthfully, attributed to each other in the Balkan War of 1912. He described meeting Marshal Pilsudski, dictator of Poland, who at once became friendly when Noel admitted that he had served as a soldier as well as a journalist. He had written about the bitter 'troubles' of Ireland and had taken part in the long struggle for Indian independence. In India his friendship and his books championing independence are still widely remembered; there was an outburst of applause in Delhi when I mentioned his name in a public lecture in the late fifties. One of his most interesting memories was of his meeting with Lenin in 1902, when a group of Russian revolutionaries were stranded in London for lack of the return fare to Moscow. Noel persuaded a rich Englishman to pay their fares and recalled that the Bolsheviks honourably repaid their debt in 1919 after they came to power. He learnt Russian and stayed in a Soviet village in the early days of the Revolution. Though, as usual, he was over-optimistic and was later accused by the Communists of every bourgeois vice, including Trotskyism, his book on the Soviet village remains one of the few historically valuable accounts of village life in the early days of the Bolshevik revolution.

In his books he seldom allowed himself reminiscences, but I have never forgotten his description of a victorious battlefield in Thessaly, where he realised that the dead Turk at his feet might have been his friend. A few of his books achieved success. His *Shelley, Godwin and their Circle* and his *Voltaire* are minor classics; his *War of Steel and Gold*, published at the beginning of the First World War, was one of the seminal books of the century, and his *League of Nations*, which appeared in the middle of the war, was one of the books which, with Leonard Woolf's *International Government*, inspired Woodrow Wilson to advocate the one constructive idea that came out of the war. Noel's love of Germany, where he had been a student as a young man, made him a vehement critic of the Versailles settlement, but did not prevent his being an uncompromising fighter in the struggle against Hitler and a champion of the Republican cause in Spain. Some of his articles against Fascism might be reprinted today. I recall an article about Mussolini, whom he called 'a knight clad in shining blackmail'—a remark commonly afterwards attributed to Winston Churchill.

Noel never got over his assumption that he must be aloof and un-popular. Perhaps this was one reason for his special affection for cats, over whom he had an inexplicable influence. When he was working for the *Guardian*, he had a cat which waited in a crowded Manchester street every day so that it could accompany him during the last part of his journey home. One day, I witnessed this influence for myself. I asked Noel to summon a stray cat that was walking in the opposite direction some fifty yards away. He said nothing, but the cat turned round, walked back to him and rubbed against his legs. Outside public affairs, his chief passion was music. In this field, as in so many others, he was deeply learned and his friends never thought of a better way of pleasing him than when they presented him with an up-to-date gramophone in place of his ancient E.M.G. with its enormous horn.

Noel spent the last years of his life in bed, with a failing heart. He was writing a long book on the Levellers, for which he had done the initial research in the British Museum. He did not live long enough to complete it; Christopher Hill edited it and it was published after his death. He wrote in bed, surrounded by seventeenth-century pamphlets and source-books. When I saw him a few days before his death he was wondering whether he could finish his book. Though he would never admit it, I thought I saw in his eyes the knowledge that the necessary strength was leaving him. I came away, wishing there was some way of letting the world know how great a man it had forgotten; how whimsical and full of fun and unexpected knowledge he was; how brave and great-hearted his life had been, and how much love and disinterested work he had achieved in return for so little recognition.

My relations with C. E. M. Joad were very different. The first thing I remember his saying was that his job, like that of Socrates, was to corrupt youth. By that he meant that he would show by his writing and example that the Victorians were wrong and that Bernard Shaw and Bertrand Russell (his twin heroes in those days) were right. He often annoyed them both by too obviously imitating them. He spoke with the authority of pre-war Balliol to young men and women who went to universities after 1919. At that time the gap between those who had known the war and those who were too young to have been in it seemed immense. We were on holiday in the Lake District, climbing all day and endlessly arguing. Joad's exuberance was contagious. He was the jolliest and most candid of hedonists, and there was nothing bad about himself about which he did not confess—or should I say boast?—in one or other of his books. In the twenties he was thrown out of a Fabian Summer School by a puritanical manager who objected to his habit of every night seeking out the prettiest girl he could find and, if possible, seducing her. He minded very little, since the choice was large and the Fabian Society was by no means the only organisation which had Summer Schools where he could display both his intellectual brilliance and his virility.

Cyril was not, I think, a great philosopher, but he was a most readable and clear-headed populariser of both philosophy and science. His swiftness of mind and clarity in explaining difficult ideas later made him one of the most famous men in England as a Brains-Truster with Julian Huxley, with Commander Campbell and W. J. Brown. For some reason he is remembered as the man who always began his answers by saying, 'It depends what you mean by . . .' Every philosopher begins by telling a questioner to define his terms. He was, in fact, extraordinarily good on the 'Brains Trust', on which I was often lucky enough to be a guest member. He answered, for instance, a difficult question like 'What is love?' in so neat and perfect a package form that the next member of the 'Brains Trust' found it hard to follow or controvert him. There were no loose ends to pick up, no untidy phrases left for controversy. It was hard to follow Joad without being a bore and starting the whole discussion again.

Up to 1930 he was a Civil Servant, but mainly interested in writing books on philosophy and science. He admitted to having taken an unconscionable amount of leave to write them. His most revealing weakness was his fear of being alone. In one newspaper article he explained that this fear led him to pack every day with organised activity from early morning to late at night. At nine o'clock each morning he played the pianola, which he believed responded to his skilful touch. He required frequent exercise and, if possible, every day good conversation with young people—he was an admirable teacher—between luncheon and dinner. He preferred to lunch with someone distinguished. He admitted that his greatest fault was gluttony and was much troubled by the rotundity of his figure. After dinner he wanted bridge or chess and I recall an occasion when he was really angry with me when I returned tired near midnight and refused to enjoy a final hour of chess. At least once a week he insisted on listening to serious music, to which, in spite of the pianola, he was genuinely devoted. For many years he always played vigorous and good tennis on Saturdays and hockey (he had been a Blue and maybe an international?) on Hampstead Heath with a mixed team of students and friends. This was incredibly strenuous, for there were usually only about seven a side and

Cyril went on playing centre-half until he was well over fifty. He once imparted to me, as though confessing a secret vice, that he really and truly loved hunting. In the days when I knew him best he would go to the country and ride the toughest horse he could find. He had one or two bad falls. He needed, in one way or another, continuous reassurance of his own virility.

Love affairs, of course, were among his constant activities and he made no secret of them. His friends often compared him to a faun. His stiff, bristly beard and bright roving eyes suggested an immense physical vitality and insatiable appetite. He made no secret of his success with women and said he was not interested in talking to any woman who wouldn't go to bed with him. He found a surprising number who would. In one of his books he described how, as a young man, when he was fiercely anxious to work, sex buzzed round the room like a bluebottle. When he found the distraction too great, which was often, he arranged a weekend with a young woman of whom he was almost invariably tired after a day or two. In his own disgusting phrase he wrote that 'when the bluebottle was swotted' he would arrange for a telegram to come from the office summoning him home.

One who knew Joad all his life remarked to me that he always disapproved of Cyril when he was away from him, but found himself greatly liking him when they met. This was true of me and, I expect, of many people. His egotism was forgotten when talk began. You only laughed when you were told that at a Summer School where he was sharing a room with a friend, he threw his rucksack on the bed, put his hand on the sheets and said, quite seriously to his companion, 'By the way, do you mind changing beds with me, I think these sheets are rather damp?' Such stories gathered round him and were only subjects for jest. He was so disarmingly frank. He wrote, for instance, naively assuming that none of his friends would think it applied to them, that when he had asked people to dinner he soon became bored with them and desired them out of the way. But, of course, that never applied to any particular friend. The truth was that he had the charm that belongs to a perfect digestion and a never-failing appetite for life.

After we had been bombed out a couple of times Dorothy and I took refuge in an empty part of his house in Hampstead. On the second night after our arrival—he had been away the first night—the air-raid warden made a fuss about Joad's very inadequate blackout. The light from downstairs showed through the upper windows and had to be suppressed. Joad, in some annoyance, said, 'It really is bad luck for me that this should happen the first night I am back. If it had been last night you would have had to look after it.' I could tell many such anecdotes about Cyril, but the odd thing was that I went on enjoying his companionship; I was fond of him and his intense vitality was contagious. I always wanted to be with him again.

Cyril's last days were sad. He lost his job on the B.B.C. and suffered greatly in reputation when he was convicted of travelling without a ticket. I asked General Slim, who was then Deputy Chairman of British Railways, if it had been necessary to prosecute. He said he had done so with great reluctance and would not have destroyed a man's reputation for a single offence. But the railway authorities had convinced him that Joad made a habit of defrauding them and that he had no alternative but to make an example of him. The fact was that Cyril enjoyed the game of tricking the railway company; he was not only trying to save money. In one of his books he cites this habit to illustrate a principle of ethics. If an individual defeats the law, he says, by not paying for his ticket, no harm is done; it would, however, be unethical because if everybody evaded the law the railways would be bankrupt. He never recovered from this blow to his reputation. He died painfully from a cancer which he refused to acknowledge. One day he described to me his illness; would I advise him? He had already changed his doctor more than once, should he try a Swiss doctor? To me and everyone else it was obvious that no medical care would prolong his life. I advised him to assume that he only had a year to live and to get any book he hadn't finished off his mind and to make up any friendship which he had neglected, and, if it proved that he would live longer, anyway, no harm would be done.

The last time I saw him, shortly before his death, he was very ill, but played his usual game of chess with every sign of enjoyment. Some time before this he had written to declare his belief, if not in Christianity, at any rate in God. He told me jokingly one day that God was the Coming Man. Many years before I had heard a lecture announced as 'Joad on God'; one of his audience remarked that they would have preferred hearing God on Joad. He decided at last to take God seriously and he collected round himself a group of friends with whom he shared the Communion Service. He repented, he said, not so much the sins of the flesh he had committed, but he deeply regretted occasions on which he had been unkind. He confided to me that he did not really believe the doctrines which he was supposed to hold, but he found great comfort in the experience of communion together with people of whom he was fond. I was always critical of Cyril, but I could always tell him so without loss of friendship and I greatly missed him when he died.

These two friends were working companions whom I constantly saw in London. The third friend, Dr. Harry Roberts, I mainly saw in the country. His home in Hampshire was the only place which I regularly visited when I was not at the cottage. I did not, as a good editor no doubt should, spend my weekends in the houses of the great, learning at these centres of English thought the real lowdown of British politics. I very seldom spent a weekend at All Souls, where the politics of appeasement were effectively hatched. I once paid a visit to Lord Lothian in his enormous palace at Blickling Hall in Norfolk, the very stateliest of British homes.[1] My host, Lord Lothian, was so welcoming that I did not feel out of place, even if my clothes were not what the valet assigned to me would have expected. Lord Lothian had a clear, unexpected and strangely in-

1. Other guests that weekend included Tom Jones and Norman Davis, America's roving Ambassador. Tom Jones recalls the following conversation about him with Stanley Baldwin. (*A Diary with Letters, 1931–1950.*)

'T.J.: I had an hour and a quarter at Claridges with Norman Davis the day before he sailed, but all it amounted to was that our two Admiralties should consult together before the next London Conference. He took seventy-five minutes to say what most of us could put in five minutes.

'S.B.: He's just a peripatetic windbag, without authority, getting into the way of busy men. I managed to keep him away.'

coherent mind. When he came back from Russia, which he visited
with Bernard Shaw and the Astors, he was an enthusiast for the
Soviet Union. He changed his opinions too easily and too fast. He
always hoped that his own good will would conjure away the
illusion of evil in others. Perhaps it was his Christian Science (plus
some guilty conscience about Versailles, where he had been Lloyd
George's secretary) that made him believe that Hitler could be easily
appeased. He was blindly credulous about the Nazis. I have a note of
a lunch with him two days after the German seizure of Vienna. He
arrived in the best of spirits. While the rest of us were picturing the
fate of Jews and Socialists in Austria and discussing whether Hitler
had begun the conquest of Europe envisaged in *Mein Kampf*, Lothian
held that things had taken a turn for the better now that the Treaty
of Versailles had been wiped out; perhaps Hitler would be satisfied
and rejoin the League of Nations. I tried an enfilading attack and
suggested that Hitler's aeroplanes were not only meant for Guernica
and that the aggression in Spain would be followed by other interventions. A few days later Lothian made a speech which included a
strong passage emphasising the danger of Fascist aggression in Spain
and urging the need of maintaining its independence.

Lothian had good brains, a well-developed social conscience and
an open—a too-open—mind. He had the natural optimism that so
well suits the English gentleman and aristocrat. Given a little goodwill and tact, the right influences and friends, a readiness to hear the
other fellow's point of view and all would be well between Capital
and Labour, the Chinese and the Japanese, Germany and England.
His final speech as Ambassador in the United States dealt with the
one cause about which he was always consistent; friendship with the
U.S.A. He died unnecessarily young, I believe, because as a Christian
Scientist he refused medical help.

In this belief he was at one with Lady Astor. I remember calling
at her house for lunch. She arrived rather late and at once sat down
and said, 'For ten miles in the car I have been trying to purge my
mind of all malice and uncharitableness. Have I succeeded for ten
minutes? No. For one minute? No. It's all human nature.' All my
recollections of her are essentially comic. When she returned from

the Soviet Union with Lothian and G.B.S. and her husband, G.B.S. described a meeting between her and Lunacharsky. 'It was like this,' said G.B.S., waving a long index finger before my eyes, 'She said, "Now, Minister, do you not really wish you had not made that revolution?"' Lunacharsky's reply is not recorded; it should have been, 'Madam, I didn't make the revolution, the revolution made me.' On the day after Hitler invaded Czechoslovakia, Lady Astor gave a big lunch in St. James's Square. Garvin and other established appeasers had made a *volte face* and were demanding that we should at once declare war on Germany. The guest of honour was Maisky, the Soviet Ambassador. As he left the room after lunch, Lady Astor said, 'Of course I hate the Russians, but I've got to be nice to that little man because he may become our ally in the war.' This seemed very odd to me. If she was abruptly changing sides, surely she ought not to have announced to some forty guests that she was insincere in doing so? On another occasion which I recorded in my private diary, she came up to me in public and hit me in the chest with her fist because of some sin she thought I had committed in the *N. S. & N.* Her agreeable but always helpless husband, Waldorf, was excessively embarrassed. No doubt that was often the case. Perhaps it was just inverted snobbery that prevented my accepting an invitation to Cliveden to meet Edward, then still Prince of Wales.

But to return to my less-exalted weekends. When I was not in my own cottage I often used to stay with Harry Roberts at the house he had constructed in the woods of Oakshott Hanger, near Petersfield in Hampshire. He was a tough Cornishman with a broken nose, the result of his championship of a suffragette at a meeting where she was constantly interrupted by an enormous brewer's drayman. Harry described the occasion something like this. 'He wouldn't be quiet, so I decided to do something about it. I must have known what was coming to me, because I found afterwards I had taken off my glasses before I hit him. When I got up from the ground, my face streaming with blood, I pretended there was nothing the matter and swaggered away with much dignity and my handkerchief over my face.'

In his young days Harry had been a student at, I think, St. Mary's

Hospital, where he had studied under a famous surgeon who, working in the days before Pasteur was accepted, used to operate in a
frock-coat which was so stiff with blood that it would stand up by
itself. He would say, 'Any more operations before I wash my
hands?' Harry had begun practice in a remote district of Cornwall
where the only methods of transport were on horseback or foot. In
London he went to the early Fabian lectures, became friends with
Bernard Shaw and other reformers and Socialists in the last decade of
the nineteenth century. He knew H. G. Wells when he was an
emaciated lad studying at Kensington and enjoyed a meal with him
on half a scone, a pat of butter and a cup of coffee at an A.B.C. tea-
shop. He never felt like G.B.S., who said that his only interest in the
poor was to abolish them. He didn't want things tidy; he enjoyed all
the racy muddle of life, and politically was like a modern Cobbett.

He began his first London practice in Stepney among very poor
people. In those days the custom was for a pregnant woman to
present the doctor with ten shillings, which entitled her to visit him,
if necessary, during her pregnancy and to summon him for her
delivery. The doctor was an immensely important and dignified
person whom the poor were not accustomed to thinking of as one
of themselves. Winifred Stamp, who lived for many years as his
wife and died soon after him, explained, in a short book she wrote
about him after his death in 1946,[1] the beginning of his immense
popularity. On the first occasion after delivering a child, Harry
made the mother a cup of tea. This made a profound impression and
the name of the new kind of doctor spread throughout the neighbourhood. On another occasion, he found a woman in the last stages
of labour cooking kippers over an open fire. When he insisted that
she must lie down she protested that she had never yet failed to have
her husband's supper ready for him when he came in. Half an hour
later Harry had solved the problem; he presented the father with a
baby in one hand and kippers in the other.

In those days it was comparatively easy to acquire country
property cheap and Harry managed to purchase a stretch of Hampshire woodlands for £10 an acre. He built himself a house in a

1. Winifred Stamp, *Doctor Himself* (Hamish Hamilton, 1949).

clearing three hundred steps below the road and otherwise un-approachable. The main purpose was to provide huts where tuber-cular and other patients from the East End could recuperate. They were dotted amongst the woods: I spent many happy weekends in one of them. The house itself was a jolly wooden affair with no water except from the rain, which Harry filtered for domestic use. It was lit with oil lamps and consisted mainly of two huge rooms, one of which was Harry's bedroom, with small bedrooms for guests. The downstairs room where we had our meals and talked was comfortably furnished and Winifred, who slept in it, saw that it was free of litter. In the course of years this house became the centre of what I can best describe as a community, though it had none of the characteristics usually associated with this word. Harry was able in time to buy a shop in the centre of Petersfield where one member of his team did fine work in jewellery, another was an admirable portrait painter and a third looked after the stock, which largely consisted of books. Nothing could prevent Harry buying books and he could always supply the shop from his own house if it ran short. In his house they were stacked from floor to ceiling, apparently promiscuously, though he seemed always able at a moment's notice to provide you with the best book on any subject you could suggest. A number of close friends used frequently to go down for the week-end, eat sumptuously, walk in his woods and argue with him at nights. Everything in the house except what he made or grew him-self he had carried down the three hundred steps on his shoulders.

There was always an argument going on, salty and serious, until about midnight when Harry would turn to one of the women round him and say, 'Who's going to take down an article tonight?' In the days I knew him best he was writing five articles a week. They were admirable accounts of life in the East End or articles explaining in popular but accurate phraseology some aspect of medical science. He also reviewed books on such varied subjects as crime and punish-ment, piracy and gardening for *The Times* and the *Times Literary Supplement*, wrote regularly for the *Spectator* and even more often for the *New Statesman*. He was our medical correspondent, and his arti-cles about doctoring always included a vivid side-light on some aspect

of poverty in the East End. He used to say that he had to be dead
sober when he contributed to the *N.S.*, but liked to be a little drunk
when he wrote his two popular syndicated articles which appeared
in many local papers. He called them 'hogwash', but in fact they
were nothing of the kind; they were simple, sensible pieces, designed
to rectify common errors about health and stop people buying
dubious patent medicines. I notice in one letter he says, 'I took up
drinking again three weeks ago. Abstinence showed no results.' He
was that rare kind of man who can drink rather heavily for a time
and then by act of will give it up and return to a life where you just
have a drink before dinner. He wrote when the war was starting,
'After 1939, I am going to turn over a new leaf and start again at
thirty-five. I've done it once or twice before and I think I can do it
once more.'

After we had gone to bed on one of these Saturday nights he
would dictate an article for a couple of hours and then go into the
pantry, help himself to a large plateful of cold meat and potatoes,
draw himself a pint of bitter and take it up to bed with him. At 7.30
in the morning he would wake the household with cups of tea,
having already done an hour or two's digging in the garden. The
garden was made of chalk mixed with the manure which Harry
saved from the household, and Harry made a paradise of it. There
was always plenty of vegetables and flowers and I don't think he had
much help. He wrote about a dozen books about gardening, as well
as innumerable useful works about medicine and kindred subjects.
In one letter he described his life like this: 'I am just doing my usual
round of doctoring, digging, emptying the dub-pail, popularising
philosophy and science and talking through my hat.'

Harry was a completely unconventional man. He was never
Bohemian, for Bohemianism is by its nature wasteful of time and
effort. He was, on the contrary, practical and full of common sense.
He once stood for Parliament, but decided that he really couldn't
bear the Labour Party. He wrote to me towards the end of his life,
during the war, that I must have a talk with him about all this:

'You'll find that, though a little critical of some bits of my earlier sentimentality (as all of us ought to be as we get older), I am far from being a reactionary, property-loving Tory. I have known no one less than I who wants to regulate other peoples' affairs for my own material gain. That, I think, has been an eccentricity of mine all my life—that I have never been able to give orders.'

Property-loving! Oakshott was never locked up, and sometimes casually inhabited by uninvited guests, not because it was unconventional to leave it open, but because it was convenient for other people to be able to go in and help themselves if none of the family was there. He was so practical and so fond of people that he could easily have committed a murder (he may have done so for all I know), provided that he felt sure that it would make people happier, cause no particular suffering to the victim and that he was unlikely to be found out.

I suppose Harry's secret was his overflow of affection and vitality. He was devoted to his friends, almost you could say he fell in love with them, but was not lacking in the other kind of love, for the other sex. When he was about seventy he fell head over heels in love with a girl in her twenties. I shall not forget my astonishment when I saw them together, sitting in the big room of their house, with Winifred and all the rest of the guests and family milling round them. They were completely absorbed in each other and reading Shelley or Wordsworth—I don't know which—to each other.

When I last saw Harry his heart had finally given way. His neighbour, Lord Horder, popped in regularly, partly to discuss such matters as a joint book about the ethics of Jesus Christ and about the progress of the less-obvious plants in their gardens, and partly, as by an after-thought, to take soundings of Harry's cardiac murmur. Climbing three hundred steps from his home, carrying every article of food and drink on his back for thirty years, daily digging in the garden and doing several men's work as a doctor had not, apparently, tired him. But when he was just turned seventy he was bowled over by the destruction of the great achievement of his life.

He had created, in the days before the First World War when such things were not heard of, a prototype health centre, the type of

L

clinic in which you may be examined for your heart or lungs, for
your head or your rheumatism by a different doctor in a different
office.[1]

I have here a letter from Harry dated 23rd March 1941, just after
the two final raids in the first Blitz:

'Just at the moment, I am not in very good fettle for writing
crisp articles; nor have I very much time on hand. I am down here
for the day, and am trying to clear up as much as I can. You see,
when I went up on Thursday morning, I found all my five houses
in Harford Street reduced to a heap of rubble by a high explosive
that happened to drop there on Wednesday night. I've been building up our rather elaborate clinic for thirty-five years; and it was
reckoned rather an illustration of what could be done in a slum
district. It was equipped with everything necessary for all the work
that can rightly be done outside hospital—dentistry, gynaecology,
minor operations and all the rest of it. The Ministry of Health
used to send American investigators to see our show in Harford
Street, as illustrating what could be done under the Health Insurance Act. You will, I am sure, understand that it's a little bit
depressing. Materially, not only the houses, which had all been all
knocked together and adapted to the several purposes, but also all
apparatus, instruments, every kind of drug and quite a lot of rather
valuable furniture and equipment are just dust and ashes. Unfortunately, the material loss—very great as it is, measured by my
standard—isn't the worst of it. I have spent the whole of two days
this week trying to find a possible house or other building in
which I could temporarily carry on in the hope of gradual reconstruction of something like the thing I had built out of rather
unpromising materials. In the whole district, there isn't a possible
building to be had with a roof on it, and its wall uncracked. Still,
luckily, the young men staffing the organisation known as the
Pacifist Service Unit had just secured the Vicarage attached to a

1. It is largely due to the failure to set up such clinics or health centres, envisaged for general use by the Beveridge Report of 1944, that the National Health
Service has reached its present crisis.

bombed church. And they put at my disposal two large rooms, which enabled me, without any break, to carry on at any rate in a sort of skeleton form (never mind about the metaphors). My London address for the present, therefore, is The Vicarage, East Arbour Street, E.1. It is well-situated—being next door to such a locally well-known landmark as The Thames Police Court, Arbour Police Station. I am not yet on the telephone. But why don't you run down there on Monday morning and take a twenty minutes' stroll round the district with me; and then have a bite of what we can get in a pub? Anyway, I shall be up and down at least ever other day this week and, if I can possibly fit it in, I'll run up to the office in the hope of catching you. But if you love drama, this is the place to see it. Of course, it's a silent drama.

'Quite apart from myself and my concerns and personal interests, I find it very hard to be optimistic about the immediate future. I hope my judgment is wrong. I should be more optimistic if my previous anticipations had been negatived by events. Do let us keep in touch with one another while we can.'

When I last saw Harry he was in bed in his study-bedroom, a big raftered room in which all his immediate activities were centred. He was surrounded by bookshelves containing thousands of works of reference on special subjects, particularly medicine, scientific philosophy, criminology, penology and vagabondage. The books overflowed in great stacks from floor to ceiling. There was an old-fashioned, big E.M.G. gramophone and a library of records. There were shelves for medicines and, on some free space of the floor, sheets of brown paper on which were drying various herbs and rose petals which he was turning into *pot pourri*. By his bedside were sweets for him to suck in the night and a pile of books which he had selected for that night's reading. There were also pills and medicines for use in emergency. He had taken his teeth out and was obviously tickled by the odd picture he presented. He pointed, chuckling, to all the different objects he had collected for his comfort and amusement. He knew that he was quite likely to die in the night and that I knew it, too. His eyebrows went up high and he shrugged his shoulders in the characteristic gesture. His look and his laugh said, 'Yes, it's all very odd. Here I am doing just what I wanted to do, as always. Tomorrow I may be dead, in the meantime I'm allowing no scrap of life to go past unused and unenjoyed.'

CHAPTER SEVEN

The Fight Against Fascism

NOTHING is so characteristic of England as the small, independent, usually bankrupt society which sets out to look after one or other of our liberties or to champion some great cause. In the thirties, many such societies joined together in a Federation of Progressive Societies. Their chairman was C. E. M. Joad, who was never so happy as in the centre of a group of young admirers, especially girls. They met together in Summer Schools to assert their rights as ramblers, to climb mountains, to demand easier divorce and the reform of the homosexual and abortion laws. They included nudist and other nature cults and they demanded the right to libel people they didn't like. Some of these societies still exist and they are not to be despised. Public opinion about our antique sexual legislation, for instance, would have been less advanced than it is today if they had not been agitating for the last thirty years. Any success they had was usually due to an energetic, devoted and not-too-democratically minded Hon. Sec. I never joined the Federation, but I used sometimes to mention its activities in my *Diary* and I suspect most of its members read the *New Statesman and Nation*.

Any member of any of these societies would have told you in those days that she or he were fighting against Fascism. It was a loosely used word. The common social analysis at that time was that Britain was a Capitalist Democracy which we wanted to turn into a Socialist Democracy. That really meant a welfare state. By Fascism, we might merely mean that as more and more people became Socialists, Capitalists would become increasingly afraid for their property and find a way of destroying our civil liberties. Or again we might mean that there was a risk of Britain falling under the rule of Blackshirts controlled by Mosley or some British imitator of Mussolini or Hitler. This was not a foolish fear in the mid-thirties; the danger only disappeared after British Fascists were forbidden to wear uniforms. Like Germany, we had millions of unemployed and dissatisfied people who wanted a leader. The Fascists were making provocative marches and shouting anti-Jewish slogans in order to exploit violent resistance. The middle class in England, as in Germany, was apathetic about these danger signals and British foreign policy was to make Mussolini into an ally and to avoid saying anything to annoy Hitler. *The Times* censored every anti-Nazi despatch from their correspondents in Berlin; Norman Ebbutt was the outstanding example of a brilliant journalist who lost his job because he told the truth. The Rothermere press for a period actively and, indeed, vociferously, supported Mosley and the Beaverbrook press pretended there was no danger of war. In my private diary in May 1934, I noted a conversation with a colleague who expected a Fascist revolution or at any rate a period in which 'all the old things are stirred around, like the ingredients of a pudding, until nothing one has liked individually will be left'. He talked about 'machine-guns and revolution before long'. I scouted all that because traditional British Liberalism was still strong and I doubted whether the *Daily Mail* was all that powerful. But I thought the Labour movement was absurdly complacent about the gathering strength of the Blackshirts.

When the horror of war was imminent peace societies increasingly included the whole spectrum from the purely Liberal or non-political organisations which passed pious anti-war resolutions, to bodies in which Communists co-operated with Liberals and sometimes with Tories. The International Peace Campaign which flourished for a short time before the war was a Popular Front organisation which was led by Lord Robert Cecil, who worked with a Communist like J. D. Bernal because they both hoped to revive the League of Nations and become allies of Russia. Lord Robert, holding the moneybags, knew that he was managing the Communists; the Communists hoped to increase middle-class support for the Soviet Union.

Margaret Gardiner, who was a member of this I.P.C. executive, recalls a story which illustrates the problems of this strange alliance. How formulate resolutions which all the Popular Front would accept? One day she said to Lord Robert, 'But isn't that resolution rather ambiguous?' to which he replied, 'My dear, when you have had as much experience as a lawyer as I have had, you will know the advantages of ambiguity.'

Margaret was also the secretary of an organisation founded in 1936 called 'For Intellectual Liberty'. It met first in Leonard Woolf's house in Tavistock Square and appealed mainly, I think, to Liberals who were deeply troubled about the danger of Fascism and the extensions of their power both in England and France. It was really a British offshoot of a French movement for the preservation of civil rights. I remember it best for the wholehearted co-operation it won from one of the most remarkable women of our time.

Margery Fry is chiefly remembered on the radio, perhaps; she was a Governor of the B.B.C., and for a period the Principal of Somerville College, Oxford. If you knew her well you would have met the Chinese girls whom she adopted as daughters and you would have found that everything Chinese was close to her heart since her visit to China as a Kahn Fellow in the twenties. She was, of course, one of the Quaker clan who came from Bristol. Her five sisters all did important public work and all remained unmarried. She was utterly devoted to her brother, Roger Fry, the painter and best of art critics. She was, I believe, often lonely, and she told a friend of mine when she was seventy that she was still thinking about marriage but felt it would look rather ridiculous at her age. In fact, men fell in love with her almost as easily at seventy as at seventeen. She was never a feminist, though she fought for causes which involved the emancipation of women. Her most permanent memorial is her work for penal reform through the Howard League, and she scored a triumphant success in initiating the Criminal Injuries Compensation Board, by which nowadays persons injured by criminal violence are compensated from Government funds. She argued that such compensation would be the best reply to people who continuously say that those who wish to abolish capital punishment cared only for the criminal and neglected the victim. It is an interesting example of her thoroughness and intellectual grasp that her propaganda for this cause included her own actuarial calculation that the cost to the state of compensating the victim would be something less than a quarter of a million pounds annually. The cost for several years was, in fact, about £200,000.

I was a member of the executive of 'For Intellectual Liberty'. We did other things as well as sign the all-too-familiar letters to *The Times*. The society did something to save a few refugees from the Nazis and at one time it penetrated an Austrian concentration camp where it managed to distribute presents, the most important of which were students' textbooks. Pathetically, the only thanks which the organisation could receive was a small book of woodcuts which the prisoners managed to smuggle out to us. It consisted of pictures of men and women attempting to study under concentration-camp conditions.

The two organisations which most occupied my spare moments were the National Council for Civil Liberties and the Union of Democratic Control. The N.C.C.L. was founded in 1934 and our first meeting took place in the crypt (or, some say, the vestry) of St. Martin-in-the-Fields. The initial impetus for its foundation came from the official publicity given to the reception of a great hunger-march which came from Jarrow and other parts of the country. Sir John Gilmour, the Home Secretary, warned the public to be as careful on the day of the hunger-marchers' arrival, as if they had been a concourse of wild beasts and not a disciplined body of very tired men—tired out even though they had usually been well received during their long tramp. People in London were told to keep their children off the streets and the police even advised shop-keepers to put up their shutters because of 'possible bloodshed'. Children in schools were to be solemnly warned of the approaching danger 'before prayers'. Disquieting allegations were made that the police intending to use *agents provocateurs* to cause trouble and justify arrests. Two eye-witnesses, one of them Ronald Kidd, who became secretary of the N.C.C.L., swore affidavits about the use of these *agents provocateurs* on a previous hunger march. Lord Trenchard, Chief Commissioner of the Metropolitan Police, made a personal investigation which exonerated the police but left a nasty taste behind it.

The executive of the N.C.C.L., which included a most remarkable set of well-known names, decided to take action. A letter was published in *The Times*, which I signed along with C. R. Attlee, A. P. Herbert, Harold Laski, D. N. Pritt and H. G. Wells. It said that a vigilant committee would be present to keep a watch on the behaviour of both marchers and the police. When the marchers arrived in Hyde Park on Sunday, 25th February, the observers actually included H. G. Wells, Julian Huxley, Harold Laski, Henry Nevinson and two novelists, Winifred Holtby and Vera Brittain. There was, of course, no disturbance. Large crowds watched the processions arriving in the Park to the tunes of Scottish bagpipes. It was generally believed that the knowledge that responsible and well-known people were on the watch had something to do with the restraint shown by the authorities on this occasion. This technique of arranging for public figures to be present at working-class demonstrations became part of our regular routine.

As I remember it, one of the chief personalities in the early days of the N.C.C.L. was Claud Cockburn, editor of the weekly broadsheet called the *Week*. Respectable people who read it with avidity called it a scandal-sheet; certainly its idea was to give you all the dirt about people on the Right Wing of politics. Claud invented the 'Cliveden Set', or, at any rate, gave it its name. He had the great advantage over other editors in being obviously too poor to be worth suing for libel. The *Week* arrived on your breakfast table by the post just before you caught a train with your business friends, who would be envious of the excellent gossip you could retail on your journey. Everybody, as they say, read the *Week*. It circulated in Buckingham Palace as well as in every flat in Bloomsbury. Claud was a member of the Communist Party, but was welcomed everywhere because he always had news and was a delightful conversationalist with a most engaging stutter. He remained a member of the Communist Party throughout the war and is the only prominent member of it I ever knew who has succeeded in leaving it without acrimony on either side. He was never an orthodox party man, but thought that the Communists were more right than anyone else. He once told me that he joined up with the Party much as a soldier enlists; the time came when he felt he had 'done his bit', might reasonably be demobbed and live quite a different kind of life in Eire.

The real brunt of work for civil liberty, of course, fell not on an executive of eminent people but on Ronald Kidd. He came from a medical family, originally well-to-do, and he broke off his studies at London University to volunteer for the army in 1914. He was discharged on grounds of ill-health, joined the Ministry of Pensions, but after the war resigned from the Civil Service in disgust when army pensions were cut. He began work with the N.C.C.L. in a characteristically sordid mews just off Piccadilly called Dansey Place. One room served as his living quarters and office. It contained, to start with, a table, a chair and a cupboard. Kidd seemed never to care about money and received a wage of £4 a week, out of which he paid the rent. I have heard him called the last Edwardian Bohemian. The odd world of the theatrical costumier surrounded our executive meetings and it was not until several years had passed that the urinals just outside the door were removed. Close by was the base from which all the sandwich-board men in London, or so it seemed, passed in and out on their peripatetic profession. Few weeks passed in which I did not meet Ronald or talk with him on the phone. I never met a more disinterested man, and it was this selfless devotion which persuaded E. M. Forster to become president of the N.C.C.L., and moved him to write a finely-phrased obituary of Kidd when he died in 1942. Though this faintly theatrical flavour clung to him from the days when he was a journalist for the dramatic press, he seemed to have no ties, to be without the handicap of a past or ambitions for the future. He was one of G. K. Chesterton's Englishmen, with a quixotic desire to maintain our rights just because they were our rights.

One of our greatest successes was our campaign against the Incitement to Disaffection Bill, popularly known as the Sedition Bill. This measure sought to impose severe penalties on anyone who had in his possession any literature which could be considered likely to seduce a member of His Majesty's Forces from his duty. That could be applied, as far as the wording went, to the Sermon on the Mount. It proposed to give the police general powers to search on suspicion any premises, providing a single J.P. signed the search-warrant. It was a preposterous Bill. Forty-eight hours after its publication the N.C.C.L. circularised every M.P. with a detailed analysis. During the next weeks, conferences and public meetings were organised; the London Trades Council, representing an enormous membership, joined up with the N.C.C.L. in opposition to the Bill. I took the chair at a mass meeting in the Central Hall, Westminster; the speakers included the Bishop of Birmingham, E. M. Forster, Hannen Swaffer and H. G. Wells, who had recently come back in a very bad temper from a visit to the Soviet Union. He had decided to talk not so much about the Bill as about the threat to freedom of expression in Fascist and Communist countries, particularly Communist. It was surprising how effective his rusty little squeak of a voice could be in annoying the militant proletariat in the gallery. A score of Cockney voices barracked him and for a moment I had some difficulty in procuring a proper hearing for him. The effect of his speech was to enable newspapers to report the meeting as a battle between him and the Communists, who were, in fact, a very small minority.

Another occasion in the same campaign was a Mock Trial in Friends' House, Euston Road. The prisoner was David Low, who was accused of having drawn the cartoon which had seduced me, a private soldier, from my allegiance. Miles Malleson was the comic policeman who had arrested me, when, he said, I was 'not exactly drunk or sober, but at about the amber light stage'.

Our agitation against the Bill had found support all over the country. Eleanor Rathbone, a very industrious and independent M.P., presented a national petition in Parliament and other sympathetic M.P.s introduced destructive amendments. We did not succeed in getting the Bill thrown out, but I think we were responsible for emasculating and so discrediting it that the act has only been used in a very few relatively unimportant cases.

Ronald Kidd was always accused of having an animus against the police. He wrote, in a book called *British Liberty in Danger*, that he had no quarrel 'with the rank and file in the force, but with the departments—Scotland Yard and the Home Office—which on

occasion appeared to instruct police officers to exceed their duty'.
This was a mild stricture about police behaviour in some of the
rough-and-tumble fights at Fascist demonstrations and meetings in
the streets. Kidd found that the police tended to back the Fascists, and
he frequently made good his case in court. He took trouble about the
facts and a panel of able young lawyers was ready to help him. On
14th July 1937, for instance, at the peak of the b.u.f.'s anti-semitic
campaign of intimidation in the Jewish East End of London a small
group of Fascists were escorted by the police into Stepney Green.
The inspector, anxious, no doubt, to prevent violence, allowed no
heckling, but made nine arrests of anti-Fascists, one of whom had so
far disregarded the inspector's ban on heckling as to emit a loud
whistle. The magistrate commented: 'I think it would be a sad state
of affairs if it were a criminal offence for some irresponsible young
man to put two fingers to his mouth and whistle.' Another local
man, who was only trying to bring home his ten-year-old daughter,
was arrested on a charge of blowing his nose 'in an offensive manner'.
Kidd won this case and also that of two young men who were
treated in hospital for head injuries. No one ever discovered why, on
this occasion, the police used their batons.

No one could seriously believe in police impartiality between the
uniformed Fascists and the poorly dressed youngsters who looked
like hooligans and shouted subversive slogans. Inevitably the
Fascists seemed patriotic and disciplined and peaceful, and those they
provoked forfeited police sympathies. At the big Albert Hall Fascist
rally, for instance, the police escorted the Mosleyites to the hall and
even went so far as to close two main roads to traffic during the
evening. Half a mile away—the distance stipulated by the police—a
peaceful anti-Fascist meeting was addressed by a Labour M.P. and a
Liberal candidate; it was broken up by a police baton charge without, as far as one can make out, any excuse.

The issue of Fascist violence was first realised by the public at the
Fascist demonstration at Olympia in 1934. I happen to know much
about this occasion because Dorothy had decided to run the risk of
pretending to be a member of Mosley's organisation. She gave herself a fine, aristocratic, double-barrelled name, entered their head-

quarters and on one occasion stole from their notice-boards written instructions to Mosley's followers about how most efficiently to deal with a recalcitrant opponent. She learnt, too, all the secret plans for the Olympia rally and no doubt helped to plant hecklers at convenient places round the hall. In the event, every heckler was seized, beaten up in the passages and thrown violently into the street. Many were taken to hospital. The police watched from outside; they were not invited into the meeting, but should have interfered when the violence inside had become obvious. Such thuggery was new in British politics and hot denunciations followed at once in the press and on the radio from disinterested observers such as Gerald Barry and Geoffrey Lloyd, the Baldwin's Private Secretary. The B.B.C. published a pamphlet giving the sworn testimony of many spectators of this violence. Dorothy had discovered that the Fascists were armed with pieces of lead piping, knuckledusters and other useful weapons which they had been instructed to leave on the floor so that they could claim that their interrupters had meant to use violence. Photographs of these weapons and a story of Communist hooliganism was to appear in the Press next day. It happened that the journalist who was expected to write up the story was a friend of Dorothy. When he learnt the facts, he refused to write it and was sacked, but the story was never written.

It will be seen that the Union of Democratic Control, under Dorothy's management, was very unlike the body which had been originally founded in 1914 by men with a reputation as pacifists and pro-Germans, such as Ramsay MacDonald, Charles Trevelyan and Norman Angell. By 1933 when Hitler seized power our main objects were to attack the private manufacture of arms and to expose the policy and the secret rearmament of Germany. Dorothy was not, like me, full of fear and speculation about Fascism, she instinctively threw herself into working against it. When the Nazis staged the Reichstag Fire Trial, she was chosen by the Communist-controlled Committee for Relief of Victims of German Fascism to go to Leipzig to look after Dimitrov's mother and sister, and to see what we should do to discredit the trial. One day she heard from a friendly contact in the Ministry of the Interior that Dimitrov was

to be moved; she did not know whether he was going to be shot.
It was essential to find out. Dimitrov's mother and sister were
allowed some minutes of conversation with him every day, and
Dorothy always accompanied them and was allowed to remain in
the waiting-room. Leaving them downstairs this time, she dashed
past the guards, who were too surprised to stop her entering the
room where Dimitrov sat. She threw her arms round his neck and
the guard, assuming that they were lovers, allowed them to talk
quietly for some ten minutes. She had with her a letter signed by a
British peer; she asked Dimitrov to write something on it to show
in England. He wrote in German—it is a good souvenir to possess
today—sending greetings to the British working classes. They
planned the next stage of the campaign. On a subsequent visit to
Russia after Dimitrov's acquittal she met him again. He demanded
the reason why she did not greet him so warmly as she had on
their first meeting. He took off his astrakhan cap and put it on
her head.

In a tiny attic office in Victoria Street which no longer exists
Dorothy accomplished a prodigious amount of work. The U.D.C.
became the central power-house from which much of the fight
against Fascism was organised. The work was done by volunteers.
Almost every region in the country, for instance, had members who
would write letters to the local papers replying to any Fascist letter
which appeared. Meetings were arranged all over the country and
the U.D.C. published many pamphlets which did not reach the
bookstalls, but were widely read throughout the Labour and trade
union movements and sometimes discussed in Parliament and the
national press. The chairman of the U.D.C. at that time (before I
took over) was J. A. Hobson, a remarkable economist whose
influence was great, but who was never properly recognised in his
lifetime and is now almost forgotten.

He had been a correspondent of the *Manchester Guardian* in the
Boer War and, I think largely as a result of his observation in South
Africa, evolved a theory that during the period of Imperialist
development war arose because of the economic clash of national
interests abroad. Like H. N. Brailsford, who was his disciple, he

assumed that the causes of war in the nineteenth century were not likely to be quarrels about frontiers, but about the economic control of African dependencies. This, in my view, was broadly correct during the last days of the nineteenth century and at least partly true about the origins of the 1914 war. It was clearly untrue about the Second World War, but the importance of Hobson's formulation was that Lenin seized upon the truth that it contained, attacked it as fallacious and then elaborated it into the Communist theory of Imperialist war which played so large a part in determining Marxist theory and behaviour subsequently. Even now, I don't know to what degree Marxists have modified this tenaciously-held doctrine to meet conditions in the 1960s. But now there is no longer one Marxism, but many sects. Hobson was non-academic and studiously cold-shouldered by men with university standing. He laid down the basis of the Keynesian doctrine that many of our troubles come not from shortages, but from over-investment and under-consumption. Keynes made a belated acknowledgment to Hobson. When I knew him, he appeared to be rather a dried-up old gentleman, particularly noticeable for the odd click which punctuated his sentences and which was due, I fancy, to the imperfection of his dentures. He was one of those rare persons who was completely unspoilt by the neglect of his contemporaries, never sour and superlatively honest. He possessed a sharp, staccato wit and everything he said—a most unusual tribute—was well worth listening to. At each committee meeting of the U.D.C., which was, of course, always insolvent, he would survey the accounts and say, after a judicial survey which included a calculation of how long the printer could be expected to wait for his bill and what subscriptions were likely to come in, that we were likely to be poor enough to survive until the next war.

Money, of course, was always the main U.D.C. problem. Some arrived from old-fashioned pacifist supporters, who may not have noticed how very unpacific our policy had become. Endeavouring to fight non-intervention in the Spanish War amounted to a whole-time job. There was only one regular typist, but there were innumerable volunteers, many of whom would have been more trouble than they were worth if the secretary had not had a genius for seeking out which of them would be useful in addressing envelopes and who could be valuable in organising the many meetings we held in almost every part of the country. She herself seldom appeared, but at one period was personally responsible through contacts with M.P.s for something like a third of the questions on foreign affairs which were asked in the House of Commons and which had to be so worded as to be accepted by the Speaker.

During the early period in which I worked with Dorothy, one of our principal activities was to expose the methods of men like Sir Basil Zaharoff, who made vast fortunes out of selling arms. Today our activity seems somewhat absurd, because states themselves rely financially to a terrifying extent on selling arms to countries, particularly in backward areas, which make war on each other. It is a strange reflection that in 1966 a Labour Government should have appointed at a salary of £8,000 a year an official whose job it is to make money for Britain by selling out-of-date arms, and persuading less industralised countries to buy our modern equipment, so that we can more easily afford to manufacture it. In Dorothy's pamphlet called 'The Secret International' and the one following it called 'Patriotism Limited', she was able to gather together the materials for an indictment which proved, amongst other things, that the Green Hell war between Paraguay and Bolivia (1932 to 1935) would have been impossible but for this trade. The 'Secret International' had remarkable impact. It was shown to the conscientious Senator Nye, who managed, in the U.S.A., to organise a full-scale public enquiry into the activities of armament makers. I recall that he sat up into the small hours of the morning reading this pamphlet, scoring it with red ink and at the end remarking that he could not, in conscience, allow this trade to continue unchallenged. The American Enquiry attracted much public interest and led to a similar enquiry in this country, where counsel for the prosecution, if one may use the term, was Sir William Jowitt. By that time, the question of private manufacture was dwarfed in importance by the vast increase of government arms in Europe and the manifest re-armament of Germany.

U.D.C. pamphlets were startlingly well informed. Dorothy persuaded M.P.s and other people of eminence to take shares in Armstrong Vickers or one of the other armament firms. This gave them the right to demand the facts and to ask awkward questions at shareholders' meetings, which were expected to pass without any question unless it related to dividends. In fact, the directors were much embarrassed by shareholders who took so much interest in their activities and had to admit shamefacedly that they advertised arms in Germany and promised to withdraw these advertisements. These awkward questioners insisted on having the details of the interlocking of armament firms and on at least one occasion the directors had great difficulty in meeting a charge that some of their agents abroad employed dubious methods in persuading foreign governments to buy their wares.

There can have been few issues of foreign policy on which the U.D.C. did not produce accurate and informative literature, which found its way into the Press because of Dorothy's close contacts at that period with journalists throughout the Press, Tory, Liberal and Labour alike. She organised a China Campaign Committee in the two years before the war and organised opinion against Japan, which in 1937 began its second great onslaught. One of our less-successful activities was to advocate the boycott of Japanese goods; people like Mrs. Noel-Baker, and others whom you would not expect to see parading in the streets, walked about carrying sandwich-boards urging people not to buy Japanese goods. On one occasion, I recall, Dorothy refused a tin of fruit made in Japan and explained the reason to the grocer. 'Oh,' he said, 'no reason to tell Mr. Martin about that; it can remain a secret between us.' One odd result of our activities was that through our close contact with Madame Sun Yat Sen and other Chinese leaders, I was immediately welcomed by the Chinese Government when in 1955 I asked for permission, then rarely granted, to enter the country. I ceased to be welcome in China after two articles that contained criticism of Chinese brain-washing.

Looking back on the U.D.C. at that period, I suppose that the most effective work we did was for the liberation of colonial

M

countries which eventually won their independence after the war. We worked continuously with the India League, which was run with immense enthusiasm by Krishna Menon. Krishna has since become famous everywhere, and infamous in the eyes of many people, most of all in America. He is a man of extraordinary ability, who was not in those days accused of intrigue and personal ambition. He was always eloquent, and had the advantage of a legal training. I had first known him at the L.S.E., where he was a passionate follower of Harold Laski. He had already developed the strange technique whereby he seemed to live on nothing except innumerable cups of weak tea. He had been rescued when apparently starving in a lodging in St. Pancras. When, many years later, he was Indian High Commissioner in London, one could still visit him and find him, apparently at death's door, living on the same non-intoxicating diet. But I must say something more in another volume about Krishna, when later on I knew him at the United Nations and on my frequent visits to India.

Another constant visitor to the U.D.C. offices was Jomo Kenyatta, who provides one of the best examples of the follies of colonialism and the advantages of being vilified and imprisoned by stupid authorities. When he came to England after the First World War, he had already been in Russia and was a passionate advocate of African rights, but not a Communist. Nothing so embittered him as the suppression of Kikuyu schools, which were held by the Whites to be subversive—and no doubt often were. He was not, as I remember him, a brilliant man, but a plodder who saw that education was the key to African freedom. I helped him to write the first of many letters to the *Manchester Guardian*. He was a cheerful, friendly and endearing man, who won the hearts of those who worked with him. He studied under the great L.S.E. anthropologist, Malinowski, who was probably responsible for teaching him to use his mind in a rational way. Under his supervision, he wrote a remarkable study of the Kikuyu tribe, their customs, way of life and religion, based on the worship of Mount Kenya.[1] When he returned to Kenya after the Second World War he found that men of his own age group—a

1. Jomo Kenyatta, *Facing Mount Kenya* (Secker and Warburg, 1938).

dominant factor in tribal politics—had come to believe in violence
as the way to freedom. It may well be that he did not stand up to
them as firmly as he should have done, but he was certainly not the
initiator of Mau Mau or the 'power of darkness' which the Governor
of Kenya, Sir Patrick Renison called him, or the blackest of
black villains, fit only for lynching, as the settlers declared him
to be.

The Mau Mau resurgence was only in part a rebellion against the
Whites, of whom, I believe, thirty-two civilians were killed in the
entire affair. It became a civil war, mainly fought between modernis-
ers, Western-minded, and those who were determined to maintain the ancient religion of Mount Kenya. About a thousand
Africans were hanged; some forty Europeans in the Security
Services were killed, and thirty thousand Mau Mau died in the
civil war fought between Mau Mau and the Africans whom we
armed.

Kenyatta came out of prison in the waste land of northern Kenya
seven years later and was made Prime Minister when Kenya won
independence in 1963. I saw him again during negotiations in
England. His hair was white, he carried the official fly-whisk of an
African ruler, and he was a disciple of Gandhi. Dorothy arranged a
party for him at which old champions of African freedom such as
Lord Faringdon, Leslie Plummer, Lord Listowel and many others
were present. An incident in which Kenyatta was insulted in the
street gave the Colonial Office an excuse to 'protect' him, and
Dorothy had to resort to the device of borrowing the big car and
chauffeur from the Burmese Ambassador, one of the guests at the
party, to winkle him out from his hotel and get him to our
flat.

Today, as I write, he is the ruler of Kenya, much revered not only
by the Kikuyu but also by the settlers and white merchants who
have found it possible to collaborate with an African Government.
It is only too likely that his regime will be succeeded by a less
moderate one and that Kenya will be riven, like other parts of
Africa, by tribal disputes. But about Kenyatta himself. No one seems
to remember what once was said. Flourishing his whisk of office and

benignly explaining how important it is for the development of the country for white settlers to be well treated and for Europeans to help Africans who otherwise lack know-how, he rules with much dignity and stands fiercely against African extremists who threaten his power. It sometimes seems as if the Whites who clamoured for his death only a few years ago will end by canonising him.

In our anti-war activities and fight for colonial freedom Dorothy was prepared to act in alliance with anyone, Liberal, Conservative, Labour or Communist, as long as they honestly sought the same ends. Naturally, in this period when Marxism and the Left Book Club flourished in England, many of her collaborators were Communists. That lasted until the Nazi-Soviet Pact in 1939, when the Communists declared that, after all, the war against the Nazis was another Imperialist war, and began, in loyalty to the Soviet Union, to behave with the utmost disloyalty to those with whom they had collaborated. Dorothy was only able to continue working with members of the Communist Party on the issue of China, where the Left Front included people like Margery Fry and where no issue of spying on the Labour Party or becoming 'objectively', as the Communists would say, allies of the Nazis ever arose. But the breach in 1939 was decisive.

As for me, I had never been closely associated with them, either personally or in policy, but I was always willing to work with anybody, whatever their political views, for an object which we had, at least for the time being, in common. My problem was to decide whether the immediate object—getting an anti-Fascist out of a concentration camp, for instance—was their real object, or whether they regarded him as an expendable item of propaganda. Once I received an official letter from Arthur Henderson complaining that I was co-operating with a banned Communist Front organisation when I appeared on the platform of the Committee for the Victims of German Fascism. I replied that this Committee appeared to be doing a necessary job of work, and that if the Labour Party was also doing it I would much prefer to co-operate with the official organisation, but that if nobody else was doing the job, I would collaborate with Communists or the devil himself. I heard no more, though of course this Committee was banned by the Labour Party under what was called the Solar System, that is to say, it was an organisation not directly Communist, but radiating from it.

CHAPTER EIGHT

Betrayal

IN 1935 a group of journalists were discussing the coming invasion
of Abyssinia. One of them was Vernon Bartlett, then a famous
broadcaster and diplomatic correspondent of the *News Chronicle*. He
had had an interview with Mussolini and found him, to the surprise of many of his friends, a constructive and likable statesman.
I said to Vernon Bartlett, 'Well, here's your chance. I could not get
access to the Duce, who has banned the *N. S. & N.* in Italy ever
since we said that he was responsible for the murder of Mateotti.
But you can interview him any time you like and, since this is the
rare case of one man's war, it is surely your duty to shoot him and
save many thousands of lives.' No one had any answer to this, but
Bartlett did not fall in with my proposal and the war went on,
according to Mussolini's plan.

I recall this conversation because it reminds one how comparatively easy it then was to prevent a war. If Mussolini had died,
Abyssinia would not have been invaded. Unlike the Nazis, the
Italian Fascists were not warlike; Mussolini alone dreamt of making
ancient Romans out of modern Italians. No one seriously believed
that the Italian Navy was a match for the British, let alone for the
joint French and British fleets. The Italian Army was not taken very
seriously. When Italy became an ally of Germany, Mussolini was
careful not to enter the war until Britain was hard-pressed and
France defeated. Just before the war General Gamelin even remarked
that if the Italians could be induced to enter the war it would require
five French divisions to defeat them; if Italy remained neutral ten
divisions would be necessary to supervise them, but if they came
into the war on the French side fifty divisions would be needed to
support them against the Germans.

Britain was not deterred from stopping the invasion of Abyssinia
by any military considerations, but to oppose Mussolini was not
British policy. Vansittart at the Foreign Office and the British

Government as a whole hoped to make friends with the Duce at almost any cost in the fantastic belief that he could be permanently prevented from reaching a settlement with Hitler, with whom he was at loggerheads for the moment over the control of Austria. Any journalist could have told them a different tale. The walls of Rome were plastered with huge maps showing the Mediterranean as an Italian sea, and I remember a conversation with a typical Italian Fascist who took me for a drive in his car outside Rome so that we should not be overheard. He explained that he and his friends did not believe in Fascist doctrine, but that he was a party member because otherwise you couldn't get a job and that anyway the democracies were on the way out and the totalitarian countries about to inherit the earth.

It will be seen that this was a golden opportunity for building the League of Nations and showing that it could work. None of the later difficulties of making collective security into a positive method of dealing with the world problem was present in 1935. The League powers were still operating at Geneva and they represented an overwhelming strength if they acted together. Economic sanctions would have worked, or if, as was extremely improbable, Mussolini attempted warlike action he would have been at once defeated. Secondly, no problem of treaty revision existed. Mussolini had no serious case in Abyssinia, he merely wanted to build an empire in Africa. The result of seriously opposing Mussolini when he began his preparations for the Abyssinian campaign would have been the end of his bombastic pretences and probably the end of his regime in Italy. In an article in the *Spectator* in April 1967 Enoch Powell precisely misrepresented the situation. He made the usual excuse of the Conservative Party when he spoke of 'collective security' as a mere 'opiate', a slogan which was an excuse for failure to act. In 1935, it was, on the contrary, a dynamic policy, as Churchill recognised; it was accepted by the overwhelming majority of public opinion, as the revolt against the Hoare-Laval Pact was later to prove.

It will be seen here that there was no real comparison, either, with the Manchurian crisis of 1931, when Japan occupied Manchuria without any serious excuse except that it would suit her interests.

On this occasion the demand for a League policy of collective action against Japan was limited to a few individuals and a few newspapers, which understood that the principle of collective action against the aggressor was at stake. I recall, for instance, a debate in the London School of Economics when Professor Theodore Gregory drenched with cold water Philip Noel-Baker's confident prophecy that League of Nations sanctions would be applied to Japan and that Tokyo would be quickly brought to its knees. The *New Statesman and Nation*, with C. M. Lloyd writing the leading articles, never shared this optimism, but week by week demanded sanctions against Japan and cursed the Government for failing to realise that the whole League idea would be permanently undermined if economic sanctions were not applied in the first test case of world machinery for keeping peace.[1] In particular we were furious with Sir John Simon, then Foreign Secretary, for finding excuses in China's weakness for Japanese aggression and magnifying every risk to us if we took strong action against Japan. He argued his case so well that the Japanese spokesman in Geneva declared that he could not have served their cause better if he had been in the pay of Tokyo.

I never could reconcile myself to Sir John Simon and attacked him more viciously than any other politician. But, perhaps characteristically, I did not like hurting his feelings. In 1933, when Low did a singularly unflattering cartoon of him, we printed side by side with it an equally unflattering profile. These profiles were written anonymously by people with intimate knowledge of the victim. In this case there is now no harm in revealing that the author was Terence O'Connor, a well-known barrister who had worked closely with Simon. I did not want to appear personally malicious, so I cut out two sentences which seemed certain to hurt his feelings. The first, I found out afterwards, was adapted from a famous jibe made by Daniel O'Connell about Sir Robert Peel. It read: 'His smile

1. In his careful study of British opinion during the Manchurian episode, R. Bassett points out that two papers were almost alone in advocating sanctions in 1931, but suggests, for some reason not altogether clear to me, that the *Manchester Guardian* was more sincere in its advocacy than the *N. S. & N.* R. Bassett, *Democracy and Foreign Policy* (Longmans Green & Co. Ltd., 1952).

illuminates his countenance as the nameplate does a coffin.' The
second sentence, perhaps even more wounding, began, 'Many of
those who have shivered as he took their arm . . .' Poor Simon! He
always wanted to be loved, but lacked the knack of being lovable.
On the whole, I do not regret the sacrifice of these two wounding
sentences.

The Manchurian episode was too remote to force Labour to face
its dilemma. Nor was Hitler's invasion of the Rhineland in 1936 a
test of opinion about collective security. Today it is common to
refer to this incident as an example of British weakness and to suggest
that if we had been less blind then we could have prevented the war.
It is remarkable how many people talk as if that was their view in
1936. We know now that the French were not prepared to act and
that if the Allies had stood together Hitler would in fact have withdrawn in view of the overwhelming strength against him. But that
was not how it looked at the time, though there were already
German refugees in England who warned us of the danger of making any concession to the Führer. I had at that time a German-Jewish
secretary whom I recall protesting that it would be fatal to yield an
inch. Edgar Mowrer, author of *Hitler Puts the Clock Back*, and
Knickerbocker, also a famous and outspoken American correspondent, met in my rooms an important group of British intelligentsia
and argued forcibly that when Hitler complained of being encircled he was in fact encircling himself. They declared that at all
costs we must not be misled into believing a word he said or in trying to appease him. These warnings, which sound so sensible today,
passed unheeded then because it seemed impossible to fight a war or
even threaten it in order to prevent Hitler from re-entering 'his own
back garden'. The phrase was Lord Lothian's; it was an entirely
representative sentiment and I am sceptical nowadays when people
say they wanted to intervene against Germany in 1936. Why, we
asked ourselves, should we try to prevent Germany occupying
German territory, knowing full well that if Hitler was forced to
withdraw he would merely wait for another day when he was
stronger or, if he was thrown out, would not another German
government insist on the same revision of Versailles?

I had been present at the Saar plebiscite in 1935 and seen the overwhelming enthusiasm of German nationalism. The Communists had tried to make an issue by the slogan '*Für Deutschland gegen Hitler*', but since all the Saar inhabitants wanted to rejoin Germany and Germany was now Hitler's, their total defeat was a foregone conclusion. Then, too, we still remembered the fiasco of the French occupation of the Ruhr and no one really believed it possible to prevent Germany again becoming a great power. No, this was not a case where British consciences were divided or even troubled. Sooner or later Germany would obviously occupy the Rhineland; we were merely sorry that it was done without ceremony or legality and, above all, done by Hitler.

The Rhineland was not the issue on which the League foundered. It had already been destroyed by Mr. Baldwin and Sir Samuel Hoare in 1935. Mussolini was obviously preparing for the invasion of Abyssinia when early in 1935 Sir John Simon and Ramsay Mac-Donald went to Stresa to confer with the Duce, but were anxious not to offend him. The Foreign Office hoped to keep Hitler and Mussolini hostile to each other and thought it tactless to mention the Abyssinian war. There was a pretence that the reason for not intervening was the pacifism of the British public.

The facts are widely misunderstood. The Disarmament Conference, which had been dragging its weary course along year after year, was obviously petering out, and the League of Nations Union, in an attempt to arouse public opinion about the danger of war, organised a house-to-house canvass which came to be called the 'Peace Ballot'. The results were surprising. Eleven million people voted, of whom more than ten millions demanded economic sanctions against the aggressor and less than 640,000 opposed them: 6,750,000 had voted for military sanctions, if necessary, and only 2,360,000 were against.

Winston Churchill in *The Gathering Storm* wrote that the Peace Ballot:

was regarded in many quarters as part of the Pacifist campaign. On the contrary, Clause 5 [on Sanctions] affirmed a positive and courageous policy which could, at this time, have been followed with an overwhelming measure of national support.

The same false deduction was drawn from the Fulham by-election, in which John Wilmot, the Labour Party candidate, won a resounding victory against the Government. He was supported by a much quoted pacifist speech by George Lansbury, but Wilmot was no pacifist. He ran his victorious campaign in 1935 almost exclusively on the issue of sanctions, or, if necessary, war with Mussolini.[1]

The issue of sanctions and the preservation of the League machinery were vital, the one policy that could prevent the World War. I decided then and there that even if sanctions led to war I could no longer be a pacifist but would have to go through with it. I remember sitting late in my room one night, agonising over an article supporting the policy of collective action; the only condition was that it should be genuinely international and not merely a disguise for the old type of national war.

There was, of course, a pacifist minority which refused to believe that the League offered the best chance of peace. I remember speaking at a meeting at Birmingham Town Hall that autumn. It was a combined Popular Front platform and was summoned to show support for Abyssinia. The first speaker urged that we must carry out economic sanctions, but in no circumstances must the Labour Party support a war. I followed next and said that, though there was good ground for hoping that economic sanctions would be enough, there was a risk that war would follow, that we should be committed to it if there was war and that we ought to run the risk. The next speaker thanked me for my frankness and said that since sanctions might lead to war, he was altogether opposed to them. The fourth speaker demanded that Britain should at once take drastic steps, including blocking the Suez Canal, but that there must in no circumstances be a war. The next speaker was the luckless son of the Abyssinian Minister in London, who was killed shortly afterwards

1. In his TV interview in 1966 R. A. Butler emphasised how much the pacifist mood of the period influenced Baldwin. He specifically mentioned the Fulham by-election as an example of this pacifism.

fighting for his country. He must have found the speeches perplexing and somewhat discouraging, especially as the meeting ended with an eloquent expression of the Christian pacifist case by Canon Stuart Morris, who was later to be chairman of the Peace Pledge Union.

At its annual conference at Brighton the Labour Party finally decided to support the League. I wrote to a friend that it had been 'the biggest thing I was ever at'. I was then in correspondence with Konni Zilliacus, who was publicity officer at the League and who had just written an eloquent pamphlet for the *N. S. & N.* over the signature Vigilantes. He and I were apparently hard at work doing some effective lobbying. I wrote that I had succeeded in persuading Herbert Morrison, then President of the Conference, a pacifist in the First World War and quite ignorant of foreign affairs, to support sanctions. I had given him a memorandum at breakfast:

> He produced it complete in his speech—which was a consummate piece of oratory, brilliantly designed to get the maximum vote and to please everyone—and he said afterwards that, to be fair, he ought to have acknowledged his debt to me in the course of his speech.

I then added, characteristically:

> If, after all, sanctions turn it into a big war, I shall wish I had been with Ponsonby, who made a splendid [pacifist] speech. As you know, I thought it a legitimate gamble that would not end in war and that we could get a real League victory. If we do, there is a chance of taking the world a step further in the direction that you and I want it to go in.

Another letter shows that I was discussing the matter with Hugh Dalton, who had no doubts at all that we ought to give full support to the League. He was clearly much less troubled than I was about the danger of war, and much more ready to assume the honesty of the Government. His letter is of considerable historical interest:

West Leaze,
Aldbourne,
Wiltshire.
24th September, 1935.

'My dear Kingsley,

'Many thanks for your letter. I look forward to a talk with you at Brighton.

'I agree with much of what you say, but much the most important thing to stress at this moment is that the Labour Party demands that the Covenant shall be applied, with whatever degree of vigour the circumstances may require, against Mussolini if he makes war. This, to my mind, is completely elementary. Any alternative course leads to sheer ruin, and that very soon. I am strengthened in this opinion by the attitude of the Soviet and the Scandinavian Govts and by the unanimous declarations of the I.F.T.U. and the Socialist International.

'This attitude is perfectly consistent with continued attacks upon our own bloody Govt, and more than half my speech on Saturday was devoted to this. Particularly to their responsibility for letting this crisis develop at all. They couldn't do themselves much good in a "League of Nations election", if our speakers and publicists know their case. I regard as quite fantastic the idea that any of our leaders should join a Coalition Govt, in the event,— still I think an unlikely event but one which must, of course, be envisaged as among the possibilities—of *armed* sanctions becoming necessary. My view that this idea is fantastic leads me to dissent from the suggestion that we should advertise such fantasy by *repudiating* it in advance. The doubting Thomases would then say "no smoke without fire".

'As to Stafford. He *is* naive, often to the point of sheer imbecility. And many of us have bridled our tongues in public with an iron control these last four years, thinking that public squabbling was undesirable, even in face of great provocation and damage to the prospects of our candidates. But now he must be argued with and answered. What you say about him in your letter seems to me much more damaging than anything I said on Saturday.

'You say, in effect, that when he advocated in Parliament action against Japan, he did it with his tongue in his cheek, knowing the Govt wouldn't act. I said, in effect, that, as distinguished from G.L. and Ponsonby, he was a quick change artist, that he had often, and as lately as a few months ago, put the Party's policy in the House "with lucidity and with every appearance of sincerity and understanding", and that he had never, till a few weeks ago, spoken against his policy in the Executive. Why this sudden change? But I agree with you that the less personalities at Brighton the better.

Yours,
H.D.'

In the event Labour made up its own mind and decided by an overwhelming majority to support sanctions, even at the risk of war. There was still a pacifist hangover which rallied behind George Lansbury. This emotional and almost religious element in the Labour Party had only gradually realised that the League involved sanctions which might ultimately, in some circumstances, lead to war. In the twenties they had voted in favour of a General Strike against all wars and did so as late as 1933, when Hitler had just seized power. In that year this resolution stood incongruously side by side with another vote demanding full co-operation with the League of Nations. But this contradiction became blatant after the arrival of Hitler, and the Party was now fully pledged to support of the Covenant.

The debate at Brighton had all the qualities of great drama. It was a battle of ideas, expressed with deep sincerity and maintained at a surprisingly high level. Some of the speeches, including one by Dalton which ended with a classical peroration about Great Britain having to choose between comradeship with the League powers or behaving with the treachery of a Judas Iscariot—assumed that the National Government would carry out its pledges. But Philip Noel-Baker, Attlee and Morrison pointed out the dangers that the Government would use the occasion merely to justify increased armaments and would betray its word. Morrison, as I hoped, laid down con-

Mussolini's heart touched by Old George's peroration

Mussolini revolted by coarse brutality of Bevin.

Mussolini, George Lansbury and Bevin

ditions for Labour's support of sanctions and pointed out that the
Covenant meant not only the restraint of the aggressor but also disarmament, international instead of imperial control of the colonies,
and that it involved serious consideration of treaty revision and of
the problems of sharing markets and the distribution of raw
materials. Stafford Cripps, and other members of the Socialist
League were against all sanctions on the ground that a Capitalist
government would never genuinely oppose another Capitalist
government, and Lord Ponsonby rubbed in the point by saying that
this call to support the Government would merely prove another
trick to get us into khaki.

The important pacifist speech came from George Lansbury, who
attempted to swing the Party round to its old position of opposing
any policy that might lead to war. He was answered by Ernest Bevin
in one of the most powerful speeches that I have heard. He accused
Lansbury—the Party Leader—of disloyalty, and, to the accompaniment of an apposite hailstorm which beat a tattoo on the Dome
above us as if to emphasise Bevin's torrent of eloquence, said that
Lansbury had been 'hawking his conscience' round the country long
enough. He added afterwards: 'Lansbury has been going about
dressed in saint's clothes for years waiting for martyrdom; I set fire
to the faggots.' His great bulk filled the rostrum and I can see him
now, shouting over all interrupters, 'Who am I to let my personality
protrude as compared with this great movement?' It was far too late
for the Labour Government to go back on its past resolutions in
favour of the Covenant. 'You can't be both in and out of the
League, not if you're honest,' he roared. The great majority of the
Labour Party Conference agreed, and voted for him and against
Lansbury.

I have no doubt whatever that if the Government had seriously
pursued the policy of sanctions that autumn it would have carried
behind it the overwhelming support of the British public. For a
moment it appeared that it intended to follow an honest League
policy. In September Sir Samuel Hoare, the Foreign Secretary,
declared at Geneva that Britain would offer 'unrelenting opposition
to unprovoked aggression', and he even went on to state a full

League policy about permitting the 'have-not' powers a fair share of
the world's raw materials.

I was among the excited spectators at Geneva when Sir Samuel
made this speech, which seemed to contradict Britain's earlier policy
towards Mussolini. There was intense excitement among the delegates and I fully shared it. Instead of Sir John Simon explaining why
the Covenant should not be invoked, here was a plain-speaking
Foreign Secretary boldly declaring that Britain favoured collective
security. I rang up my paper and reported that Britain after all intended business. I was not alone in believing that the British Government meant what it said. When Hoare, instead of opposing aggression, agreed with Laval on a partition of Abyssinia designed to satisfy
the Duce without war, the disillusion was general and complete.
Later Sir Samuel told me that he found himself in an impossible
dilemma after his speech. He put most of the blame on Laval, who
would not in any circumstances annoy Mussolini. Labour, of course,
declared that his speech had just been an electoral trick, while a deep-
throated growl condemning the Hoare-Laval Pact was heard in every
Conservative Club and National Government constituency. The
British Government was not only breaking its word but was climbing down to a Wog: Mr. Baldwin was apparently surprised; he
recognised this tumult of opinion, he said, 'as the conscience of
England', and on this high ground threw over the proposals, and his
Foreign Secretary with them.

Economic sanctions were then imposed, but never seriously. They
would never have had a chance of success unless the British Government had been sincere and had genuinely tried to persuade other
countries to work with it in preventing the war. Half-hearted sanctions have never been successful; their only result is to unify the
nationalism of the country upon which they are imposed. In fact,
the League members, as well as the United States, thought only of
their own interests and sanctions fizzled out.

That was the end of the League, and it was a deception and confusion from which the British public have never recovered. It marks the
dividing line in the thirties. After that the one hope that England
would stand for a constructive world policy came to an end and the

N

Left were divided between those who were determined to stop
Hitler at all costs and those who fell back into one or other of the
various brands of pacifism.

Internationally, the results were wholly disastrous. If sanctions had
been difficult before, they were now impossible. Britain blamed
France and France Britain, and both blamed America. A French
cartoon showed the British lion refusing to allow the Italian wolf to
consume the Abyssinian lamb without allowing Britain its share.
The word was passed round that the British lion had once again
threatened to bite with its false teeth. The Abyssinians were
massacred more quickly than the experts expected. It was generally
known that Ras Tafari, Emperor of Ethiopia, had been encouraged
by Britain to maintain his resistance, but not to provoke a fight,
because he should wholly rely on League action. The sanctions
imposed were not serious and Mussolini finally decided that the
West was negligible and that it would pay to rely wholly on Hitler.
The Fascist powers felt safe to go ahead in Spain and the last chance
of making a reality of the League had faded out.

The one person who gained by the discredit of the League and the
confusion of English thought was Stanley Baldwin. He ambled
along, dilatory always, but instinctively astute. He misled everyone
but responded quickly to popular moods. I learnt from close friends
of his that fear of war was always a principal motive of his policy, or
lack of it; this view of him is fully borne out by his conversations
with Tom Jones, his close friend, and one of the Cabinet Secretariat.
He knew, like Chamberlain after him, that rearmament was the first
step to another German war, and there was truth in the accusation
made by his Right-Wing critics that he and MacDonald obstructed
the increases of British defence that would normally have been
considered necessary if Britain was to defend the Empire without
powerful allies.

Baldwin was never an Imperialist. At the same time, he did
nothing to make the Disarmament Conference a reality and everything to destroy the alternative policy of collective security. His fear
and hatred of war were perfectly sincere and he ended his famous
'the-bomber-will-always-get-through' speech by an earnest appeal to

youth to prevent such a horror. Yet when, in 1933, the Oxford Union had voted against fighting 'for King and Country', he spoke in the severest tones of this youthful response to his warning that modern warfare involved the 'monstrous wickedness of bombing the women and children of another country lest they should bomb yours first'. He could, if he had thought or cared to enquire, have noted the resolution was carefully phrased to include all those who were in favour of running the risk of a war arising from sanctions, though they rejected support for another old-fashioned national war. This interpretation was quickly endorsed by an overwhelming Cambridge Union vote in favour of fighting 'for the League and sanctions'. As the *Isis* pointed out at the time, and as the Oxford President remarked, the two resolutions were not contradictory, but supplementary. The *Isis* added that it welcomed 'the clearer thought and higher ideal implied by them'.

What was the key to Baldwin? If you look at his volume of speeches, *The Torch of Freedom*, the subjects are significant. 'Our Freedom is our own', 'The Love of Country Things', 'The Bible', 'Shakespeare', 'Scott', 'Old Sarum' and 'William Morris'. It was the Worcestershire countryside and the works of Mary Webb, a warm-hearted populariser of country life, not the ideas and values of his cousin, Rudyard Kipling, which appealed to him. In short, he was a 'Little Englander'. He disliked foreigners and believed that England could not survive another war. Big ideas like the League were dangerous, but the British people would fight for their interests if sufficiently hard-pressed. They might have to arm against Hitler, and though he did not much care about the Empire, he thought it treasonable to talk, as many were doing, about returning the colonies to Germany.

It is wise, but very unusual, to retire at the height of one's success. Statesmen always talk of making way for the younger generation, but they usually stand immovably on the upper rungs of the ladder. Gladstone announced his final retirement in 1871, but lived to be twice again Prime Minister, to split his Party and to die an object of detestation, as well as awe, to younger men who for twenty years had kicked against his domination. In the summer of 1936 Baldwin's stock stood at its lowest. His famous statement that he could not begin a policy of rearmament in 1933 because in view of pacifist sentiment he would have lost the election was neither forgiven nor forgotten, and his responsibility for the betrayal of the League in 1935 and for jettisoning Sir Samuel Hoare had destroyed his reputation as a trustworthy and honourable Prime Minister. Yet by the end of 1936 he had raised himself to the pinnacle of popularity and again proved himself a grand master of political manœuvre.

The story of the abdication of Edward VIII, and of Baldwin's part in engineering it, is too well known to need repetition, but, as it happened, I was oddly concerned with it in a small way, which casts a light from an unusual angle on what was certainly a unique event. For months, like other people in Fleet Street, I had been aware of the scandal widely publicised in the United States and on the Continent, but carefully hushed up by agreement between the press barons and Buckingham Palace. I was not deterred from talking about it by any agreement or censorship, or even by the fact that one could not, at that date, discuss rumours about Edward VIII and Mrs. Simpson with any honesty without running risks under the law of libel. There was a more important reason which influenced me; skilful journalism can usually get round the law of libel. One day I saw a friend of the King and asked him whether I ought to 'blow the gaff'. He entreated me not to. He said that Edward was for the first time in his life happy and satisfied. It was Edward's own affair; Why should I interfere? Then, a few days later, I was informed that the King insisted on his right to marry Mrs. Simpson. This, of course, made the issue one of public importance. Obviously the question who is to be Queen of England cannot be a secret. I learnt from D. N. Pritt, K.C., that the King would much appreciate an article supporting his right to marry whom he pleased: he lived in fear that some popular news-sheet would break the silence with sensational headlines. He wanted it stated in a serious paper that he intended marriage and was only prevented by Cabinet opposition. He might welcome an article to this effect in the *New Statesman* if I supported his view. I quote from my personal diary at that time:

24th November 1936

I hear that the situation re Mrs. Simpson is reaching a climax. I tackled Pritt on 18th November about whether it is true that the Cabinet threatened to resign if the King insists on marrying Mrs. S., and whether it is true that leaders of the Labour Party (some, I don't know which) have also promised to refrain from exploiting situation in that case—which would mean forcing the King to abdicate. Pritt does not definitely confirm the last rumour, but tells me it is true that a crisis is reached between the King and Stanley Baldwin. I suggested in that case, if the King is determined to marry, that there is no reason why we should not have an article supporting the King as against the aristocracy and the smug people. The only doubts are whether Mrs. S. can be put over as a Queen now, in view of the American newspaper scandal, and whether it is true that she is a pro-Nazi and likely to lead the King in a Fascist direction, or even get him into a generally irresponsible crowd who would be dangerous not so much to the Monarchy as to the rest of us. Pritt tells me that Walker Monckton (the eminent barrister who was advising the King) is in intimate touch and might, he thinks, in the circumstances welcome an article supporting the King's right to marry as he pleases.

Friday evening. I see Monckton at 11.30 p.m. at Wyndham's Club. He tells me much good gossip (or rather truth that would be lovely gossip if I spread it), and welcomes the idea of the article because the King and he have talked over the possibility of flying a kite to see how the public would react.

The situation is (a) that the King is determined to marry openly; and (b) that the Government is divided about the possibility of making Mrs. S. Queen, but most think it impossible and Baldwin completely opposed; (c) the King very obstinate and neurotic. Keeps saying his private life his own and won't be interfered with. S.B. says King can have no private life. S.B.'s strongest card is feeling in Canada, where great shock from U.S. newspapers.

Important point is that King holds as point of honour to announce his intention openly before the Coronation. He does not think it decent to be crowned and then marry later.

King did not say 'Won't come to your bloody Coronation.'
Asked if he did, he said ,'No, he bloody well wished he'd thought
of it.'

26th November 1936.

I saw Monckton again on Monday and Tuesday nights. On
Tuesday he was just back from a long conversation with Baldwin.
We discussed the constitutional issue and the possibility of a compromise in which the King should marry without making Mrs. S.
Queen. Would require Act of Parliament, otherwise she would
become Queen Consort automatically. Another awkward legal
question is whether the King can make any announcement before
the decree is absolute.

Monckton had conversation with the King and Mrs. S. She
behaves well. Calls the King 'Sir' and occasionally 'His Majesty'
and curtsies. Mrs. S. very pleasant and good-looking, but, according to Monckton, does not move like a queen and would need some
lessons in deportment. She is upset about the situation, quite un-push-
ing and realises the trouble she is in for. She is willing and anxious
to leave England for the period of the Coronation. My *N.S.* article,
written on Sunday, dictated to Dorothy, is in the King's hands.

On Tuesday, Monckton tells me that Baldwin says he will be
patient. Was patient in the General Strike and so got through.
(Monckton thinks 'old hypocrite!') King also tries to be patient
and not force issue. He is disinclined for immediate publication of
my article. I urge that the situation will not have changed in a
week and ask why we should wait, with a risk of someone butting
in? *The Times* may come out on the other side. M. thinks not.
Beaverbrook and Rothermere are completely nobbled, and *The
Times* will do what S.B. wants them to. Conference between the
King and S.B. is put off, each trying and hoping to wear the other
down. Looks as if I shall have to hold my article, much to my
annoyance.

Wednesday morning, Monckton rings me. King delighted with
article. For first time, feels his point of view appreciated. Wants
us to hold it. Fears it will be obviously inspired, and I had better

wait until next week. In the meantime, I might like to see him? Probably arrange it at Monckton's chambers. I naturally express my gratification. Later: All went phut. Had message Edward was away for week-end. Row reached height on Tuesday, but incident ended by the Bishop of Bradford. Very annoying. Should have cherished that interview as historic occasion and have got a clearer view of what little man was really like.'

At the end of 1936 I wrote a short book called *The Magic of Monarchy*, in which I argued that Ernest Jones, the psychoanalyst, was right in seeing an advantage in having a fixed president or monarch who would ensure continuity even when we needed, as people do, to work off our grievance by psychologically killing the king. In England we had a General Election instead of a revolution. But it seemed to me unnecessary to deify the monarch and pretend he was something more than human. I particularly picked up a phrase in which William Temple, then Archbishop of York, spoke of the king as being 'the incarnation' of his people, which suggested a primitive theory of a royal person who, as a scapegoat, bears the sins of the people and whose ritual death is a condition of tribal prosperity. This led to a considerable correspondence with the Archbishop, who wrote:

> Bishopsthorpe,
> York
> 16 April 1937

'Dear Mr. Martin,

'It was very kind of you to send me your book *The Magic of Monarchy*, but if you will forgive me saying so I cannot find it equally intelligent of you to be so perplexed at that very innocent remark of mine. It is so evident that the function of the Crown is primarily symbolic that it never occurred to me that anyone could suppose that my use of this phrase referred back to the outlook of primitive tribes or the rest. On the other hand most English people's conception of a symbol, when that word is used, is so meagre that it seemed more advisable to leave it out.

'What I was concerned about had two main points: (1) the distinction between the State and the Community, which seems to me one of the most important, and is often ignored; (2) that in respect of that distinction what the King embodies symbolically is not the State but the Community. It is obviously the abolition of all political power that has made possible this function, and it is a function of the highest social value because it is good for any country—unless its injustices have gone so far that the sense of national unity only perpetuates evil—to have a universally acknowledged focus for its communal emotion. That is what the King provides. Also as being the Community, of which the State is an organ, he represents the reserve powers which can in a sufficient emergency modify the activities of the State. The extent to which all this becomes actual will of course depend on the extent to which the individual monarch is in personal sympathy with the judgement and feelings of the great mass of his subjects. That was where George V was so good. His political notions were in many respects deplorable, but his sureness of judgement, which was instinctive and not intellectual, with regard to the prevalent national feeling was quite remarkable, and it enabled him to be an embodied expression of the communal spirit.

'I do not know why I should bother you with all this, except that I think you have a slight penchant for supposing that ecclesiastics talk nonsense, and I should therefore derive some private gratification from persuading you that there was some sense in this particular phrase that you object to.

Yours sincerely,
William Ebor.'

He wrote again on April 23:

'It is monstrous of me to keep it up, and I do not in the least expect you to do so. But I am intrigued—as we say now-a-days—by the fact that your mind draws the exactly opposite conclusion to that which mine draws from the inadequate conception held by most of our fellow countrymen concerning a symbol. They usually think that a symbol is anything to which some conventional association has been attached, and that there neither is, nor can be, any real identity between the symbol and the thing symbolised. It is all part of our grossly inarticulate habit of mind. For it seems quite clear that a good work of art is what I once ventured to call "an essential symbol", i.e., a symbol of the whole range of qualities or whatnot which is effective because it is an individual instance. And it is in this kind of way that a King can be, and is really called to be, a symbol of the Community. If he is, as I think you called him in your book, the Chief Executive, or something of that sort, he is absurdly expensive. What we pay for is precisely his symbolic value; but this is useful to the national life only so far as it has in it something of substantial identity and not merely conventional association. Of course in the old Kings there was this idea alongside of actual direction of the nation. Then came the long struggle in which the Kings lost political power, and during which their symbolic value was reduced to nearly nothing. The power having gone we have been re-discovering the symbolic value, and it seems to me worth while to look out for language which expresses that rather startlingly so as to make people face it. What is ridiculous and hurtful is the supposition that because kingship means this the individual man who is King is endowed with all human perfections. I thought I saw in your book an inclination to disparage the kingship through fear of deifying the King. It seems to me that the vitally important thing to do is to keep alive a sense of distinction between them so that kingship is a vocation which the King in fact fulfills in greater or less degree. It has all become complicated because George V filled the part so completely with hardly anything left over so to speak either on the side of kingship or his own personality.

'But don't bother to answer all this. I am sending it only because I am interested in the sharply divergent reactions of our two minds to the same consideration.'

These letters never seemed to me to justify his point of view about 'incarnation'. On the whole it seemed to be true that the effect of

Edward's abdication was to undermine the deification of the monarchy, which had troubled me in the later days of George V. The new king and his successor were seen as human beings, and far more open to criticism than George V had ever been. The Coronation of George VI was a great occasion; the monarchy regained its popularity under a singularly modest king and attractive queen, but even those who tried hardest never succeeded in again making the Coronation a superhuman occasion.

Stanley Baldwin did not resign before the coronation of a new king. In the ceremony itself, a feudal and religious affair in which no statesman, however distinguished, could compete with the bishops, the soldiers, and the older Peers of the Realm, Mr. Baldwin, who was only one of six equal Premiers, was yet to a discerning eye the central figure. Had it not been for him, another king would have been crowned, and perhaps another queen. But in that case would the crowds have cheered? Would the Crown have stood, as it undoubtedly did after its brief eclipse, once more established in the affections of a vast majority of the British people? No one acclaimed Mr. Baldwin as kingmaker, but many whispered that he had saved the British monarchy.

During the few weeks after the Coronation, before Baldwin's retirement, I heard him make a very characteristic speech. It was an after-dinner affair—a vast dinner, given by the Federation of British Industries to about a thousand guests. He began with a pleasant touch about 'growing old peacefully', and then, in a voice full of feeling, went on to warn us of the dangers of excessive speed in our generation, and of the loss of values involved in mechanisation. 'Fifty years ago,' he said, 'no one ever heard of a nervous breakdown, now . . .' He drew a contrast between the tranquil, old-world life of the countryside, when work was done at a pace natural to man, and the dire results of a civilisation of mechanical speed, ruthlessly binding every worker to a conveyor belt, regardless of the strain on muscle and brain. His real philosophy, no doubt. Humane, kindly, the outlook of a genial country gentleman, not of Kipling, and not—no, certainly not, of the Federation of British Industries. I looked round me. There they sat, these prosperous manufacturers in their white waistcoats, with their ties just the least off straight after an excellent dinner, served with excellent wines, applauding, delighted to pay tribute to the Prime Minister, and happily agreeing with him that life was much too strenuous, too exhausting, and likely sooner or later to bring them all to duodenal ulcers and nervous breakdowns.

Mr. Baldwin had the right qualities for leading a coalition government. He acted like a Conservative, spoke like a Liberal and was always in words and actions a true representative of the great British middle-class—a category which psychologically included many who were paid by the week and did not wear collars. He was not a great orator, but I remember Lloyd George making a characteristically dramatic comment on this. 'When Mr. Churchill gets up,' he said, 'the House of Commons quickly fills; each quip is savoured and repeated, the eloquent passages form the subject of admiring discussion for days, the carefully-prepared phrases stand out like jewels and are recorded by gossip writers and lobby correspondents. Every listener is conscious of the occasion, of being part of an audience, of being present at a great occasion. At the end of the speech they are applauding, as when the curtain falls at the opera. They listen to Churchill, but *they do not go along with him*. They are outside critics in the auditorium, not colleagues weighing the arguments of a trusted leader. Now if you want the man for a common jury, get Baldwin every time. He seldom utters a sentence above the commonplace; not a memorable phrase, brilliant passage or original idea. There is no occasion; only a conversation, a statement of the case that helps people to make up their minds.' In politics it is better to be persuasive rather than brilliant. 'Weight' is more important than brilliance. It so happened that history gave Churchill weight as well as intellectual opportunity in the war. Lloyd George was speaking in the thirties, when Churchill was also still in the doldrums. In 1940 I should say he was the most persuasive speaker England ever knew, for in 1940 he spoke not so much the thoughts of the audience, but its feelings. In the thirties Baldwin was on top; it was he who had the capacity to enter the public mood and soothe its conscience. It responded by saying that here, at any rate, was a

man to be trusted. His speeches were as effective as they were dull.
I remember a conversation with Keynes:

Keynes: Neither you nor I, Kingsley, will ever be Prime Minister.
K.M.:   I certainly shan't. But why not you?
Keynes: Because neither of us has the capacity to write out a speech
        of impossible dullness, full of clichés and obvious truths,
        then learn it by heart and repeat it so slowly that everybody
        believes every word of it.

CHAPTER NINE

Rival Ideologies

Things fall apart, the centre cannot hold,
Mere anarchy is loosed upon the world,
The blood-dimmed tide is loosed, and everywhere
The ceremony of innocence is drowned.
The best lack all conviction, and the worst
Are full of passionate intensity.
Surely some revelation is at hand?
Surely the Second Coming is at hand.

And what rough beast, its hour come round at last,
Slouches towards Bethlehem to be born?
                              'The Second Coming,' W. B. Yeats

AFTER the 1935 betrayal, things fell apart; the centre could not
hold. For a moment the Government had seemed to support the
League and although there were many individual pacifists among
Labour members, the Party had decisively voted for sanctions, even
if they led to war. But now collective security had been abandoned;
there was no longer any resting-place for the minds of those who
were pledged 'never again' to fight in another nationalist war.
Another 1914? Not on your life! That is what we had all sworn not
to fall for again; we thought we knew the tricks used to inveigle
Social Democrats into fulfilling their traditional role, first swearing
to oppose war and then proving, when the test came, as nationalistic
and bellicose as the warmongers themselves. Nothing now seemed
left for people caught in this trap but to demonstrate against Government foreign policy, to oppose national armaments, and only to
support rearmament if it was to rebuild a collective system. This
meant, in practice, making an alliance with Russia and the Scandinavian powers. Churchill was to call this a 'Grand Alliance' and Left
called it an 'International Popular Front'. This remained the dominant policy of the Labour movement until 1938, in spite of the
existence of pacifist factions. A few Labour leaders such as Hugh

Dalton fought fiercely behind the scenes for rearmament; how could you win an electoral victory, Dalton asked me in a letter of 26th July 1937, with a slogan of 'Arms for Spain, but no arms for Britain'? He went on:

'The ordinary voter simply does not understand the parliamentarian's argument that a vote against all provisions for the Army, Navy and Air Force is not really a vote against all defence, but only against the Government's foreign policy. It is quite impossible to win elections unless we cease from the "symbolic" opposition to all rearmament . . . the most fatal form of "collaboration" with the National Government, to prevent a Labour victory, is by putting a gun into the Government's hands by which they could shoot down all our candidates by the most deadly fear of misrepresentation. Courage or judgment? Which is the best? What good in politics is either without the other?'

The question, Dalton said, was not one of principle but one of tactics. Attlee, leading the party, argued the Labour case differently. No doubt he was compromising with the pacifist group on the Executive and in the country. He wrote, in *The Labour Party in Perspective*, a Left Book Club choice in 1937:

'If Labour came to power, it could with France and the U.S.S.R. and the smaller states, which are largely governed under Socialist inspiration, pursue a policy of international economic co-operation, based upon the utilisation of abundance instead of restriction, which would rapidly have its effects on world economic conditions.

'The League must maintain its forces strong enough to resist any attempt at aggression . . . under conditions of co-operation an all-round reduction of armaments would be possible. But Labour is not in power and the question is how far it should support the National Government's rearmament. Hitherto, the League has consisted of a number of different states without any unity of command. They have pursued national aims and commanded purely national forces ... the present weakness of the democratic states in face of fascist aggression is not due to their actual superiority in strength. On the contrary, even today they are actually stronger and immeasurably better off in war potential—that is, in resources of personnel and material.

'The Labour Party is opposed to the policy of the National Government in seeking security by piling up huge competitive armaments. It can only tolerate armaments as a necessary support for a policy of collective security. It is fully alive to the dangers which exist in Europe, owing to the aggressive policy of the fascist powers, but it has no confidence in the will of the capitalist government to oppose them. There is every indication that the policy pursued is an attempt to play the old game of "alliances", based on the maintenance of the balance of power, to say that what the Government is doing is necessary for the defence of the country is to beg the whole question. I do not believe that the entry into a competition in arms would give security. On the contrary, I think that it is leading us straight to the disaster of another World War. The Labour Party, therefore, has steadily opposed rearmaments, the policy of the Government, not on the grounds that the level of armaments of two years ago is adequate or even that the present scale is excessive, but because it is impossible to tell what the scale of armaments should be in the absence of any sound foreign policy.'

The strength of this argument lay in the perfectly true assertion that so far from rearming, the Government were in fact rapidly disarming the forces opposed to Fascism. However great our armaments might be, they could never atone for throwing away the alliance with Russia and other countries which could act in unison against the totalitarian bloc. Sir Stafford Cripps and his followers of the Socialist League put the point even more strongly; they were convinced, not without reason, that the rearmament proposed was not intended for use against the Fascist powers, though it might be used against the Soviet Union. I myself wrote a long article in the *Political Quarterly* arguing that all the other threats of war were unlikely to be realised, but that a combination against the Soviet Union was the probable upshot. I proved wrong in 1939, but my prophecy was almost correct. Even in the winter of 1939, when Russia attacked Finland, the forces making for war against Russia rather than against Germany were almost successful in switching the war to one with Russia.

Since Chamberlain was, in fact, ultimately pushed into war with Hitler, historians have ridiculed this Labour attitude and even pretended that Britain's comparative lack of preparation for war in 1939 was the fault of the Labour Party. Labour did, of course, support the war when it came and would have been glad in 1940 if we had been more fully armed. They were never convinced until 1939 that we really intended to go to war, and could always argue that rearmament was unnecessary for a policy of appeasement.

This issue of whether or not, with a Government which did not oppose the dictators, it was wise to use opposition to rearmament as a tactical weapon against the Government's foreign policy was exhaustively examined in the columns of the *New Statesman and Nation*. Numerous people, distinguished and obscure, contributed to this argument, either from a pacifist or Marxist point of view, and during 1936 Keynes wrote letters in reply amounting altogether to some eight columns. The question was put to him whether he would, for a good cause or a bad, simply support Britain in any war? Was not Chamberlain's real position that Britain would only fight for the Empire and not for any more ideological cause, however vital it might be for the world? His final letter is worth repetition:

'Civilisation and liberty are a fairer cause than the integrity of our possessions. But today it is these, and not the Empire, which are in immediate danger. Because the Prime Minister does not register strong emotion about them, he tends unfortunately to gather support from the many people in this country who, rightly perhaps, prefer peace to any cause whatever. That he registers strong emotions about the Empire is overlooked, at present, by these supporters. And when danger in that direction does arise, the issues will probably be so inextricably tangled that those who love civilisation and liberty will not find it easy to stand aside. So we look like enjoying the best of both worlds. Meanwhile, protests are in vain. "The immediate job," in Mr. Kingsley Martin's words, "is to overcome the Party participation which stands in the way of a union of popular forces." '

Maynard Keynes' most distinguished opponent in this argument was Bertrand Russell, who represented a utilitarian form of British pacifism. He was a pacifist because he regarded war as a worse evil than any alternative. He had been in prison in the First World War because he argued publicly that Sir Edward Grey's policy was wrong, that England should have remained neutral and that it was the duty of all citizens to speak their mind, whatever the consequences. He had been deprived of his lectureship at Trinity College, Cambridge, and had spent most of a valuable year writing philosophy in gaol. He remained a pacifist in the thirties, and his state of mind in 1935 is admirably illustrated by a letter he had written to the *New Statesman* in August. It is very characteristic of the thought of the period:

'In all the densely-populated countries of Western Europe, it seems almost certain that, within a few days of the outbreak of war, panic will seize the surviving inhabitants of the capitals and the industrial areas, leading to anarchy, starvation and paralysis of all warlike effort. The only sensible course, therefore, is to prevent war if possible and to remain neutral if war occurs. The neutrals will be the only victors and the only powers whose policy will have a chance of prevailing. . . . In the late war it was arguable that victory, being possible, *might* do some good. With the modern technique of gas attack, no *belligerent* can hope for victory. Absolute pacifism, therefore, in every country in which it is politically possible is the only sane policy both for governments and individuals.'

In writing this letter Russell was chiefly concerned about the psychological results of the Government's Civil Defence circular,

o

which he thought liable to soothe people into acceptance of war. He was supported in this view not only, as some people have thought, by Communists who had ulterior motives, but by orthodox Labour spokesmen who held that this circular was 'a direct incitement to war-mindedness'. No one, I think, at that time challenged Russell's view that Civil Defence preparation was mainly a form of propaganda; we all recalled Baldwin's statement that 'the bomber would always get through'.

I wrote to Russell when I had decided that we ought to regard a League war as a police action on the analogy of a medieval king whose duty it was, even though it meant fighting, to suppress the robber barons. He replied in a private letter on 7th August 1935:

> 'I am against a League war in present circumstances, because the anti-League powers are strong. The analogy is not King v. Barons, but the Wars of the Roses. If the League were strong enough I should favour sanctions, because the effect would suffice, or the war would be short and small. The whole question is quantitative.'

Strangely wrong, Russell seemed to me then, just because the barons were reapidly getting stronger and the king's powers fading out altogether. In 1937 he wrote a brilliant book *Which Way Peace?* I reviewed it sympathetically, but saying that I was no longer able to hold war the worst evil, as I had done in the days when it took two to start a fight. The bombing of an open town such as Guernica had convinced me that the democratic powers must unite to defeat the Fascist bloc. In June 1940 Russell, who had been living in America for the last eighteen months, wrote to me:

> 'The news from Europe is unbearably painful. We all wish that we were not so far away, although we could serve no useful purpose if we were at home. Ever since the war began, I have felt that I could no longer go on being a pacifist, but I have hesitated to say so, because of the responsibility involved. If I were young enough to fight myself, I should do so, but it is more difficult to

urge others. Now, however, I feel that I ought to announce that I have changed my mind, and I would be glad if you could find an opportunity to mention in the *New Statesman* that you have heard from me to this effect.'

Russell was always candid and more courageous about admitting that he had changed his mind than any other man I ever met. He was to change it again more than once. Soon after the war, when America had atom bombs and Russia was not nuclear armed, he argued, to quote his own words:

'Pressure should be put upon Russia to accept the Baruch proposals and I did think that if they continued to refuse, it might be necessary actually to go to war.'

In 1953 he described in the New York *Nation* as a Communist invention the suggestion that he ever favoured a policy of threats against Soviet Russia which might lead to war, and referred to the fact that he had induced the *New Statesman and Nation* to publish a long letter from him refuting 'the slanderous report' that he had ever contemplated any such policy towards Russia. This had been, indeed, an amusing occasion. He solemnly called on me with his lawyer, demanding that I should withdraw a statement that he had favoured threatening Russia with war. I had neatly settled the matter by offering to publish anything he liked over his own signature. The letter which followed was a piece of excellent 'copy' for me. Three columns of Russell for which I paid nothing! But the aftermath was even more odd. When the evidence was brought to his attention he admitted having advocated this warlike policy against the Soviet Union and wrote in a footnote in the *Listener* (28th May 1959):

'Although it may seem incredible, I believed this statement [i.e., that he might have been willing to bomb Russia] to be entirely correct at the time when I made it. I had, in fact, completely forgotten that I had ever thought a policy of threat involving possible war desirable. . . . I have no excuse to offer.'

Even the greatest minds have forgetful moments and during his last years Russell has moved steadily to the Left. He had at one time argued that since the nations would not voluntarily agree to keep the peace, one power had better possess the strength to prevent a war that would destroy all of us. At one time he believed that the lesser evil would be for the dominating power to be American because, little though he liked American civilisation, he thought that their way of life offered the rest of the world a chance of liberty, whereas Communist world rule would clamp down on freedom everywhere and be almost impossible to modify. Later, he became wholly one-sided, strongly supporting China against India and the Vietcong against America. I do not myself take so simple a view of the Sino-Indian dispute, although I share his furious misery about U.S. policy in Vietnam—but his are no longer the views of a peacemaker, rather of a Chinese doctrinaire. The amazing fact remains that Russell was the only individual in the world able to make an impact on the Cold War situation. He was in a position to write and receive answers from both the Secretary of State of the United States and the Premier of Russia in the nuclear dispute, and he is listened to by thousands all over the world who still regard him—or until recently have still regarded him—as the one philosopher who speaks with authority, a dedicated intellect which devotes itself wholly to saving mankind from its most deadly peril,

Only the religious pacifists maintained their attitude unchanged even in the war itself. They were not affected by any argument about a 'lesser evil'. They were forbidden by their Christian or Tolstoyan faith to take part in war, and as long as they based their case on this conviction they were invulnerable. But pacifists cannot take part usefully in international affairs. A refusal to fight may have the effect of increasing the likelihood of war. I discussed this often with Dick Sheppard, who, in October 1934, had asked for postcards from men saying that they renounced war and would 'never again' directly or indirectly support another. He received some 40,000 pledges in reply and at its height the Peace Pledge Union, which resulted, numbered some 135,000.

Canon Sheppard, universally called 'Dick', was a most unusual

parson, whose reputation did not at first recommend him to me. He
sounded like a very hearty Christian. He was a member of the
aristocracy, and a buddy of all the 'bloods' and anti-rationalists.
He was Vicar of St. Martin-in-the-Fields and afterwards Canon of
St. Paul's Cathedral, a popular preacher and religious journalist;
also a good cricketer, often mistaken for a sporting character, and,
worse still, he was a famous practical joker. He was a man of the
world about whom all the world spoke well. On the other hand,
he had made St. Martin-in-the-Fields a centre where tramps
and vagabonds were welcome, and his books were outspoken
in their condemnation of the religious Establishment. He was
certainly greatly loved by the poor as well as popular among the
rich.

When I met Dick Sheppard I found that all the things I had heard
against him were trivial. He had a great gift of sympathy, seemed
totally uninterested in himself, and made you feel you were the only
person in the world he wanted to talk to. Shaw spoke of him as a
superb actor, and no doubt he would have been successful as a
comedian in the West End. But he had a humour of a quite different
kind. One would not expect a famous cleric at a religious conference
to tell the assembled company at breakfast that he had met an
elderly lady when he was going to the bathroom, that in horror she
cried 'Mercy' and locked her door on seeing him coming. His comment was, 'Either she must have stolen my Service Book and had a
guilty conscience, or in spite of my years I must still look a bit of a
lad in pyjamas.' His conversation was full of spice, which was not
diminished in his later years, when asthma and other troubles were
obviously killing him. He worked himself to death, could not take
holidays, and was overwhelmed when separated from his wife. As
parish priest of St. Martin-in-the-Fields he was chaplain to Buckingham Palace. George V instructed him to admonish Edward, Prince
of Wales. Sheppard was furious when he heard that the King had
rendered the interview futile by telling Edward that they were to
meet by command. On another occasion a little girl was sent to him
by her mother because she wouldn't say her prayers. Sheppard was
making a bonfire of leaves in the garden when the little girl arrived,

and won her confidence by saying that one ought to make one's own prayers and throwing her prayer book into the bonfire.

He endeared himself to me not at all by his religious journalism, which I thought poor stuff, but by his honesty and desire to get at the truth. Once he said to me that he had very little faith left and not much hope, and he had to rely on charity. I think it really was a fact that he felt love for almost every human being he met. His love had an infectious quality. Some people's lives were changed when they discovered that he really cared about them.

This selfless and affectionate quality did not make him a wise politician. It was enough for him that an increasing number of people joined his Peace Army; perhaps it might become so big that it could prevent the next war? He would write little postcards recording the growth of his movement. One of them which I still possess says that his latest meeting had gone well 'and it was amusing to see Osbert Sitwell and Beverley Nichols walking away from it wearing our new Peace Badge'. In the summer of 1933 when Mussolini was preparing war against Abyssinia he rang me up to ask my advice. He had, he said, a Peace Army some thousands strong who were prepared to obey his orders. What should they do? Would it be a good idea for them to go to Geneva to protest against war? I explained that in Geneva the League would be discussing sanctions against Mussolini as a way of stopping him from attacking Abyssinia. There was, of course, some risk that war would result from sanctions, but if the pacifists protested at Geneva they would be lining up against the one policy that might prevent the war. If they wanted to make a relevant protest they had better go to Rome as tourists and demonstrate there. Some of them would no doubt be arrested, but they would really be opposing the war, not impeding those who were already trying to stop it. Sheppard replied that he had never thought it out like that. The Peace Army did not go to Rome; I never heard of it doing anything.

When Dick Sheppard died his place as leader of the P.P.U. was taken by Max Plowman, a religious pacifist if ever there was one. He was a poet of the First World War who found his highest pleasure in interpreting the prophetic writings of Blake. He was a craggy, difficult and lovable creature; he found me cynical and exasperating. His correspondence, in which he did most of his thinking, dated from 1913 until his death in 1941. It was edited with meticulous care by his wife.[1] He was the type of man who from the days of George Fox and John Bunyan has given British Protestantism its peculiar character. In his first letter from the Front in 1916 he described himself jabbing bayonets into sacks, which was so much lunacy, but inescapable. He had made, he said, no protest against British policy while we were at peace and had no right to complain when the result was war. By October 1916 he had got to the point of writing:

'I want to exploit the fear of war. . . . After the war, millions of men in every country will have one dominant conviction—that war is a loathsome inanity to be avoided at any cost. But they will be inarticulate in their knowledge. I want to start an International League of Individuals, sworn never to take up arms.'

Couldn't pressure be brought to bear on governments? Working men never wanted to fight. 'Can't someone start an International League to give that one and only tenet a voice? . . . A pretty theory, coming from an instructor in bayonet fighting.'

In 1917 he was arguing furiously with his brother, who thought the Germans must be 'taught a lesson'. He had tried logic, Max said, for three or four years, now he must begin to do what he thought right. Shortly afterwards he was hit in the head with a piece of shrapnel; he was never sure, he wrote, whether it was this that finally knocked sense into him. Anyway, he resigned his commission and informed his embarrassed superiors that he had developed a conscientious objection to war. They were all very nice, obviously in no hurry for a court martial, and he was still awaiting trial when the Armistice made it unnecessary.

Sheppard's Peace Pledge Union was exactly the army of objectors to war that Max had asked for. By that time, he had formulated for

1. Max Plowman, *Bridge into the Future* (Andrew Dakers, 1944).

himself a position in which Socialism and pacifism were a single religion based on revolt against materialism and state coercion. It was typical of him that he disliked the P.P.U. almost as much as he did other organised bodies. He used sometimes to ask me to join him, explaining that among the sponsors of the P.P.U. there was no more real agreement than among the first dozen people one might happen upon in Piccadilly. His own book *A Faith called Pacifism*, was far more deeply felt than scores of other pacifist affirmations of that period; these were mainly written by people whose faith did not outlast the beginning of the war. A few of them became 'pro-German'. If you were a pacifist in the sense that you thought anything might be better than war, you might be brave enough to say, as a well-known literary figure did in the Albert Hall, that what was called 'dishonour' was far better than war, or you might, like George Lansbury, full of goodwill, and Lloyd George, full of guilt about Versailles, make personal contact with Hitler and find him wonderfully persuasive. After all, Hitler always gave sound, patriotic reasons for each of his aggressions and he could always sting the conscience of the West by talking of the follies of Versailles, and right up to the end he persuaded many Englishmen that he desired nothing so much as friendship with Great Britain.

It was this pro-Nazi tendency among members of the P.P.U. that finally broke up the organisation. Max, for whom Fascism stood for everything he hated, was horrified. He was almost equally opposed to Communism and replied to his friend Middleton Murry, who was trying to reconcile Christianity and Marxism, that Marxism was an unconstructive philosophy in which there is 'no love, no admiration, no hope, just a dull, objective sense of fact, and we hope to reconstruct the world on the basis of this. As well might a man hope to beget a giant race out of the knowledge of feminine anatomy.' Marxism was at best a half-truth, which omitted man's capacity to break away from himself as a purely economic animal. In fact, 'all human history has been the history of the creative efforts of mankind to live in increasingly wide circles of amicable community'. He wrote shrewdly that Murry's fallacy in accepting man as an economic animal led him into writing 'the word "disinterestedness" where

he means "love", because he has no object for love and "disinterestedness" will stand without an object.'

With this faith in his belly there was nothing to do when the war
came but to attempt to build a community of people with a common
faith which would survive the war. This led to the formation of the
settlement at Langham, where again only disappointment awaited
him. The quarrels among pacifists in community only repeated the
sorry, usually comic, story of many such experiments in the past.
They nearly drove Max off his head. But he persisted that the really
disruptive thought which led people astray was their fear of the 'nag
of consequence'. A wrong is not made right by contemplation of the
possibly evil results of trying to do what is right. Were this not so,
'such an item of history as the Crucifixion would never have
happened', and our moral code would be altogether different from
what we profess:

'Don't you see that the "swopping of horses" that goes on between the personal ethic and the social and political ethic is the
root of all the trouble, and that unless we tackle that trouble at
the root in *ourselves*, the present irresponsible position of things
simply must persist.'

Only imagination could break the vicious circle that follows from
'virtuous wickedness'. Unless we leave off arguing about hypothetical consequences we must fall into an ever-deepening morass.

Max died in June 1941, before his prophecy was fulfilled by the
British and German policy of indiscriminate civilian bombing. We
had not then burnt 40,000 people to death in Hamburg, 80,000 in
Tokyo and an even larger number in Dresden. The nuclear bomb,
which completed Max's argument about the 'nag of consequences',
came later still.

I was so interested in Max's effort to solve this apparently insoluble
ethical problem that I examined with great care a book which restated the same pacifist argument at some length, in the *Political
Quarterly*. I took as my text Aldous Huxley's *Ends and Means*, which
was published in 1937. Its central argument was that all real progress

is progress in charity, that no violence could increase the amount of charity in the world, all politics included violence and the only solution was the formation of groups of individuals who had refused to add to the miseries of the world. I thought the argument unconvincing since, in fact, somebody had to go on trying to make the world better, even though it might be true that they would necessarily fail. I remember Dick Sheppard once, in one of his surprising moments, putting his head round the door and saying, 'Do you agree with Aldous Huxley that one cannot built rightly with the wrong materials? It so often seems that one can.'

One of the greatest difficulties of Huxley's position was that the pacifists were likely, willy-nilly, to help the thugs rule the world. Without meaning it, pacifists supported the most violent people in society because, in the last resort, they would be compelled to give way to those who were willing to use force. Mahatma Gandhi, much quoted by pacifists in those days, was aware of this problem and never certain that any group of his followers would present a non-violent resistance front when it came to the crunch; they might be willing from cowardice to suffer violence rather than return it, but could they ever reach the point of *ahimsa* if their nation or those they loved were threatened? For the politician, politics are always a choice of evils.

I used to tease my pacifist friends with the case of the good Samaritan. We know from the parable that Christian behaviour if a man is left for dead at the roadside is to tend a man's wounds, put him on a mule, take him to an inn and give the innkeeper tuppence to look after him. But Christ gave no guidance about the proper conduct if the good Samaritan arrived while the robbers were still beating the man up. Should he go to the rescue, using what weapons he might have, even if they involved the most extreme form of violence? Or should he 'pass by on the other side', of course preaching a sermon on the wickedness of violence as he did so? I once asked Sheppard what Jesus's answer would have been; he shook his head and said he wished Christ had been more explicit. International affairs are always, of course, infinitely more complex. No war is fought for purely humanitarian reasons, yet getting rid of concentra-

tion camps and ending Nazi cruelty were important subjects in the
minds of many people in 1939. If you took the case of war in Spain
were we not 'passing by on the other side' if we allowed ourselves to
be blackmailed into refusing the Spanish Government its normal
rights of commerce and import of arms?

I wrote to Aldous Huxley because I had heard that he and Gerald
Heard were setting up such a community in California. I quote his
reply:

> 701 S. Amalfi Drive
> Pacific Palisades
> Calif.
> 30th July 1939

'Dear Kingsley Martin,

'Many thanks for your letter, and apologies for not having
answered it before—a delay due to pressure of work.

'I don't know where you got your information about Gerald
and myself being about to start a community; it doesn't happen
to be true. I can't speak for Gerald; but certainly I don't know
nearly enough about many things to be able to embark on such a
venture with any prospect of success. This doesn't diminish my
interest in such ventures; for I become more and more firmly convinced that it is completely pointless to work in the field of
politics, in the ordinary sense of the word—first, because one can't
achieve anything unless one is in a key position, and, second,
because even if one were in a key position, all one could achieve
would be, at the best, a deflection of evil into slightly different
channels. The existing system seems to be even less viable than
previous social systems (because more efficient and therefore capable of achieving greater evil in a shorter space of time than
previous systems). One is forced to the conclusion that the men of
religious insight were right in insisting that society at large and
men and women as they are on the average, in the "unregenerate"
state, are doomed to perpetual self-frustration and self-destruction.
Every great religious leader has been profoundly pessimistic about
society at large and men and women as they are. (Generation of
vipers. Many are called, few chosen. The needle's eye. From those

that have not shall be taken away even that which they have.
Unless your righteousness exceed that of the Scribes and Pharisees.
Maya. Fallen World. Etc. etc.) On the other hand, they have been
profoundly optimistic about the potentialities of individuals and
very small associations of such individuals. (The kingdom of
heaven. Nirvana. Non-attachment. *Sub specie aeternitatis*. Dying to
the ordinary life of personality to be reborn. Etc. etc.) Nineteenth-
century humanists (who were members of the more prosperous
classes in the more go-ahead countries of the West) reversed the
traditional attitude and were optimistic about society at large and
men and women as they are (social reform, compulsory education,
Utopia, evolution. Etc. etc.) At the same time they were so pessimistic about the things that every religious teacher had been
optimistic about that they were simply unaware of the possibility
that human beings could ever transcend their miserable little egos.
This attitude is becoming less and less acceptable, even in the West
and among the prosperous. It is obvious now that the religious
teachers were right and that nothing can be achieved on the
exclusively political plane except palliation and the deflection of
evils. So long as the majority of human beings choose to live like
the *homme moyen sensuel*, in an "unregenerate" state, society at
large cannot do anything except stagger along from catastrophe to
catastrophe. Religious people who think that they can go into
politics and transform the world always end by going into politics
and being transformed by the world. (E.g. the Jesuits, Père
Joseph, the Oxford Group.) Religion can have no politics except
the creation of small-scale societies of chosen individuals outside
and on the margin of the essentially unviable large-scale societies,
whose nature dooms them to self-frustration and suicide.

'It seems a dismal conclusion; but it is the one that every
religious teacher has always insisted on as unescapable.

Yours,
Aldous Huxley.'

Clearly if you believe in this extreme form that the end never
justifies the means you must be an absolute pacifist. You must not

lie and cheat and murder, even to save your country being overrun. I get annoyed by people who denounce Communists and Jesuits for holding that ends justify means if they themselves condone the bombing of open cities in wartime. Were they not themselves willing to profit by every kind of Secret Service 'cloak and dagger' activity and the foulest kind of 'black' propaganda in order to defend themselves against the Nazis, who were, of course, doing exactly the same things? These moralists are prepared to do evil to prevent worse if they are sufficiently hard-pressed. The difference between them and Communists on this point is that the Communists do not make the same distinction as other people between peace and war. They are fighting a class war all the time, believing that the only way to permanent peace is what they call the dictatorship of the proletariat.

In England the Left was affected by Marxist thought, but for the most part only allied to Communism because it became increasingly difficult to believe that pacifism was any reply to the Nazi movement. The Left Book Club became the principal instrument of Marxism and persuaded a large proportion of the educated youth of England to the doctrine that Capitalism created war, that Fascism was the last, most dangerous form of Imperialism and that the motives for war would disappear when Socialism was achieved. Marxism also meant the economic interpretation of history and the belief that, sooner or later, a proletarian victory was inevitable. They thought that just as Feudalism had given way to private Capitalism, so Capitalism would develop into Imperialism and Fascism; if they were brave and resolute, Fascism might be overthrown by the proletarian revolution, even in their time. An exceptionally able man like Victor Gollancz, always primarily a moralist, made up his mind that war could only be prevented by an alliance between the U.S.S.R. and all the Democratic countries. He threw his whole remarkable organising capacity into propaganda for Socialism here and on behalf of Communism in Russia. With Strachey and Laski as joint sponsors of the Left Book Club, he went to surprising lengths. Though occasionally publishing books from people such as Orwell and Attlee, he would, at this period, try to persuade non-Marxist writers to cut out any word that could be offensive to the Soviet

Union. In every part of England Left Book Club groups were
formed and they came mainly under the influence of Communists
or near-Communists. Between 1936 and 1939 their influence, particularly in the universities, was enormous.

The Nazi-Soviet pact destroyed the myth that Russia was somehow morally superior and aloof from the world of *realpolitik*. Victor
Gollancz was only one of thousands who was outraged by what he
felt was a monstrous betrayal which made war inevitable. Though
he made many speeches in praise of Russia after 1941 when the
Soviet Union was in the war, he was at heart relieved by the 1939
break with the Communists. His *Betrayal of the Left* was a powerful
indictment of Communism. He had parted company from allies
whose philosophy was the opposite of his own. He realised that he
had really always been a Christian pacifist. After the war, he spon-
sored the 'Save Europe Now' campaign, which was designed to
relieve starvation in Germany and he was bitterly opposed to the
Peace Treaty which divided Germany. The more terrible the sins of
the Nazis, the greater their need for forgiveness. He became a
mystical Christian, while retaining the appearance of an Old Testa-
ment prophet, and he was as interested in compiling learned and
unusual religious anthologies and books about music as he had been
when he made publishing a political force in the thirties.

When war was inevitable, the numerous peace societies from the
National Peace Council downwards were pitiably divided. Their
basic membership was usually pacifist and their funds came from
Quakers and others who did not believe that any League threat
would result in peace or that it was moral anyway. They were penetrated by Communists who tried to persuade them first to use sanctions against Italy and then to line up in a Peace Front against Hitler.
If you look at the proceedings of the National Peace Council at this
period, you will find that they passed resolutions about the wickedness of war and the bad policy of Mr. Chamberlain. So far, they
were all agreement. When they went on to discuss the methods by
which Hitler could be stopped, they were so divided that they often
abandoned any effort to say anything. Thus the one really effective
result of Marxist propaganda in England was the final confusion and

defeat of the pacifists. Many of them had abandoned their absolute pacifism by 1938. When in 1939, after the Nazi-Soviet Pact, the Communists suddenly decided to oppose the war as 'Imperialist aggression', and created an organisation called the 'Convention' to organise peace propaganda, the unfortunate pacifists who had been recently converted to accept the war were utterly routed and bemused. Many of them had given up their most cherished principles as a result of Marxist pressure. They now had no leadership and were reduced to impotent misery or angry patriotism.

The Convention, as the Communists called it, never had deep roots. The pacifists discovered that the Communists were really Soviet nationalists, though they might not go so far as the 'revolutionary defeatism' which had ended the war in Russia in 1917. As a matter of fact, I do not believe many of the Communists would themselves have maintained their own doctrine to the end. If we had been invaded in 1940 most of them would have taken up their hammers and sickles to defend the beaches with Winston Churchill.

And then the spectrum changed again. Nothing, in the view of the Left, was so impossible as an *entente* between Stalin and the Nazis. Only a few days before the Nazi-Societ Pact, I attended a great meeting organised by the Left Book Club. The platform included Lloyd George as well as John Strachey. I still recall the confident, resonant voice of John Strachey as he said: 'Nothing is so certain amid the shifting sands of politics today as the absolute knowledge that the Soviet Union will never yield an inch to Nazi Germany.' In 1939, when war with Germany seemed certain, Harry Pollitt's pamphlet 'How to Win the War' declared:

> 'To stand aside from the conflict, to contribute only revolution-ary-sounding phrases while the fascist beasts ride roughshod over Europe, would be a betrayal of everything our forbears have fought to achieve in the course of long years of struggle against capitalism.'

He declared that 'the Communist Party supports the war, believing it to be a just war which should be supported by the whole

working class and all friends of democracy in Britain'. But after the
Pact in November 1939 Pollitt was pushed aside and Palme Dutt,
the high priest of the Communist movement, produced a pamphlet
'Why this War?' in which he wrote:

> 'This is an Imperialist war like the war of 1914. It is a sordid
> exploiters' war of rival millionaire groups, using the workers as
> their pawns in the struggle for world domination for markets,
> colonies and profits, for the oppression of peoples. This is a war in
> which no worker in any country can give support.'

In June 1941 Hitler invaded Russia. The Communists, like good
Soviet nationalists, again right-about-faced. It may well be, as I said,
that they had really always been half-hearted in 'revolutionary
defeatism' and felt, as Stalin was later on to say, that from the
beginning the war against Germany had always had 'an anti-Fascist
character'. Now they threw themselves into the struggle with un-
exampled enthusiasm. Harry Pollitt was again popular with the
Communist Establishment. He said: 'We must go on increasing our
production and must throw all our weight into the fight so that we
shall batter hell out of Hitler and Fascism.'

Perhaps a conversation I had with Lord Beaverbrook, who had an
experience of Communist workers when he was Minister of Supply
and had produced aeroplanes for the Battle of Britain, will best
illustrate the point. Sitting high in a top suite in the Savoy Hotel,
Beaverbrook shouted:

> 'That fellow who has just left is afraid of the Communists. I tell
> you we want the wings of the morning. We want a bellyful of
> wind in our sails. Who are the people to put a bellyful of wind in
> our sails? Who will give you the wings of the morning? The
> Communists! The Communists!'

His words with their Biblical flavour floated over the roof-tops and
could have been heard in Trafalgar Square.

Personalities by Low: Ernest Bevin, Sir John Simon, Walter Elliot, and Stanley Baldwin

League personalities by Kapp: Dr Beneš and Viscount Cecil

CHAPTER TEN

The Spanish War

In September 1937 I visited a great Paris Exhibition which symbolised national aspirations. It was dominated by the German and Soviet pavilions. The German building was no temporary affair, but huge, built of solid stone to be removed block by block and rebuilt in Hitler's Reich. Immediately facing the German eagle was the Soviet pavilion with two colossal figures of a young man and woman of the New World standing on top of it. When you had done staring at these immense erections and admiring the fairy fountains playing beneath them, you realised that there were quite a lot of other countries represented. Spain, for instance, then immersed in the horrors of civil war, had a small building containing Picasso's expression of his anger and there were also a number of vigorous paintings by the younger artists of democratic Spain. On the other side, Britain was modestly housed in something that looked like a white packing-case. When you went in, the first thing you saw was a cardboard Chamberlain fishing in rubber waders and, beyond, an elegant pattern of golf balls, a frieze of tennis rackets, polo sets, riding equipment, natty dinner jackets and, by a pleasant transition, agreeable pottery and textiles, books finely printed and photographs of the English countryside. I stared in bewilderment. Could this be England? If so, it was the England of the cultivated rich or perhaps of the England foreseen by Bernard Shaw when Britain's economy would depend on the export of chocolate creams. An entirely upper-class England. Almost all the photographs were of pastoral scenes and old churches, not a single factory chimney, not a gun or battle-ship or aeroplane, not a hint that Britain had a colonial empire, not a sign anywhere of a proletariat. A nice England, unlike any that had existed or could exist; England as seen by guests in a country house-party where the servants were unobtrusively in the background, where all nature smiled and every luxury appeared as if by magic.

The curious fact was that the British upper class should have so far

P

changed as to wish to portray themselves in this way. Had they
really given up any notion of ruling the waves or were they merely
desirous not to remind other countries that Britain still had a Navy?
I wrote at the time:

> Someday perhaps before very long, British Imperialism will
> turn the tables and Labour will find itself committed to another
> national war fought for democracy, a war to end war and all the
> rest of it. In fact the British upper class is not pacifist. It is just a
> question of the kind of things it thinks worth fighting for. It is not
> for nothing that we are embarking on a vastly increased armament
> expenditure. The present Exhibition represents a phase of Britain.
> In two months' time it will have disappeared. We shall be build-
> ing another Exhibition of destroyers, big guns, Hawker and Fury
> aeroplanes, munition factories and regiments of cannon-fodder.

I wrote with some bitterness because the Spanish war which had
begun in the summer of 1936 had seemed to me the last proud
moment of hope. There seemed an offchance of defeating Fascism in
Spain instead of merely waiting until we had to fight for nothing
but national survival. A. J. P. Taylor writes off as nonsense the view
that 'the victory of the Spanish Republic would overthrow Hitler
also'. I think it was not nonsense. It might have led to Hitler finding
himself confronted with a barrier both to the East and West. Mr.
Hugh Thomas,[1] who writes with unique authority on the Spanish
War, admits that non-intervention might only have delayed the outbreak of general war, but adds:

> 'This delay, like Munich, was undoubtedly caused by a certain
> craven indolence on the part of the British Government, which
> did not profit them at all. A general war which broke out in 1936
> or 1937 or 1938 would have been fought in circumstances more
> favourable to the Western democracies than that which came in
> 1939 over Poland. One alternative to the "farce of non-interven-
> tion" was, of course—as it was to Munich, to the reoccupation of

1. Hugh Thomas, *The Spanish Civil War* (Eyre and Spottiswoode, 1961).

the Rhineland and to German rearmament—to stand firm and denounce the breach of agreements. This policy had, at least, the possibility of upsetting the dictator without a war being needed.'

In short, there was a chance of re-creating, with the aid of other League powers which included the U.S.S.R., the system of preventing general war which had been destroyed in 1935. Craven indolence there certainly was; but it was prompted partly by a preference for Fascist victory in Spain and a horror of finding ourselves on the same side as the Soviet Union.

The cause at stake seemed to many of us greater and involving fewer risks than others that lay before us. It was the hope of liberation from ancient tyranny that inspired resistance to Franco. The medieval church and aristocracy had always crushed any signs of democracy in Spain. The issue of Communism was a fake. The Communists were a small, uninfluential group in Catalonia, which was the traditional home of Anarchism ever since the days of Bakunin. Soviet policy was nationalist; no doubt some Russians had dreams of a Communist Spain, but Stalin did not imagine Spain would be anything else but Spanish and his idea was to keep the war going as long as possible. The spring of action which brought the masses from their homes to fight against Franco was hunger, reinforced by hatred of clericalism and absentee landlordism. The issue was whether Spain must for ever remain a backward, uneducated, impoverished land under the autocratic rule of the priests and army. As the war developed, fanaticism grew, and so did cruelty. Hugh Thomas gives an example of the Carlists who were 'stimulated to a greater fury and patriotic zeal when a solitary Republican bomber dropped a bomb which struck the famous effigy of the Virgin of the Pilar at Saragossa, but did not explode. It was not simply a matter of religious outrage; the Virgin had shortly before been solemnly named Captain-General of the city.' On the Democratic side, many churches and convents were burnt, though not apparently looted, and some priests, nuns and monks were killed. The worst atrocities were carried out by Franco's Moors, but both sides often killed their prisoners. Franco ordered many deliberate massacres, and La Pasionaria, who became the very symbol of popular resistance, urged Spanish women to fight, if they had no other weapons, with knives and burning oil. The slogan which became famous among workers everywhere is usually attributed to her, 'It is better to die on your feet than to live on your knees; *they shall not pass.*'

From the very start the war took on the aspect of a class struggle. It was commonly presented in the British press as if the Reds were the Rebels and the Fascists the defenders of legality. The Rothermere press ran banner headlines about Franco's crusade for Christianity, carried out by 'Loyalists' and 'Insurgent patriots', against Communism. Much was said about Franco's praiseworthy golf handicap. In some British newspapers, old atrocity stories and photographs which had done service against the Germans in the First World War and been periodically used against the Russians were brought out from dusty pigeonholes. Even reputable papers talked as if Franco was head of a government, and hundreds of thousands of readers were persuaded that the fight in Spain was the result of a Bolshevist rising. On the other side the principal advocates of the Republican cause were the *News Chronicle* and the *New Statesman and Nation.* No doubt the Left was often deluded by the propaganda of Willi Muenzenberg, who ran a Communist publicity bureau in Paris, but the *New Statesman and Nation* had excellent reports from Spain itself. Our regular Spanish correspondent, Geoffrey Brereton, was reinforced by Cyril Connolly. They both did their best to establish the truth.

Non-intervention sounded reasonable enough in theory, but in practice it meant support for the Fascist side. While Britain and France were carrying out their pledge not to aid either belligerent, Italy and Germany poured out supplies and sent Franco the troops and aeroplanes he needed. In the House of Commons the pretence of non-intervention had to be maintained by lies and evasions. In 1937 there were some 30,000 German and 80,000 Italian troops in Spain and as the war went on it became clear that Hitler was trying out his aeroplanes in Spain in preparation for the European war. He also assured himself of an adequate supply of Spanish iron ore. On the French side Léon Blum, as much a pacifist as any premier can be, was much troubled by the danger of a struggle between Fascist and Popular Front forces in France and, above all, was frightened of war. But nobody seriously thought that world conflict would result if Britain and France defended their right to send ships to Spain and continued normal trading with the Spanish Government. Though Blum accepted Anthony Eden's warning to be cautious about sending aid to Spain and was ready to discourage the French workers from helping their comrades there, he later repented his decision. The French Government did, in fact, allow foreigners and Frenchmen to cross the Pyrenees during the larger part of the war. There were also periods in which the frontier was shut and aid cut off from France as well as from Britain. This did not prevent M. Cot, the Minister for Air, arranging for air support of a very limited character to reach the popular forces in Spain.

The Right as well as the Left in Britain were roused when they learnt that twenty-two of our ships had been attacked by Fascist planes, eleven of them sunk or seriously damaged and twenty-one British seamen and several non-intervention observers killed. Hugh Thomas remarks that 'even the subtle vocabulary of R. A. Butler, Under-Secretary to the Foreign Office, was taxed to explain why the Government would not permit the export of anti-aircraft guns to Republican Spain, nor our merchant ships to carry their own arms'. Churchill, usually on Franco's side, said, 'I understand undergoing humiliation for the cause of peace. I would have supported the Government if I felt we were making towards greater security for peace, but I fear this abjection is woefully misunderstood abroad. I fear it will actually bring us nearer to all those dangers which we desire above all things to withhold from our people.'

Though fear of war no doubt entered Chamberlain's mind, it was not that which prompted British policy. Even when events as ghastly as the German bombing of the open town of Guernica took place we refused to sent anti-aircraft guns to Spain. Roosevelt, who for a time relaxed the American blockade of Spain, was driven by Catholic pressure into renewing it. Joseph Kennedy, U.S. Ambassador in England, played his pusillanimous part in influencing U.S. policy. He was horrified at any suggestion that America or Britain should help in any way the 'bunch of atheists and Communists' which he believed the Spanish Government to be. In the House of Commons Labour made speeches on the side of the Spanish Government; Noel-Baker and others, particularly trade unionists, criticised the farcical character of non-intervention and organised meetings demanding the provision of medical supplies and food to the Spanish people. No one but a Tolstoyan pacifist could hold that a democratic government should be deprived of its normal rights because it was attempting to suppress a Fascist rising. Mr. Attlee even visited Spain and gave his name to a battalion of the International Brigade. Some Independents, like Eleanor Rathbone, spoke with even more fervour than Labour members. The Labour Party in the House did not come near to representing the mood of the Left. The Left on this issue did not mean a few intellectuals, but a very large section of the British public. The agitation on behalf of Spain was far larger and more serious than any similar mass movement in my experience.

The strength of this agitation was greatly increased by the part played by the International Brigade. It came from every part of Europe and America and provided a focus for popular feeling. The Brigade played an important role in the fighting, especially in the defence of Madrid when everyone expected Republican resistance to be quickly squashed. I remember that the *Observer* actually announced that Madrid had fallen and had to eat its words next week. The Brigade contained some weaklings, and some who had joined only for the sake of adventure or because they were out of work. But the great majority were frustrated young men who desired to stand up to Fascism and believed, since their governments were on the wrong side, that they could show by their example that such a thing as international working-class solidarity existed. About half the 40,000 volunteers were Communists or near-Communists, but they had with them the whole Byronic tradition in which enthusiastic idealists had enlisted abroad to fight for liberty. They included a large body of unindoctrinated working men who believed they were fighting for a good cause, and a sprinkling of university students such as John Cornford, Ralph Fox and Julian Bell, who were all killed. Of the British contingent, 543 were killed and between 2,000 and 3,000 wounded. The fact that they were ready to die for a cause in which they had no material interest had an important effect on the morale of the Spanish workers and it inspired audiences in innumerable mass meetings to contribute money in every part of Britain. About a million pounds was collected, largely in donations from people who could ill afford to subscribe. A few rich men also gave larger sums. Students demonstrated in the streets and often their parents supported them. There was no device for raising funds from jumble sales to whist drives which was forgotten by the organisers of 'Aid to Spain' and the Popular Front of Labour, Communist, Liberals and even some Conservatives became a reality. Threats of expulsion did not deter a minority of Labour M.P.s from appearing on the same platform as Communists. Liberals, Labour men and ex-I.L.P.ers had found a common cause with the extreme Left, which most of them detested. I recall one meeting at the Albert Hall when Nehru spoke and Paul Robeson sang, with innumerable encores, to the delight of a great enthusiastic audience. One found oneself speaking on the same platform with Harry Pollitt, James Maxton, Wilfred Roberts of the Liberal Party, the Conservative Duchess of Atholl and independently minded clergymen. This Popular Front did not fade until Barcelona was captured in the spring of 1939.

Much has been made of my refusal to publish a series of articles from George Orwell, who was outraged by his experience in Catalonia, where many so-called Trotskyites had been gaoled or murdered by Communists. I am not surprised that I did not publish the articles.[1] I knew and liked Orwell and would in the ordinary way

1. Orwell's letter to Frank Jellinek late in 1938 seems to support my decision He wrote:

'I entirely agree with you that the whole business about the P.O.U.M. has had far too much fuss made about it and that the net result of this kind of thing is to prejudice people against the Spanish Republic. . . . [In my book] . . . I've given a more sympathetic picture of the P.O.U.M. line than I actually felt, because I always told them they were wrong and refused to join the party. But I had to put it as sympathetically as possible, because it has had no hearing in the Capitalist Press and nothing but libels in the Left-Wing Press. . . .'

have published anything he offered. In fact, he continued to write for the paper throughout the war with Germany. But in rejecting these articles I was for once a realist; nearly all the papers were full of attacks on Negrin, the humane and liberal Prime Minister, and I objected to adding my venom for much the same reasons as I should have hesitated about doing propaganda for Goebbels in the war against Germany. I had never been one to withhold criticism against my own side, but in this case when almost any other paper would have accepted his articles I decided there was no need for them to appear in the *N. S. & N.* I knew that whatever else was true the war would certainly be lost if its direction fell into the hands of the Anarchists, many of whom were admirable people and abominably treated—I did not then know how abominably—by the Communists. I did not love the Communists, but I knew that the Spanish Government was compelled to give them too much power because no country except the Soviet Union was aiding the Republican cause. I probably underestimated the Communist atrocities; it was not an unnatural fault when every day brought me news of tortures and shootings carried out by Franco and his Moors.

This was the mood of almost all the political and literary figures who at that time contributed to the *New Statesman and Nation*. Some were more committed than others; a few like Spender and Auden paid only short visits to Spain and wrote memorable poems about it. I well remember Auden in those days; he was the most accomplished of the poets of the thirties, was a regular contributor to the paper and I have never been able to understand why he does not feel respectful to his own youth. He now describes these poems as 'tosh'. I well understand how a man may change his basic attitude to public affairs, but that he should wish to change the wording of what he wrote earlier, because he no longer approves of it, is to me incomprehensible. He wrote then with obvious sincerity of the guilt men must feel about the 'necessity of killing'. In later editions he has altered 'necessity' to 'fact'. Does he no longer believe that in war men must kill and suffer from the guilt that they feel as a result of outraging their nature? Whatever his answer—it must surely be a completely pacifist one— I want to put it on record that at this stage of his life Auden was an engaging, sincere and committed man and it is a period of his life, whatever conversion he has suffered since, of which he should be proud.

I visited Spain twice during the Civil War. On the first occasion I went out with Louis Fischer, who was not yet disillusioned with Stalin and was, I think, responsible for seeing that some Soviet arms reached their destination. It was then, too, that I got to know Otto Katz, a Czech Communist who worked with Willi Muenzenberg at his Paris office. Muenzenberg was an inspired propagandist who later developed independent ideas and was murdered, if one accepts Arthur Koestler's account[1] by Stalin's agents. Otto Katz, alias André Simon, was a fanatical and ruthless Commissar; he was ultimately executed in the Stalinist purge in Prague on the nonsensical charge of having consorted with such Western Imperialists as Claud Cockburn and, it may be, me. I do not think I was deceived by Muenzenberg's propaganda; I did not need propaganda because I was committed and ready to overlook much that was evil on the Government side in Spain in the certainty that this was a war that had to be won. Maybe if I had known more, I should have been revolted by Communist behaviour, but were not Western liberals ready to endorse bombing of civilians in the Second World War?

On my first visit the Government's H.Q. was in Valencia. We drove through the narrow strip of territory in a convoy of trucks to Madrid. The Government managed to keep this contact with their hard-pressed capital. Physically, I remember the overpowering smell of unrefined oil which pervaded everything else in a Madrid hotel, the meals which consisted of bread and grapes—satisfactory when there were grapes—the bullets which screamed over our heads as we walked through the University City where the fighting had been fiercest and the ruins were unlike anything I had seen since 1917. The Spanish people were grim and proud; they did not hurry over-much as they made their way into air-raid shelters when Franco's planes flew low over the undefended city. There I met Ernest Hemingway, in his element where there was danger, and Herbert Matthews, the courageous correspondent of the *New York Times*.

1. Arthur Koestler, *The Invisible Writing* (Hamish Hamilton, 1954).

One of my companions was Dorothy Parker, who died in 1967. She was already famous in New York for her witticisms, but was in Spain sad and rather silent, weeping often at the desolation which she saw around her. I remember the long journey back through the night to Valencia where I won the friendship of the Prime Minister, Dr. Negrin, and of Señor Del Vayo, the Foreign Secretary, both men who were not dishonoured by the miserable intrigue and treacheries which are, no doubt, an inevitable sequel to defeat.

I formed a high opinion of Negrin. He was a *bon viveur* as well as a distinguished scientist and doctor, and he accepted the premiership in a crisis because, as a Socialist who hated poverty and tyranny, he thought it his duty to take a place that no one else seemed able to fill. I could not find that he was inspired by ambition or that he ever shared in the fanaticism which surrounded him. Later he was much criticised for the self-indulgent life he lived as an exile in Paris. But when I knew him in Spain he was a brave and liberal-minded man who resisted Communist pressure as long as he could. There is evidence that he tried to rid himself of Communist agents when the P.O.U.M. was 'liquidated' by them. He might have succeeded if the West had given him a modicum of aid. He was conscious that Russian help was precarious; Stalin was cautious in the extreme. The U.S.S.R. sent money to the Spanish Government and provided it with some of its ablest international advisers, such as Togliatti. There may have been as many as two thousand Russians altogether in Spain and I recall the excitement there when some Russian aeroplanes, apparently faster than the German, were said to have arrived to help the Democratic cause. But even before the end of 1937 Soviet interest in Spain had slackened and Stalin showed that he was unwilling to plunge more deeply into the war lest he lose the goodwill for which he still hoped to win in the West.

It was not until long after the war that we learnt to what lengths of treachery to his own supporters Stalin was prepared to go. In one way and another he liquidated all the Russians who had fought in Spain, perhaps because they knew too much, perhaps because he wished to wipe out the memory of the Spanish episode. Those who had fought had become Trotskyites in his diseased mind. He decided long before the war was over that he must play for respectability if he was to keep on good terms with the Western democracies which in the long run surely must also become frightened of Hitler. The fate of the men of the International Brigade was tragic. In Russia its members were shot or exiled; in the United States, long before the McCarthy period, they were debarred from employment, and, even in England, when the war started, their invaluable experience in Spain was rejected. Tom Wintringham, a captain in Spain and an expert in guerilla warfare, was long cold-shouldered before his services were used at Osterley Park in the training of Commandos. Others were not even allowed to volunteer for the armed forces or Civil Defence.

I had some prevision that this last demonstration of working-class solidarity in Spain would be brought to nothing (with Russian connivance) when I went to a conference of the International Peace Campaign in Brussels in 1937. This I.P.C., as I have explained earlier, was an alliance between the Communists and those in the West who were still working desperately for collective security. Communists were pleased with their success in penetrating a committee on which sat Lord Cecil, Philip Noel-Baker, W. Arnold-Forster and other equally distinguished figures in the Peace movement. The I.P.C., therefore, worked as a sort of League of Nations Union or, if you belonged to the other camp, the Popular Front in action. It sounded a hopeful development and so I thought, when I attended the *Rassemblement Universelle pour la Paix* in Brussels in September 1937. The effect of the Conference on me, and no doubt many others, was to induce something like desperation, and I wrote:

This Congress came at least ten years too late. Ten years ago a peace congress of common people from all over the world—for the Congress was really world-wide—might have been the beginning of a League of Peoples which could have superseded the League of Nations. As it was, the proceedings only recalled H. W. Nevinson's brilliant phrase about 'the stage army of the good'. And this was the more pathetic because the delegates included a host of faces not known at Geneva, working-class people who had

come often in spite of official discouragement, in spite of the cool-
ness of Transport House and the League of Nations Union to any
congress which was to include Left-Wing and Communists as
well as professional pacifists. In some factories working men had
clubbed together to send delegates. There they were, the cannon
fodder of the next war, waiting for leadership and knowing, as
their cheers showed when they had the chance, that the next war
had something to do with Fascism and with Spain. But neither
Fascism nor Spain could be mentioned. An American organisation
'against war and Fascism' had to suppress its too provocative title.
Twice the rank and file tried to express its feelings. On the first
night when a Spanish delegate appeared, a host of fists went up
and shouts began 'Les avions pour l'Espagne'. The demonstrators
were at once informed that this was an entirely non-political
congress. It was about peace, not about politics, not about the
actual war which is now raging, but about the prevention of some
war that might happen some time. A strange division, but one
maintained throughout the Congress. At the final demonstration
the Spaniards again appeared, and 'Pasionaria', the eloquent and
beautiful deputy from Oviedo, who had evoked ardent sympathy
for her cause in France, arrived on the platform. Shouts of 'Les
Espagnols au micro' broke out spontaneously. It was not Lord
Cecil but Marcel Cachin, the veteran French Communist, who
checked this demonstration. They must not introduce politics.
'Pasionaria' remained silent. Marcel Cachin pronounced an eloquent and unexceptionable speech on liberty, democracy and
peace. 'Admirable discipline among the Communists', I heard a
League of Nations Organiser remark. A promise had been given
to the Belgian Government that there should be no political
demonstration. Yes, the Communists behaved admirably. They
kept their word. But what was the use of promising not to discuss
realities? What was the use of a 'united front' if the price was
worn-out platitudes and the murder of honesty, enthusiasm and
faith?

I quite lost my temper at this preposterous conference. I looked at

Lord Cecil's superb profile in the chair, and at Philip Noel-Baker at his side, drafting, translating, dauntless and always optimistic; I heard professional League of Nations speakers talking about the value of congresses helping us 'to appreciate each other's difficulties and points of view' and courageously pretending that there was still such a thing as collective security, even while the bombers which I foresaw would soon be attacking French and British towns were destroying my friends in Spain. The Congress even invented a Peace Day, a Peace Fair and a Peace Penny and it voted to nationalise the manufacture of arms, though the Fascists had already nationalised theirs. There was a Peace Oath, too, but the Oath, like everything else, carefully avoided the only question that mattered—whether pacifists would or would not fight against aggressors. If they did not mean to fight, I wrote after the Conference, then they should have been at Dick Sheppard's meeting next day, where George Lansbury and Aldous Huxley were speaking. If they did mean to fight, then the only subject to discuss was 'Les avions pour l'Espagne', since their cause and their last chance was even then disappearing because the Spanish Government had no aircraft to defend itself against Italian legions, German Junkers and Moorish soldiers.

A great storm broke out as I left the exhibition building where the Congress was held. The fine words that had once revolutionised the world—liberty, equality and brotherhood—and which had been in some form or other the inspiration of human striving in the Western world for the last two centuries, still reverberated in my ears. Myths, no doubt, but myths that might be realised some day, and in some new form, when the pagan myths of national sovereignty and racial domination had brought us all to destruction. I had a vision, as I waited in the driving rain for a taxi, that a mighty gust of wind had taken these great buildings and the rolling phrases that went with them and whirled them up to heaven, like so many leaves of paper, like so many bank-notes in René Clair's film of the catastrophe of capitalism. There, flying up to the clouds, were the exhibition statues of Labour, Peace and Industry; there was Lord Cecil, dignified as ever in his assumption, and with him a host of others, talking about the sanctity of treaties, Article 19 of the

Covenant, even while the entire gesticulating Conference and the map of Europe with it rolled away, carrying within its folds old John Locke, Voltaire, Rousseau, Jefferson, Jeremy Bentham and Woodrow Wilson. Returning to earth, I caught the Ostend boat. The wind had not subsided and the only vision left was the huddled deck of sick humanity.

Defeat was near when I visited Barcelona at Christmas, 1938. My companions on that occasion were George and Pat Strauss, Dorothy Woodman and Ted Willis, now a peer and a well-known playwright. On Christmas Eve we stopped near the Spanish frontier and filled a car with chocolates and cigarettes for distribution in Barcelona. I have a vivid memory of being driven in the densest of blackouts to the house where Dr. Negrin and a company of officials and staff officers were silently watching an anti-Nazi film, *Dr. Mamlock*, which is still occasionally revived by film societies in this country. We talked until four in the morning. I told Negrin about a change of opinion in Britain since I had last seen him in Valencia more than a year earlier. Many British Conservatives were now ashamed of the Non-intervention Committee, had misgivings about the safety of Gibraltar and now admitted to me that they might have been wrong in supporting Franco. Churchill had just written an article to an evening paper admitting his change of opinion and even saying that it was important that the Spanish Government should not be defeated. 'Too late', said Negrin quite calmly, in the tone of one who had squared his account with destiny.

From Spain, Dorothy and I crossed the Mediterranean to Tunis where, amidst the pleasure of bargaining over rugs in the desert town of Kerouan, we met members of the neo-Desturian movement, and even on one occasion were allowed to meet their wives in the women's quarters. We also listened to a speech by Daladier, France's chief spokesman at Munich. More realistic about the value of Hitler's promises than Chamberlain, he had expected to be greeted with execration when he returned from Munich. He had said nothing about 'Peace with Honour' and was astonished when he was welcomed as a hero who had saved France from war. Now, three months later he looked and spoke, as Noel Brailsford, who had joined us in Tunis, remarked, 'Like a man who has just committed a murder'.

From Tunis I crossed to Rome in time to see the Duce meet Neville Chamberlain, who had come out to confirm the fast friendship with Mussolini that was supposed to have been achieved at Munich. We journalists stood in a phalanx at the railway station while Mussolini strutted up and down waiting for Chamberlain's train. Then the pair of them inspected the guard of honour and went off to their conference. In the afternoon a military display was laid on in the Roman Stadium. What, I wondered, did Chamberlain think of the goosestep which the young Fascists from the Military Academy performed for his delectation? He was physically tough enough for a man in his seventies; in the morning he had visited the tomb of the Unknown Soldier and had conferred with the Duce; now in the afternoon he stood for an hour and a half, side by side with Mussolini, watching the manœuvres. Little boys of eight to fourteen years of age marched like grenadiers, did their drill with great precision and ended by lying down and shooting at the Duce and Mr. Chamberlain. I wished that their rifles had been loaded.

Two things I noticed which must have been apparent to Chamberlain, too. The goosestep was new to Italy; Fascism had never been like the German article, a religion, and had always been tempered by a certain genial indiscipline in the Italian character. Italian Fascism had been cruel to its adversaries and in its treatment of natives had surpassed the brutalities of British or French Imperialism, but at home there had always been talk. Dissidents had been tolerated as long as they confined themselves to whispered criticism. Now, since Himmler had paid a memorable visit to Rome, everyone was pretending to goosestep and small officials, post-office workers and suchlike now wore something that looked like a naval uniform. Whether Chamberlain noticed how much the Italians really disliked the growth of German influence I cannot tell. Maybe he noticed that these small boys carrying their rifles talked to each other as they marched off the parade ground, and that when the girl athletes marched off the stadium, some boys in the audience actually gave them a wolf whistle. All round on the statues surrounding the stadium—they wore figleaves—boys had climbed up and perched on their heads and shoulders. Such ease and enjoyment would never have been permitted by the Germans. But that did not prevent Mussolini coming into the war when he thought spoils could be picked up cheap, nor did it prevent him from saying that 'When the war was over, he would have to find something else; the Italian character has to be formed through fighting.' But the Italian, certainly the Roman character, did not change at Mussolini's bidding. A holiday, as Shakespeare puts it, could always be culled out for Pompey or for Caesar. Now it was Chamberlain's turn.

In the evening Chamberlain received a group of journalists. He seemed very well satisfied with himself and said one thing I shall always remember. Like Sir Samuel Hoare, who just before the seizure of Prague said that Europe was settling down 'to a Golden Age of peace', Chamberlain assured us that everything in Europe was now peaceful and comfortable. The only thing, he added, that needed clearing up was the Spanish war.

It may sound ridiculous to some people nowadays that in Spain I knew the bitterness of defeat. There were many others with me. All through the Austrian and Czech crises I demanded in leading articles the re-creation of the Grand Alliance—the League revived—and insisted that its task must include the defence of Spain. I saw it as the last hope of winning the anti-Fascist struggle without general war. But that was argument and open to discussion. The truth was that I felt the defeat in Spain as a personal defeat; there was nothing left now of the idealism that was wasted there. The next phase could only be a national war which would end, as it did, in another Peace, not in essentials very different from Versailles.

Voices of Spain: the Church and the Army salute Franco, and—the other voice of Spain—Salvador da Madariaga interpreted by Kapp

War: the masks of death (Dorothy is second from the left), and myself
with Bob Boothby and Father Groser in the East End during the Blitz

CHAPTER ELEVEN

Trotsky and the Purges

IN 1937 I revisited the United States and spent a holiday in Mexico. When I came back in April I wrote:

> No one who is not a journalist can imagine the lordly sensation of visiting the United States without giving a lecture or writing an article, of staying in the devastated Ohio Valley and feeling no compulsion to describe the spectacle of this monstrous disaster, of talking to Mr. Roosevelt without reporting it, of listening to interminable discussions of the Supreme Court issue and sit-down strikes without having to form premature judgements, of flying to Mexico and taking disinterested pleasure in some of the greatest scenery in the world, of having long talks with Trotsky and President Cardenas and not telegraphing exclusive interviews to anyone, of sitting up all night watching Indian dances and just enjoying them without thinking out any apt phrases about their ethnological significance, unspoilt beauty or primitive charm.

Quite a programme! It began with seeing the Ohio River in flood on my way to stay with Herbert Agar, who was then editing the *Louisville Courier*, one of the very few Democratic papers in the United States, then fighting an almost lonely battle for civil liberty. At his home in Kentucky and in neighbouring States I saw the Negro problem at first hand. I went to an old-world Southern dinner of the kind which is called 'gracious' in the South. I drove with Herbert Agar to a hill-billy town where they were very poor, but were the proud possessors of Elizabethan names, true survivors, I believe, from the early days of British colonisation.

I wrote of the floods, which used to be an almost annual event before the Tennessee Valley Authority had drained the area, that:

Q

The scene was only comparable with Flanders or the Somme in 1917. A flood of water has much the same effect as a flood of soldiers. A wide sea of mud, draggled trees snapped off, with the roofs of the shattered houses caught in the broken branches, bed-steads, the remains of wardrobes, chairs, barns and thousands of rusted motor-cars in vast rubbish-heaps . . .

And much more to the same effect. The astonishing thing to me was that in face of such disaster, Roosevelt was bitterly attacked as a Red when he wanted the Federal Government to intervene. In a Greyhound coach the company got into argument. Everyone agreed that someone should do something for poor people who had lost their homes. Their ruin was not their fault, though it might be the fault of the authorities, who had allowed the forests to be cut down, and had not built reservoirs or river-walls to curtail the annual flood. But, a Republican asked, where does this idea of Federal relief lead to? What would happen to American democracy and to the security of ownership if people got it into their heads that they had a right to a livelihood when they found themselves, even if for no fault of their own, without food and shelter? It was not the fault of factory workers if they were suddenly dismissed because the employers wanted to cut down production. And so we got to an argument about strikes and the Social Security programme and Unemployment Insurance, which had been condemned out-of-hand by every business man a few years before, but which now, in one form or another, had come into existence through a large part of America. Mr. Roosevelt was a natural representative of this inevit-able phase of liberal reformism; the Hearst press was screaming that he was a 'Communist', and Dorothy Thompson, whom I later got to know well and who was the only woman ever considered for the White House, wrote comparing Roosevelt, because of his Supreme Court proposals, with Hitler and Mussolini!

I met Roosevelt after one of his press conferences and found him about as revolutionary as, I think, Lloyd George was in England:

There's not a thump on the tub, not a word of emotional or

even personal appeal. His technique could not be bettered. He is not afraid of the Press and uses it frankly and properly. His smile has become stereotyped, but it is still engaging. Newspaper-men like him because he is really more frank than most politicians and understands what they want with no fuss or waste of time. They know, of course, which questions are 'planted' and he knows that they know. They understand each other excellently. He says, as if by a sudden indiscretion, exactly what he means to say and never by a real indiscretion a word more than he means to say. When they ask for more, he smiles more broadly, 'No, you want to know too much. I'm not answering that.' What a pleasant contrast to the Ramsay MacDonald trick of evading an awkward question by elaborate and ambiguous phrases which could be interpreted in five ways, and all denied, if necessary, afterwards! No Jim Thomas notion that you can get away with anything if you are jolly with the boys! Afterwards, the President asked me what I thought of the conference. I told him he was consummate. He did not need telling, but I had to say something and he smiled even more broadly than before.

I went on to the sharecropper country in Arkansas, where I saw poverty unequalled except in Asia. It was a peculiarly terrible kind of destitution because the sharecroppers were, in effect, slaves; though they were paid a minute sum of money for their work, they were forced to live on the 'furnish' which the employer provided for them on arrival, at the same time compelling them afterwards to buy everything on credit from a shop which he himself owned. These sharecroppers could not read or write, and would be thrown out if they complained of the money given them, though it was never sufficient to get them out of debt with their employer. Therefore, they lived without money, without the right to bargain or to stand up for themselves; they had, in effect, no rights and lived in conditions of animal poverty. They were about 60 per cent White, and the Blacks were the descendants of slaves. Efforts to form a union to improve their conditions were met by violence; organisers were flogged and sometimes murdered.

In the disastrously wet spring of 1937 I called on a farmer who boasted proudly of his independence, but he admitted that the floods, which came every year, were unusually bad. If he was forced to plant too late he would get no crop and would owe money for the seed he had to borrow. 'Then what?' I asked. 'Then,' he interrupted, 'I shall be a sharecropper.' That clearly represented the end of everything.

Afterwards I visited a white sharecropper's home. There was only the one usual piece of furniture, a double bed, in the room on which the farmer himself lay dying of pneumonia. Round him were standing his wife and four children. The Red Cross had provided them with food for one meal and a doctor had paid a visit. As we paddled our way back through the floods which surrounded the house, the dedicated lawyer, who had been my guide and who was famous for the risks he ran on behalf of the sharecroppers, said: 'Well, you've seen a typical sharecropper's house, and those people were a little better off than most sharecroppers because there were blankets on the man's bed.'

After Arkansas I made my way to Memphis and fell into talk with a cotton merchant and boldly began to discuss my impressions of the sharecropper country. I wrote in my diary:

> There were several men present, some of them may have been planters. Anyway, the merchant said very little until it was time for us to go our different ways. Then abruptly and vehemently, as if it had been long pent up inside him, he said, 'I dislike everything Roosevelt is doing and has done so far, but I know how sharecroppers live and I tell you this. If Roosevelt succeeds in doing something to change the conditions of the sharecropper, that will more than make up, in my opinion, for every other crime he could commit.' And he turned away as if he had said too much. Opinion does move, slowly.

It has moved far since that day, but it is an illusion to think that, because the South is so much industrialised now and because the standard of living is high in the United States, there is not still much abysmal poverty within the 'affluent society'.

One other memory should, I feel, be recorded. In the Peabody Hotel at Memphis, where I spent a night, I noticed at breakfast time that a slip of paper had been pushed under my door. It read:

'Dear Guest,

'You neglected to BOLT your door last night. Our Night Manager, rather than awaken you, took the liberty of doing this for you. Just another little service that the Peabody is happy to render its guests. We trust you enjoyed a good night's rest.'

From Memphis I crossed Texas to the Mexican border by aeroplane. In those days the thousand miles or so of Texas meant four or five air stops. But at every stop there were girls with complexions that came from cosmetic advertisements and teeth that showed how unnecessary the dental advertisements were; their job was to serve cold drinks. From the border an aeroplane took me across the great Mexican desert, where you could see grotesque cacti tumbling about at strange angles, building themselves up into gigantic organ-pipes, or sometimes looking like the dilapidated ruins of castles in decay.

In Mexico City itself I stayed with Diego Rivera, then at the height of his fame as a master of mural painting. He was Trotsky's host and he made it possible for me to meet him, in spite of the heavy armed guard at the door. I think Trotsky saw very few other non-Mexicans before he was assassinated by a hireling of Stalin.

Our discussion was naturally mainly concerned with the great purges that were then horrifying the world. I had never held a para-disiacal picture of the Soviet Union. Apart from other defects, it always seemed to me that after so many years in power the Soviet government should have rid itself of the political police. On the other hand, I was inclined to remind the Press, which was full of plots, drugs, tortures and other forms of diabolism, that Russia was not the only country where civil liberty was disregarded. I had some corres-pondence with Maynard Keynes on the subject. He had visited the

U.S.S.R., with Lopokova his wife, the famous Russian ballet-dancer, in 1928, and the pamphlet he wrote on his return expressed views not unlike my own. I remember his saying that we must not be deceived by the 'moral superiority' of the U.S.S.R., but he could see nothing much worth talking about in their economic experiment. In 1933 he blew up because my article on the trial of the Metropolitan-Vickers employees, who were accused of sabotage, seemed to him—though, as he said, I may not have meant it—to amount to something like a defence of injustice. I had pointed to parallels in other countries, but he insisted:

> 'I would like to see for once the kind of leader which you would write if the Government in England were to do the kind of things in matters of justice and the suppression of liberty, or in the commission of economic errors in the same kind and scale as events in Russia.'

We must have met and talked at some length on the issue of Russia, where we did not remain seriously at loggerheads. Three years later I presume that both of us had to some extent changed our minds. He had become more puzzled about the trials and I more critical. There was really no parallel between the ghastly purges of Russians, whom the Soviet dictator feared, and the trial of English business men who of course denied the absurd charge of sabotage, but did not complain of their treatment or, I think, refuse to admit that they had broken Russian law. When the great purges began in January 1937 Maynard wrote: 'I thought your leader this week, "Will Stalin Explain?", absolutely perfect, the argument convincing, the arrangement beyond criticism and the style perfectly lucid, severe and to the purpose.' He added, in handwriting: 'I am absolutely baffled for the correct explanation. In a way, the speeches of the prisoners made me feel they somehow *believe* their confessions to be true.'

We have learnt since then from many sources the methods which the Russians used to extort confessions. In those days my own state of mind was exactly Maynard's. I went to see Trotsky, knowing that what was happening in Russia was cruel nonsense, but feeling that it needed more explanation. He was in the house which Diego had lent him in an outlying suburb of Mexico City. He never left it without a bodyguard of detectives and an escort of motor-cycles. Four armed guards were standing at the gate. Once inside, I thought an exile could scarcely hope to find a lovelier refuge. He was sitting in a long, cool room, looking out on to a patio—gay and beautiful, the walls bright blue and the bougainvillea a blazing glory in the sunshine. He was working, he told me, on his new book, *The Crimes of Stalin*. I noted on my return that:

Pictures of Trotsky are apt to suggest the stage revolutionary with fuzzy hair and a certain untidy vehemence about the neck. Nothing could be further from the fact. Dapper was the word that came into my head when I first saw him. He looked as if he had just come out of a hot bath, just had his hair cut, his beard trimmed and his suit pressed. His hair and beard are grey and his face a fresh pink. He looked like a Frenchman, not, I decided after a few minutes, a French politician but, in spite of his neatness, a French artist.

As we talked, I retained the impression of Trotsky as an artist, an intuitive and imaginative man, vain and very able, a man of fierce will and unruly temperament. If I had met him without knowing who he was or what he had done and without having read his books, I should have been impressed; but I doubt if I should have recognised his genius. In conversation it grew upon me that he lacked one of the qualities of greatness which I think Lenin had to an extraordinary degree. Trotsky, I think, had always seen events in relation to his own career; even when he was throwing his immense energy into the task of building the Soviet Army and reorganising the shattered railway system, he must even then have been saying to himself, 'I, Trotsky, am doing this great thing and doing it superbly, as only I can.' He was a dramatist and played his own title roles; I doubt if his judgment had ever been objective. But. in exile, objectivity is almost impossible. Its destruction is the worst damage that exile inflicts. Perhaps Lenin was the only political refugee who never lost his sense of proportion.

Trotsky was charming and friendly. Yes, he was pleased to talk to me because he regarded the *N. S. & N.* as one of the few honest and genuinely radical papers. I supposed he had read a recent article expressing scepticism about the evidence of the Moscow trials. I asked him at once about the 'archives' of which he had spoken in the Press. He had promised detailed refutation of the evidence of the confessions, how soon would it be ready?

This led, of course, to a long discussion of the evidence. There was plenty of proof that the trials were fakes. Much of it was obviously absurd, but often the absurdity could only be demonstrated by correspondence with the French police and other authorities.

When we had gone into all this, I told him I was still puzzled by the confessions. They were difficult to explain on any hypothesis. What possible pressure could be brought on all these experienced revolutionaries which would make them not only confess, but stand by their confessions when they had the opportunity of publicly refuting evidence in open trial?

Trotsky explained that I did not understand the methods of the G.P.U. He described how they first got hold of a woman and questioned her until she made a confession which incriminated her husband; how this was used to break down her husband's resistance and how he, in turn, was induced to incriminate his friends, all of whom were gradually persuaded by pressure of one sort or another, to sign what was required. The G.P.U. knew, he said, how to attack each of its victims in his weakest spot, this man signing from sheer nervous exhaustion, that one because of a threat to his wife and children, and the other in the hope of pardon and release. The preparation of such a case took years, and the trials were a climax of a determination which Stalin had taken in 1927 (when the split in the Party occurred) completely to eliminate all those who had sympathised with Trotsky and who might in the future swing opinion against Stalin's policy. The G.P.U. would not stage a trial until they were sure of all their men. Tomsky, it should be noted, had committed suicide or had been killed.

I still did not understand why none of the prisoners had repudiated his confession in court. I tried to think of myself in such circumstances. I could see myself breaking down and confessing to anything under pressure, but the trial itself was free and open, and I think I should have withdrawn an extorted confession when I saw the Press correspondents hanging on my words. Russians tell me that this is an English view, that confession is a spontaneous impulse of the Slav soul, 'an old Russian custom', not a peculiar invention of Dostoevsky and the G.P.U. 'Why,' I asked, 'did none of the accused men imitate Dimitrov?' It was strange that not one of them should have gone down fighting and have appealed to the public opinion of the world. Most of them knew they were going to die anyway. Trotsky grew very animated. I was wrong. Even after the example of the first trial, these men did not *know* they were going to die, there was a world of difference between the certainty of death and just that much hope of reprieve—here Trotsky made an expressive gesture with his fingers to indicate even a millimetre of hope. And in fact they had not all died. Radek and Sokolnikov and two others were still alive. He was completely convinced that there had been understanding between Radek and Stalin. Radek knew that he was to have been reprieved. As for Dimitrov, there was no parallel at all. He had never been subjected to the kind of pressure that broke the accused men in Russia. Moreover, he had had all the press of the world in front of him, while in Russia the correspondents were all 'paid prostitutes of Moscow'.

It was here that I began to demur. I had certainly been influenced by some of these 'prostitutes'. 'The arch-villain among the press men,' Trotsky shouted, 'was Walter Duranty' of the *New York Times*. How much did I think Pritt had been paid to write his account of things? I explained that I knew Pritt well, that he might have been deceived, might even be accused of credulity, but that he was not open to bribes.

Trotsky and I had a regular wrangle on this point and I am afraid I failed to convince him. To see him get up and shout abuse at Mr. Pritt was revealing. He seemed to believe that anyone who had a word to say for Stalin or who hesitated to denounce the whole trial as a frame-up must be in the pay of Moscow. He made an exception in the case of the Webbs—they were merely poor, credulous dupes.

When we had finished discussing the trials I asked Trotsky what he thought would now happen in Europe:

He said that this Trial was 'the beginning of Stalin's agony'. He paraphrased Abraham Lincoln; it was not possible 'to betray all the people all the time'. Stalin had gone too far in betrayal, repression had reached its limits in Russia and the disillusion of the workers had begun. The Russian people would throw off the yoke. Did he mean in war or before war? War, he said, would hasten things. He did not wish for it, but when it did come, its inevitable result would be to release the proletariat everywhere and in Russia most quickly of all. 'I tell you,' he said, 'that in three to five years from now the Fourth International will be a great force in the world.' The Fourth International must develop in any case. In war, its development would be very rapid.

I was much impressed with what Trotsky had said about the trials —on which, indeed, I needed nothing but confirmation, except on matters of detail. I concluded with some reflections on Trotsky's vehemence, which made me wonder whether there might not be a shred of truth in the accusation that he really was concerned in some crazy plot with other revolutionaries who had come to hate Stalin. If he was not involved, that was certainly not for any lack of desire for another revolution in the U.S.S.R.

Any doubts engendered by Trotsky's almost hysterical outburst were quickly dissipated. I was soon writing that the Soviet trials were 'appalling' and that the charges made against people like Rakowsky, who had a particularly loyal Soviet career, were utterly incredible. Like most other people brought up in the security and isolation of England, I imagined that we were witnessing a peculiarly horrible method of disposing of political opponents—a macabre sort of General Election—and we did not realise, as we learnt later, that thousands of people who could have had nothing to do with any kind of conspiracy were being murdered. As it was, I quickly became utterly sceptical about the purges and, as the months went on, not only sceptical, but angry and contemptuous. I reviewed and endorsed Gide's recantation; a Communist supporter who had praised everything in Russia, he returned from his tour of the Soviet Union convinced that the revolution had, in fact, been betrayed by Stalin and that Russia was living under a reign of terror. In June 1937 I wrote an article 'European Nightmare', which pointed out that the international repercussions of the latest batch of executions, which included the murder of Tukhachevsky and other leading Russian military figures, must inevitably arouse grave misgivings 'about the stability of the regime and the reliability of the Russian war machine'. If there was any truth at all in any of the monstrous charges made in these trials, then Russia must be in a much worse state than we had imagined. I wondered whether there could be any truth in the rumours of a Russian-German rapprochement. Were the Russians really playing a double game which might in the end, if we were not quick, lead to an alliance or at least understanding between Russia and Germany? We mentioned this danger repeatedly in our columns during the next two years. As for the trials themselves, they became so ridiculous that even the Communists who wrote regularly in our correspondence columns defending the purges sounded as if they could scarcely convince themselves. I wrote in sheer derision about the nonsense alleged concerning the death of Gorky and pointed out the damning fact that Yagoda, who had been head of the Secret Police, had himself confessed that 'he had hounded to death numerous former heroes of the Revolution', and that his execution was followed by that of his successor, Yussev, who had also been responsible for the execution of Yagoda and others. If all the former evidence at the trials had been false, then presumably the only people to be rightly executed were the heads of the Police. I chose one particular bit of the confessions which seemed to me to epitomise their nonsense:

> What do you make of this kind of dialogue? Vyshinsky asks Kamenev whether he was guilty of 'deception'.
> Kamenev: No, worse than deception.
> Vyshinsky: Perfidy?
> Kamenev: Worse.
> Vyshinsky: Worse than deception, worse than perfidy—find the word. Treason?
> Kamenev: You have found it.

Does this read as anything but ghastly farce?

To return to Mexico; from Mexico City I went on to Cuernavaca and Taxco de Alarcon, which had already been largely taken over by American tourists. That is to say, the main hotels were inhabited by Americans and there were smaller houses which had become the resorts of American bohemians, a Greenwich Village away from home. It was incomparably lovely, with its view of the towering slopes of Popocatapetl, on which one could feast one's eyes all day. I recall outside a hotel a tiny, naked Mexican baby rolling in the dust, and the disgusted comment of an American tourist when he rolled too near to her feet, about the filth of these natives. To me, it was all fairyland; my regret was that I could not talk to these primitive people. The great ornamental church decorated throughout from the Taxco silvermines gave the peasants who stood in it a picture of what they thought Heaven must be. I watched them gazing awe-struck at the God on the Cross and all the saints in tawdry splendour; here was peace, a paradise in which they could forget the grinding poverty in which they lived. I was in Taxco at a particularly enchanting moment. A great *fiesta* dominated the town. In the central square the dances never ceased until long after dark; the dance of the Moors and the Christians, with the Moors on hobby-horses, a relic from the time of the Spanish conquest, was repeated over and over again, night and day. I could not find that the words were understood; I am not sure that many of the sounds were words at all. The performers chanted and danced in relays, wearing anything bright and unusual they could lay their hands on. Many of the men were dressed in women's underclothing and wore chains round their necks made of the tops of beer-bottles. One was dressed in a pink petticoat and a felt hat with a mauve plume in it. A figure representing a jester wore a huge mask and carried the Devil over his back while he was fighting San Diego. Outside the church another dance was taking place with the daughter of Montezuma, who ends up by kissing the dead Christ—horribly dead, as Spanish Christs always are. All around were hawkers, selling tinsel objects and cooking tortillas over small fires. Many of the wares showed the usual Mexican, as well as Spanish, obsession with death; the sugar candies, for instance, were shaped like skulls. I became even more conscious of this strange blend of masochism and sadism afterwards when I saw, for the first and only time, a bullfight in the great Mexican arena.

I spent the night listening to the plangent rhythm of the music and dancing in a hotel bedroom, which I was lucky enough to find free, on the central *patio* only a few yards away from the dancers. In the day, the most exciting sight was the game, if one may so call it, of the Torillo or Little Bull. The man playing the bull charged into the crowd with a vast wicker structure on his head. The structure was jointed with short sticks, on each of which was a rocket or other type of firework, so that no one would quite know in which direction the next explosion would take place. He charged the crowd with head down and fire bursting from his horns. A mass of people followed him and the crowd in front scattered and evaded the rockets as best they could, while one of the mass behind him, much daring, would kick his behind. In mock rage he would turn about and scatter the crowd in the other direction.

A slow train also took me to Oaxaca, where I climbed some of the most impressive of the local pyramids. On one I surprised a platoon of boys and girls singing revolutionary songs. Mexico was still going through its anti-clerical and peasant revolution. At my hotel I was awakened at four in the morning by a full military band, blowing and banging at top pressure exactly underneath my bedroom window. I leaped from my bed like a hooked minnow; I could not have been more surprised if this had been the Last Trump. The most puzzling part of it all—and I think it continued for at least half an hour—was that nobody else in the hotel seemed to take any interest. Why was this grotesque serenade apparently focussed on me? If one madman had been playing the trombone in the middle of the night, a horde of porters would have rushed out to drag him away, people would have been cursing from bedroom windows, but here was I, standing on my balcony before the dawn broke, with sixty men in uniform standing at attention, blasting me with martial music and not ceasing to kick up this infernal din until nearly five o'clock in the morning. Apart from the band, the street was empty and there was not one other person except myself who seemed sufficiently interested to bow acknowledgment to this alarming tribute.

Enquiry at breakfast led to the discovery that the music was not intended for me but for the Governor of Oaxaca who had arrived during the night and was sleeping in the next bedroom to mine. Such a morning serenade, they told me, was an old Mexican way of greeting a distinguished guest. The Governor had come because President Cardenas was expected next day. 'Perhaps,' said my informant, who had been the owner of a hacienda and bore a grudge against the President, 'he doesn't give notice of his arrival because he is afraid of being assassinated; most Mexican presidents die that way if they are caught without a bodyguard. This one spends his time going round the countryside, stirring up trouble amongst the Indians. Of course they haven't an idea what it's all about; they are just tempted by the promise of land which they can't cultivate when they get it. You'll see the Indians who have been brought in to the town by party officials tomorrow when they come in from all over the countryside. We shan't get any peace here for weeks.'

I hurried out into brilliant sunshine. It was hot already by nine o'clock and the streets were full of Indians arriving on their *burros* and sometimes in motor-lorries; they wore clean white cotton for the holiday occasion and they had bright blankets over their shoulders

and carried baskets of food. They formed a great crowd at the station and as the hours went by, waiting for the train, they gradually
took up camping sites on the pavement behind the lines of soldiers.
A squad of boys dressed in white gym costume came marching past
and then some scores of little girls with white blouses and gay
rosettes, Girl Guides (or Children of Mary) turned into Comsomols,
if you prefer the Russian parallel.

The sun was high above us and we had eaten the tortillas which
women were frying for lunch when the President arrived. No, he
certainly did not seem at all afraid for his life. The crowd soon broke
through the cordon of soldiers; he was the first Mexican President,
so they told me, who had ever mingled with the people without a
bodyguard. This tall man with a black beard and heavy, impassive
face had somehow made himself loved. I could just keep him in
sight all the way back to the hotel, with only a handful of officials
round him, in the midst of a jostling, cheering crowd of Indians.
They continuously let off fireworks rocketing up into the sunshine,
invisible, but making a cheerful noise which is one of the chief
splendours of a Mexican holiday.

Later, Cardenas ate with his friends in the hotel where I was
staying. He sat at a nearby table with his officials round him. An
American sharing a table with me said, 'Just watch me. I must tell
my wife that I have shaken hands with the President of Mexico.' He
proceeded to do so. Wishing to make a more modest acquaintance
with Cardenas myself, I asked the proprietor if there was any way of
sending the President a message? 'Only one way, Señor,' he said,
'send him a telegram.' The Post Office was near by and the Governor's house where Cardenas was staying was just round the corner.
I sent the telegram asking for an interview. Within an hour a
messenger arrived to take me to the President. I cannot remember
our conversation but I formed the impression, which I have never
lost since, that he was a strong, good man who would be thinking of
the welfare of Mexican peasants and not, after the style of most Latin
American politicians, concerning himself with his own aggrandise-
ment. Since then, the revolution in Mexico has been through many
phases and more than twenty years afterwards, when I went again

to Mexico, I tried to renew my acquaintance with Cardenas. I failed, because he was still educating and organising, and travelling about the Mexican Indian villages. No one could tell me just where he was; he was lost among the Indian peasants to whom he had dedicated his life.

CHAPTER TWELVE

The Nightmare Year

I CAME back from Mexico to listen again to contradictory voices arguing about how to avoid war. It was an unhappy and inconclusive Babel. Maynard Keynes and I began a long correspondence about foreign affairs as early as 1937. His letters are more worth quoting that those of other people, who also changed their minds more than once in the two years before the war. His *Economic Consequences of the Peace*, which had delighted us all when we were young, was used as the intellectual basis of appeasement. The argument that a great country like Germany could not reasonably be treated as a second-class power and that the reparation clauses of the Treaty of Versailles were unworkable had proved true, and, though he had supported me during the Abyssinian crisis, he remained non-interventionist during the Spanish War. He was driven back to support of Baldwin when the League was destroyed. He had been fully alive to the basic issue when Hitler came to power. On 15th November 1933 he wrote to me:

'It seems to me that today's news about Germany cannot be taken too seriously. The hideous dilemma is presented—allowing them to call our bluff, and re-arm as and when they choose, with what results one can imagine, or the horror of a preventive war.'

By 1937 I had made up my mind that Fascism must be fought, and that if it came to a question of facing Hitler our best chance was to organise resistance on two fronts. This meant that the key to British policy must be an alliance with the Soviet Union. Thus, I was opposed to appeasement (with some wobbles), and Keynes supported it even after Munich.

In the summer of 1937 Keynes had become seriously ill and was convalescing in North Wales. He wrote to me on 1st July saying: 'Lying in bed, I think a great deal about foreign policy, and some

R

time this month I'd like to write you an article about it, if you'll have it.' He sent the article on 5th July, finding our demand for collective security too much to stomach. He wrote strongly supporting Baldwin, and I wrote a reply. The two articles appeared side by side, and he subsequently wrote:

'As regards Spain, I feel glad to have got a pacifist article into the paper—it must be the first for many months! And now we've each had our say I have no more to add unless something arises in subsequent correspondence. I still feel much happier with Eden as Foreign Secretary than I should with Brailsford, and so, I expect, do you.'

He added later:

'Are you quite sure—thinking twice—that you want non-intervention to come to an end? Is it your idea that the Spanish Government will be able to buy and import successfully more men and munitions than Hitler and Musso will send Franco free of charge?

'Is it your idea that the British and French Navies are incapable (or would you say unwilling) to keep out a single man or a single gun? I should like to hear the argument more fully developed—if you would stand this treatment.

'I am getting on very well here. They have discovered exactly what is the matter with me, which is a great thing, and it seems to be fairly easily curable.'

We both, as he remarked, 'had our say', his for appeasement, mine for a collective alliance against the Nazis. He interpreted his objective as the end of the injustices of Versailles, while I regarded Hitler's offensive as being part of an aggressive policy which must lead to war unless we ganged up collectively against him. In a letter of 9th August he wrote:

'My progress is slow but steady, and I am now able to drive out in the car in the afternoon. Much sympathy with your affliction—

and your bad temper. It makes you, I notice, just as cross now to think there is not going to be a war as it did before when you thought there was going to be one. There is no pleasing a really bellicose pacifist! They have got you both ways. And, as for Spain, I am not a bit sure that not making her territory the seat of a general European war is "letting her down".

'Seriously, it all depends, of course, upon whether the Fascist powers are intending to use the present negotiations as a way of getting out without too much loss of face, or whether the plot is really something quite different, not yet disclosed. Being an optimist, I am still hopeful that it may end in the division of Spain geographically into two states. But, above all, I want the war to come to an end and not to extend.'

In the meantime he had taken a strong line about resistance to Japan, and on 29th September 1937 was writing:

'As you may have seen from my letter in *The Times* today, I agreed very strongly with the article you had last week about economic sanctions for Japan. This seems to me one of the clear cases where decisive action is quite without risk, if sufficient join in, and certain to be successful: and there will be united public opinion behind it, (which last it is always necessary to remember is an essential prerequisite of decisive action). So I do hope you will go hammering on along that line. People are quite absurd, in my opinion, in underestimating the effect of economic sanctions. In the case of Italy, as we all know, they have never been honestly and decisively applied. If they had been, it would have been another story.

'I have at last escaped from my Welsh prison, very greatly improved in health; though I am not allowed to return to real life for some time yet. . . .'

In November he thought we had gone altogether too far:

'The first leader in this week's paper is apparently intended to incite China to a war to a finish, so long as any Japanese soldier remains on Chinese soil. At the same time, it holds out no hope that any effective assistance from outside is at all probable. Is there not some disastrous confusion of thought and feeling behind this? And next week, for all I know, you will be advising the Chinese to adopt the faith of Dick Sheppard.

'I feel increasingly that the paper does infinite harm by its capacity for making the better cause appear the worse, and giving an impression of imbecile confusion of mind and emotion. Garvin at least has the merit that he makes the worse cause appear the worser.'

A few days later he wrote and enclosed a letter which he suggested I should show to my colleagues.

'My own view is that we ought to have invited the United States to join us in imposing a boycott. I understand the reasons against this, though I am not convinced by them, namely (a) that we are not yet strong enough, (b) that the general position is so critical that we must on no account risk any dispersion of forces, and (c) that public action is insufficiently homogeneous. It is also extremely unlikely that, even if we had taken the action I desired, America would not have responded.

'Since, however, there seems no chance of a boycott, and China has saved her honour and her position and character as a nation, it is most advisable in her own interests that peace should be con-cluded as soon as possible, even though it involves what amounts to her ceding a large area of territory. Finally, this being so, we ought to use all our power and influence to get her the best possible terms. It seems to me wicked to encourage her to con-tinue if any sort of tolerable terms are obtainable, and our duty to get her the best terms we can.

'Turning to the wider problem, in my view, our sole and over-riding purpose should be to make quite sure of countering the Fascist powers at long last. It is precisely because I believe the position to be critical and dangerous that I believe strategic re-

treats to be necessary and the gradual consolidation of forces absolutely essential. There is no chance except by achieving an almost
worldwide consolidation of opinion on very broad issues. Such
issues as an enormous majority of the people in this country, for
example, and, one hopes, in America, are ready to agree about.
It is no time for being minority-minded, and those who are im-
penitently minority-minded are helping the enemy.

'You, on the other hand, are perpetually engaged in conducting
an indignation meeting, more often than not only secondarily
against the enemy, and primarily against friends or, if not friends,
at least potential allies, and thereby saving your soul and preserv-
ing yourself from all taints. I regard this as unserious and futile and
playing into the hands of the enemy. Every sort of motive has to
be mobilised on the right side, and the issue must be represented in
terms which appeal to the great mass of opinion, as it is well
capable of being. It is no good to spit and fume against the powers
that be and all the real forces in the world, keeping in reserve, as
the final expedient of escapism, throwing in your hand and lying
flat on your face before the advancing forces.

'I also have another feeling, which may be unreasonable, which
ought to be mentioned because it plays a not unimportant part in
my own mind. I cannot accept the policy of non-resistance, but I
have a very strong objection to sending the average man to fight
on an occasion, or at a time, or in circumstances whatever they
may be, for reasons which only appeal to a minority. There are
no issues on which the rights of the majority are so paramount as
in the case of war and peace.

'Thus if the issue is to be joined, it must be for reasons which
unite the vast majority of right-thinking men. It is this, and not
sectional differences and heresies, or too nice an examination of
selfish motives which should be one's aim.

'Well, that is how I feel and why the paper so often strikes me as
injurious to the better cause. I am not sure that I should not like
to write publicly on these lines and leave you to expound the
opposite in reply. That is, if you really believe the opposite, which
I doubt. For I believe that what I am objecting to is due to an un-

controllable minority-mindedness and the old non-conformist urge to save *one's own* soul. But we are at a juncture of the world's affairs when these virtues are vices.'

Our leader-writer, Mostyn Lloyd, would, I think, have replied in such terms as this: If we allowed each case of aggression to go by default as soon as there was danger of sanctions leading to war, then the smaller countries would cease to believe we were serious and when the world crisis came we should find that many of our allies had given up hope and were ready to make a separate peace with the enemy. (Maynard's remarks about Dick Sheppard read oddly in view of his recent boast that he had succeeded in getting a pacifist article in the paper!)

In March 1938 Maynard's views changed. No doubt he was mainly affected by Eden's resignation. Chamberlain had taken over foreign policy himself and increasingly cold-shouldered his Foreign Secretary. Neville was no weak man, frightened by dictators, but a tough, extraordinarily complacent man, who thought he could manage the job of foreign negotiation better than the Foreign Office. He saw only too clearly that Vansittart and his friends, who hated Germany and had a conventional view of the balance of power, would inevitably take us into war. He 'promoted' Vansittart, and took Sir Horace Wilson, a Civil Servant with a good record as a trades disputes negotiator, as his closest adviser.

Halifax, as Foreign Secretary, was also preparing the ground for appeasement. He had told Hitler, at Berchtesgarten in November 1937, that the British Government 'would look favourably on changes of the situation in Germany's favour'. He had no objection to a revision of the treaty in Danzig, Austria or Czechoslovakia, provided that the changes 'came thorough the course of peaceful evolution' and avoided methods 'which might cause far-reaching disturbances'.

Chamberlain permitted his relatives and friends to tour the Fascist countries and spread the news that Britain desired only friendship. The last thing he wanted was the interference, as he felt it to be, of Franklin Roosevelt; he rebuffed his approach without consulting the

Foreign Secretary. The last straw for Eden was Chamberlain's readiness to make a gentleman's agreement with Mussolini, without insisting that he fulfil his part of the bargain, which was to remove at least a symbolic number of Italian troops from Spain. Chamberlain belonged to a narrow circle of Birmingham business men and seems always to have been troubled by a desire to emulate Joseph Chamberlain's eminence in the political arena. He made the fantastic error of assuming that Hitler and Mussolini were also 'economic men'; they would obviously prefer possession without war if it were politely offered them.

Maynard wrote to me on 23rd February 1938:

'Yes, I am very glad, looking back, that I thanked heaven a few months ago that we had Eden as Foreign Secretary, and defended him from the charge of being a Fascist.

'The gravity and importance of what has happened cannot be exaggerated. But if one is to try and extract any comfort from the disaster, I find a certain amount in the fact that the fissure of opinion has taken place at the most favourable point possible, leaving the maximum of weight and numbers to the Left. As you know I feel nothing more strongly than that in an affair of this kind it is useless to be in a minority. I do not reckon the chances of escaping from that position good, but they are surely better than they could have been with almost any other split, or on almost any other issue. That seems to me the point to emphasise—the necessity of consolidating as an effective force the *whole* body of opinion to the left of the Government.

'But what a miserable figure the Labour Party cut in the debate. Not a single speech of bigness, dignity or importance. Nothing but stale debating points, and personal jibes.

'I expect that the future has big surprises for us. I do not rule out the possibility of the Prime Minister having a genuine success on the immediate issue. If Mussolini was wanting an opportunity to back out of various commitments, this is clearly a heaven-sent opportunity for him to do so without loss of prestige. If so, I do not see how one can deny that it will be a benefit on the small stage of the immediate future. If this happens, it will confuse the issue, but, of course, it will not touch the main matter.'

He wrote an article proposing a geographical division of Spain as part of a general policy of collective security. I asked him on the telephone whether he did not think that he owed me some *amende*. He replied that he agreed and had thought of putting in a reference to his conversion, but that he had not done so because he felt that it would 'damage the artistic shape of his article'. I had my little crow!

The year 1938 was a nightmare; after Hitler's invasion of Austria in March it was no longer possible to delude ourselves about his intentions. On 10th March we published a leading article 'The Inescapable Facts', which stated our own policy and on the front page said that at this late hour, five minutes to twelve, there were now only two possible lines to follow. One was the logic of Chamberlain's collaboration with the dictators. If Mr. Chamberlain, in order to avoid war, was really prepared to swallow the results of isolationism, would he go as far as allow France and the Channel ports to fall under Nazi rule? If that is what he really meant, to give up our position in the world and surrender the Empire, we would go along with him, but we did not for a moment believe that this was seriously intended. We believed that the course he was following would lead us into another national war—without allies—in which we should probably be defeated. The only other policy was to strive to regain the alliance of the Soviet Union and re-create a League of Progressive States, which was what Mr. Churchill was advocating. This essential policy, I wrote:

> must be adopted immediately if it is not to be for ever too late, cannot be carried out by the Chamberlain Government. No one believes in Mr. Chamberlain; his discredit and failure are hourly more obvious. Such a policy, with the discipline, the conscription of wealth and of British manhood which would be necessary can only be put forward by a broad-based Government which includes Mr. Eden, Mr. Churchill and the Labour and Liberal leaders. It is time the people of England told Mr. Chamberlain in

unmistakable language that for a policy of connivance and encouragement to Fascism the British nation is not prepared for more taxation, for more conscription or for discipline, but there is no sacrifice it is not prepared to undergo for a government which really intends to throw its weight on the side of democracy and against aggression, and therefore possibly even at this eleventh hour may avert the overwhelming catastrophe that threatens the world.

(19th March 1938)

I saw no alternative to Churchill, though I had all my life regarded him as the most dangerous of political opponents. At any rate, he was not for collaboration with Hitler, but saw that the Soviet alliance was essential, as only then would Hitler face a war on two fronts. Possibly if that were achieved it could be avoided altogether. Maynard was also beginning to find the Prime Minister's attitude almost insufferable. He had not yet decided where he stood, but was admitting to me on 25th March 1938:

'It is a very good paper indeed—all except Fischer's article: the object of that seems to be to cause a loss of sympathy for France and Blum, and its tendency on the whole pernicious—the sort of article which I imagine Goebbels would willingly pay for. But I agreed with all the others, and by no means least with Joad. I have very little doubt that he is right that we hate the Fascists so much and are so anxious to have a smack at them that we tend to argue that the policy is much more bound up with peace than it really is. However, the situation is admirably put by the whole conjunction of articles.

'The objection to the Prime Minister's speech is not so much what he said as his tone and the way he said it. Exactly the same things could have been said differently so as to make a very fine speech indeed. As it is, he manages to give the impression that he is not in the least moved by what has happened, that he will not live up to any of his professions, and that his sympathies are in the wrong place. And he is clever enough to spike opposition by putting forward proposals about which there is a large measure of agreement or half agreement.

'When, in the *Economic Consequences of the Peace*, I quoted a page of Shelley without acknowledgment, I was generally believed to be the author. I hope that the same thing will happen this time! There is another verse in reserve almost as apposite as the one I quoted:

> "*Then went I to a garden, and did spy*
> *A gallant flower,*
> *The crown Imperiall: Sure, said I,*
> *Peace at the root must dwell.*
> *But when I digg'd, I saw a worm devoure*
> *What show'd so well.*" '

To substitute Churchill for Chamberlain now became the object of all progressive British policy. I was myself a member of a discreet organisation designed to give support to Winston without the wrong kind of publicity. It contained members of all parties and of none. Lunches were held to advance Churchill's cause, and at one of them (in December 1937) I made a note of a speech by Anthony Eden. We were a mixed crowd; present were Lord Derby, Sir Archibald Sinclair, Arthur Salter, Norman Angell, Eleanor Rathbone, Waley Cohen, Gilbert Murray, the Duchess of Atholl, Lady Violet Bonham Carter, Wickham Steed, Maxwell Garnet, J. L. Clynes, Jimmie Mallon (Warden of Toynbee Hall), Wilson Harris of the *Spectator* and Duncan Sandys, Churchill's son-in-law. Eden was still optimistic that war might be averted and gave us a survey of Europe. Wickham Steed questioned him about our relations with Roosevelt and Wilson Harris about a possible revival of the League. After lunch I asked Eden how he interpreted the German demand for colonies. He was sure that it was mainly a bargaining counter for a free hand in the East. I asked him whether, in that case, we ought not to call Hitler's bluff by some sort of colonial offer. Eden agreed, but said that one of the main difficulties of the situation was that Hitler would never 'bargain', but said he must have everything he wanted 'as a right'. It was characteristic of Churchill that he was never above a joke. At another luncheon in honour of M. Titulescu, who had recently been thrown out from the Premiership of Rumania because of his anti-Nazi views and replaced by a M. Tatarescu, Churchill opened the proceedings by slyly remarking that Rumania was not the only country in which patriotic and potentially important public servants were excluded from the government and that he hoped Titulescu would soon oust Tatarescu, and give them tit for tat!

In May Hitler had turned his propaganda machine against the Czechs and discovered that they were resolute and brave. They were sure of French support, relied also on Britain and Russia, and were undoubtedly capable of serious military resistance if he attempted to treat them as he had Austria. After all, the Austrians were Germans of a kind and many thousands of them had welcomed Hitler's arrival. In May comparatively few of even the Sudeten Germans wished to be taken over by the Third Reich.

I was deeply emotionally involved in the Czech crisis. I had first visited Czechoslovakia in 1935 and had a wonderful holiday in the Carpathians; I was supposed to have been needing the mudbaths at Piestany and had walked far and fast to show that no such treatment had been necessary. I spent a fascinating week with my friend Vočadlo. He was one of a group of Czech Liberals the best-known of whom were the brothers Capec. Vočadlo, whom I had known at Cambridge, is one of the world's best linguists and was to prove himself, in a German concentration camp during the war, one of the bravest of men. He took me to Capec's house in Prague in 1935, when Beneš was reporting the results of visiting the Soviet Union. Beneš had already developed all the little mannerisms at which I used to smile so often on subsequent visits and when he was in exile in England. He was a benevolent schoolmaster, expounding all the difficult problems to the boys, and ticking off the points one by one on his fingers. He was an optimist, who always believed he would somehow come through and who hoped, when he eventually went back to Czechoslovakia after the war, that he could bridge the gulf between Russia and the West. 'I think,' he would say with his head a

little on one side and his index finger emphasising the point, 'I think
—but I cannot be sure—that I can persuade the Communists and the
liberal Czechs to work together. I think . . .', but he couldn't be
sure.

In 1935 he had been cementing an alliance with the Soviet Union;
it had become necessary to strengthen it because Henlein and the
nationalist Germans in the Sudetenland had already become menac-
ing. If they had looked dangerous in 1935, how much more serious
a threat were they to the composite state of Czechoslovakia after
four more years of Nazi propaganda? Though the majority of them
were loyal Social Democrats, too many of them were ready to
respond to the Nazi bait. There were three millions of them and the
Czechs were less than seven million out of a total population of
twelve million, which included Slovaks, Hungarians and Poles. I
revisited Prague in May 1938, and reported that, with the Hungarians
as aggressive as the Germans, and with the Nazis in Austria, the
Czechs well knew that their hope of survival rested on their alliances
with the Western powers and with the U.S.S.R. Masaryk, the
founder of the Czech state, had not wanted to include Germans. The
Sudetens had some real grievances, even though they were the best-
treated minority in Europe. In little ways they were treated as in-
feriors by the Czechs, but the Czech Government knew that their
real problem had nothing to do with Sudeten grievances. Frontier
revision, which seemed obviously sensible to the West, would not in
reality solve anything, since Hitler was interested not in the Sudetens,
but in destroying the Republic, and getting his hands on their great
armament works at Skoda. Further, as my Czech friends liked to
remind me, Bohemia was the centre of Europe, which traditionally
gave its possessor mastery of the Continent. It was, too, the gateway
to the East.

The British Government's response was to send Lord Runciman
to Prague to undermine Czech resistance and to persuade the Czechs
to make concessions to the Sudetens which were obviously incom-
patible with Czech sovereignty and indeed with the existence of the
state. The Soviet Union's request for military talks was disregarded;
Chamberlain, Hoare and Simon were all violently anti-Communist

and Halifax, nominally Foreign Secretary, was particularly hostile to atheistic Russia.

Another factor frightening the government into appeasement was the extremely successful propaganda of Colonel Lindbergh. Lindbergh was generally assumed at that time to be a completely impartial witness who had seen the Russian airforce at work and found it wanting and, with full access to the secrets of Goering's plans, had come to the conclusion, as Tom Jones noted in his *Diary*[1], that:

'the air power of Germany is greater than that of all the *European nations combined*, and that they could not be prevented by us or by France by laying the great capitals level with the ground. Until we can guarantee the maximum resistance possible to such a catastrophe, I don't see our Ministers—a feeble lot anyway—going to war.'

And the next day, he added:

'Since my talk with Lindbergh on Monday, I've sided with those working for peace, at any cost and any humiliation, because of the picture of our relative unpreparedness in the air and on the ground which Lindbergh painted, and because of his belief that the democracies would be crushed absolutely and finally.'

Tom Jones made sure that Lindbergh's evidence should be given to Stanley Baldwin who, he said, was for 'peace at any price'. There was a curious sequel to Lindbergh's visit. After he had lunched with some of us at the R.S.G. Club, where he terrified us all by his account of the coming destruction of London, a visitor, who may not have realised the completely private nature of this gathering, told Ellen Wilkinson of the effect that Lindbergh had had. She violently attacked Lindbergh in a Sunday paper, and for once in its history the R.S.G. unhappily became the subject of public discussion. Ellen, of

1. Tom Jones, *A Diary with Letters* (Oxford University Press, 1954).

course, was quite right. Goering had no such power as Lindbergh suggested. Unwittingly, Lindbergh did as good a job for the Nazis as any hired propagandist might have done.

By August, I had become convinced that Runciman's efforts to persuade the Czechs to make a compromise that would satisfy the Sudetens were futile, since the Sudeten Nazis, knowing that Hitler backed them, would accept nothing less than secession. War could only be prevented if Hitler was confronted with the certainty that he would be involved with the French, British and Russians. In the case of war, nothing could save the Czechs from destruction. They would be confronted with Hungarian and Polish demands as well as German; they were open to Nazi attack from Austria, as well as the Bohemian frontier, and the Sudeten Fifth Column would support the Nazis from within.

In this dilemma I wrote to Keynes for advice. It is the only occasion on which I remember doing so on an issue of public policy. I was a 'maverick' who usually paid less attention to Maynard's admonitions than they deserved. He replied on 26th August that we should 'bluff to the hilt and if the bluff is called, back out'. He wrote, in a not-easily-legible handwriting:

> 'Yes, I suffer from much gloom about Czechoslovakia. The only morsels of comfort I can offer you are the following:
> (1) *Russia* is the key to the position. She will have to be the first to lend material assistance. (Will she?)
> (2) Germany is *equally* vulnerable to air-raids.
> (3) The Czechs unaided can give a pretty good account of themselves.
> (4) The inevitable never happens. It is the unexpected *always*.
> (5) In a world war Hitler will be beaten and knows it.
> 'I agree with you that we should bluff to the hilt: and, if the bluff is called, back out. I prefer, meanwhile, meiosis and bogus optimism in public.'

The next day he bravely attempted prophecy:

'Having put on my mantic robe and concentrated, my further reflections of Cz-Slo are:

(1) Hitler's speech at Nuremberg will be violent and amount to a quasi-ultimatum demanding a revision of frontiers.
(2) After many parlez-vous this will be granted.
(3) He will again win the appearance of a major success.
(4) And it will be without war.

'What we ought to work for is a maintenance of Cz-Slo's integrity apart from frontier revisions. As a preliminary we ought formally to ask Germany her intentions and demand an international conference. If she refuses, invite collaboration of U.S.A.'

On 27th August 1938 I had already argued that:

If Hitler agrees to accept a solution with Czechoslovakia, it may still be possible, if the Czechs make an imaginative offer of partnership to the Sudeten Germans, to reconcile them to the existing frontiers. But if Lord Runciman reports that this is impossible, the question of frontier revision, difficult though it is, should at once be tackled. The strategical value of the Bohemian frontier should not be made the occasion of a world war. We should not guarantee the *status quo*.

I went on to argue that the U.S.S.R. would not move unless France moved, and the French, though they were mobilised on the Western Front, could do little to help the Czechs. 'Nothing we or anyone else could do would save Czechoslovakia from destruction; it would be a question of a counter-attack on Germany.'

I made these remarks in an editorial note a few days before *The Times* published its famous article urging frontier revision. This *Times* article was regarded as official and we believed, probably correctly, that Geoffrey Dawson was stating a policy that both he and Chamberlain had some months earlier agreed upon if the Czechs proved 'awkward'. Chamberlain, report had it, had outlined the necessary break-up of Czechoslovakia at Cliveden when the issue had first become urgent in the spring of 1938. Unlike Chamberlain,

I regarded this German occupation of Czechoslovakia as a horrible tragedy, but I held that world war was inevitable if we stuck to our pledge without a Soviet alliance and it was my duty to say so. What I said was precisely true, but I said it at the wrong moment when most English papers which had been clamouring for appeasement had changed their tune. I was carrying out a consistent policy, for I had always held that we should not in any circumstances go to war with Hitler unless we had a military alliance with the Soviet Union. I have no doubt that Maynard Keynes' advice on this occasion carried great weight with me and I believed that it was an act of courage, not of cowardice, to say what was really in the minds of most people which they did not dare to express. That, after all, had always been my policy—to tell the truth when most people were silent. I chose a disastrous moment.

This was a mistake which I was never allowed to forget. We had been the most outspoken in our policy of resistance to Hitler and naturally historians and journalists have seized upon my lapse to point out that at the crunch I had agreed with *The Times*. My Note became disagreeably public because I wrote a letter furiously attacking Chamberlain, which appeared in the *News Chronicle* on 21st September. Gerald Barry, its editor, informed me next day that a reply had reached him based on the view that I had contradicted myself in supporting frontier revision three weeks earlier and that I now called Chamberlain 'Hitler's jackal' for agreeing to the revision. What were my feelings now? I replied that I hoped that all that was forgotten and would not be revived. Gerald did not publish the letter. The reply which he rejected actually appeared as the first letter in *The Times*, which was, of course, glad to remind the public that a paper of the Left, as well as themselves, had favoured frontier revision. They published a reply from me, but the correspondence petered out when Chamberlain flew to Munich on 29th September. My self-reproach was bitter. I felt guilty towards my friends in Czechoslovakia, who refused to admit that destruction and occupation and a world war might have been worse than the loss of independence. I also realise that in my excoriating analysis of Chamberlain's behaviour, I had really been attacking myself.

Maynard Keynes had not repented. On 11th September he wrote to me, still backing the policy of frontier revision:

'Please don't imagine that I have weakened on the wisdom of frontier revision. Indeed the latest concessions are such as to make one feel even more than before that in the long run frontier revision is a cleaner and *safer* remedy. I was simply trying to be emphatic about what you say yourself—that it is plain as a pikestaff that at this juncture one must back up the Czechs, and particularly *not* suggest to Hitler that he can get what to him seems more. . . .

'I believe in living from hand to mouth in international affairs because the successive links in the causal nexus are so completely unpredictable. One does well to evade *immediate* evils.

'I cannot imagine a nastier crew than your alleged conspirators behind *The Times* article—particularly Allen who has raised my nausea for years past. Geoffrey Dawson is a very *queer* personality and with a good side to him, however nefarious his methods.

'I don't expect any resolution of these positions tomorrow. There is time yet, and there may easily be wisdom (as King-Hall suggests this week) in reserving fire—though this is very unnerving to those not behind the scenes. If only one had ultimate confidence in Neville and Halifax!—which I at least haven't, though I don't yet reject the idea that they may be doing very well. Every day the force of world opinion is gathering force and the cup filling up.'

Munich was a traumatic moment and, like other such occasions, has been the subject of many myths and self-justifications. Appeasement had been and still was the general policy of England. Churchill himself had spoken in favour of Runciman's mission to Czechoslovakia and, though he made a powerful speech denouncing the Munich settlement, he did not, nor did anyone else, prefer general war. Alan Taylor remarks that 'all the Press welcomed [he should have said *accepted*] the Munich Agreement as preferable to war with the solitary exception of *Reynold's News*, a Left-Wing

S

Socialist Sunday newspaper of small circulation, and, of course, the Communist *Daily Worker*'. Duff Cooper, First Lord of the Admiralty, resigned, and his autobiography, *Old Men Forget*, says that Chamberlain ought to have gone to Germany with a firm message that Britain and France would fight if the Czechs finally decided that Hitler's terms were unacceptable. At the same time he thought that the Czechs ought to have revised their frontier. What infuriated him was that Chamberlain and the French had bullied the Czechs into accepting Hitler's demands. We ought to have gone to war rather than allow one country dominating the Continent 'by brute force'. Looking back today, I can see that Chamberlain, hideously distasteful though I found him, was more consistent than his critics, since, once Czech resistance was undermined by Hitler's occupation of the Sudetenland, Czechoslovakia had no frontier that could be effectively guaranteed. It was a nauseating story of Chamberlain doing Hitler's dirty work for him, laughing and yawning while the Czechs were compelled to sign away their own independence. It was this that roused the anger of so many people who had been appeasers and it explains why Léon Blum, in a memorable sentence, said that he 'was divided between shame and cowardly relief'.

Maynard's main feeling after Munich was that we had been tricked. He wrote to me from Sussex on 1st October:

'These are my basic reflections so far:
(1) This settlement would not have been too great a price to pay for peace. But with any sort of honest policy peace was never genuinely at risk. The pacific impulses of the nation have been shamelessly exploited and the final piece of stage management was as wicked as it was skilful.
(2) We have suffered one of the worst pieces of trickery in history. Honourable international policy has suffered a terrific reverse by the unscrupulous intrigues, quite unsupported by public opinion, of our own pro-Nazis. But they have played their cards so damned well, that more than usual of the wisdom of the serpent is needed on our part.

(The attitude of *The Times* must have been revolting to almost everyone.)

(3) Russia (and of course France too in a different way) has been greatly to blame. Why on earth didn't she invite officers from our W.O. to inspect with their own eyes the Russian state of preparedness? There has never been any convincing evidence of Russia's reliability, and she has played straight into Chamberlain's hands, making it as easy as possible for his policy of ignoring her.

(4) It is *not certain* that the present settlement may not be a good thing in the long run. Viewed quite drily, there is a great deal to be said for it. Hitler's next move is not very obvious or easy. This makes our right reaction to it exceptionally difficult. The settlement itself cannot be rightly denounced as indefensible and monstrous. What is certain is something rather different—namely that the sympathies and methods which have brought it about cannot be safely allowed to continue in charge. This time they may, by historical luck, have carried through a necessary thing which decent men could not have accomplished. This means that a frontal attack on the settlement itself is not the wisest course.

(5) I suppose that popular emotion will shortly be capitalised in the shape of a General Election. The most important immediate political objective should be a union of forces against Chamberlain. This is much wider than a Popular Front and will require a very special kind of electoral strategy. I believe that this should be in the first instance purely *ad hoc* election, without any union or parties or much attempt at an agreed programme. It should be straight anti-Chamberlain, with Liberal give-and-take in the constituencies, the most likely anti-Chamberlain candidates being supported by all of us irrespective of his party, e.g. Winston, Eden, Duff Cooper, Boothby, Nicolson, and he should be unopposed by Liberals or Labour.

(6) One's own state of mind at the moment is painful in the way in which only a *mixed* state can be. Intense relief and

satisfied cowardice joined with rage and indignation, *plus*
that special emotion appropriate to the state of having been
swindled; the whole nation swindled as never in its history.'

He restated these views in an article in the *New Statesman* on 8th
October 1939, and concluded it:

'We and France have only sacrificed our honour and our en-
gagements to a civilised and faithful nation, and fraternised with
what is vile. This, at any rate, is in the short run, calculation. The
Prime Minister thinks it a small price to pay and can swallow with
a good conscience a week's playacting, beginning with gasmasks
and ending with bouquets, even if it involves a brief moment of
harsh plucking at mother's heartstrings.'

He wrote again on 4th October, after a debate in the Commons:

'It did not go too well for Chamberlain and today's may go
worse. A General Election looks less likely . . . the damned thing
about the settlement is that from our selfish and shortsighted point
of view there is much to be said for it. Good *may* result from what
no wise or good man could have brought himself to accomplish.
Vile and dirty work can be beneficial to those who do it—or do
you believe in the eternal justice of the world? I don't.'

CHAPTER THIRTEEN

The Mindless War

THE best case to be made for the Polish guarantee was stated years afterwards in a letter to me from Walter Elliot, who held that if your sense of justice was sufficiently outraged and your pride was sufficiently humiliated, you should go to war irrespective of its results without thought of victory or defeat. He wrote to me on 1st May 1944 objecting to the suggestion that the Russian alliance could really have anything to do with Britain's decision in 1938:

'The fact is, it was a choice of the soul (as going to war always ought to be), and the choice to be made in such circumstances is "Would I rather be dead, in every kind of shame and misery, *and have this* injustice happen, or *alive*, and that *still* it should happen". That is a very fundamental question, and nobody should ever go to war who is unable to answer it in the affirmative, for one must never go to war expecting to win, but always to lose. If one wins, so much the better, and one has no right to assume the participation of any other nation.

'That is the deep philosophical conception (which I must say I find shared by very few people). As to the upper layers of the argument, it seems so fantastic to suggest that Chamberlain's policy was an alliance with Germany as again to deserve nothing but yells and howls. It is incredible how difficult it is to get it across, even to the most intelligent and sympathetic man, that Chamberlain, seeing clearly the picture of the smashed, savage and cynical Europe which we now see as bound to develop even from a successful war, was sincerely attached to the cause of peace! He said in his Munich speech that if he were convinced that any nation would try to dominate Europe by force he would oppose any such nation. When he was so convinced (at Prague), he did oppose it. He had no more intention or desire for an alliance with

Germany than Joynson-Hicks had for an alliance with Bolshevik Russia (though he retained friendly relations with that great country). Therefore, I say, this argument seemed irrelevant. But one certain fact of our time is that nobody is going to change his or her views about Munich for any argument whatsoever.'

This highly idiosyncratic and romantic view of war is the best defence that can be made for the Polish guarantee. Elliot, of course, was right in saying that Chamberlain hated both the Nazis and war, but I think he underestimated the Prime Minister's determination to keep out of trouble, and that he still hoped for another Munich in Poland. Hitler had a strong case over Danzig. Chamberlain described this guarantee as a new epoch in our foreign policy; 'If the independence of the Polish state should be threatened, I have no doubt that the Polish people would resist any attempt on it—then the declaration which I made means that France and ourselves would immediately come to her assistance.' But this declaration was followed by a leader in *The Times* (1st April), pointing out:

'The new obligation which this country yesterday assumed does not bind Great Britain to defend every inch of the present frontiers of Poland. The key word in the declaration is not integrity, but "independence".'

The Times added that it was the independence of every negotiating state that mattered and that what Britain had done was to give an assurance of all support to Poland 'during the period of consultation with other governments'. In short, *The Times*, no doubt correctly interpreting Chamberlain's meaning, was ready to negotiate about Danzig and only minded, as it said in the title of its leading article, that we should stand for 'ordered diplomacy' and resist, or at least threaten to resist, illegal seizures.

A remarkable story, which seemed well-authenticated, may explain the next development. As Colonel Beck, the Polish Foreign Minister, was starting for England to discuss the terms of the guarantee, he was informed of *The Times*'s interpretation of it. He rang up the British Ambassador in Warsaw at midnight to say he was 'unpacking his bags'. The Ambassador at once rang up London and reached Lord Halifax in his bed at two o'clock in the morning. Halifax had no alternative but to assure the Polish Minister that the British guarantee was real and complete. Beck came to London and, in its final form, the guarantee left it to the Poles to decide whether any demand of Hitler threatened their independence. So the guarantee was made absolute because the Poles resolutely refused to surrender Danzig and to have their independence whittled away on the pattern of Czechoslovakia.

Wickham Steed, who had been editor of *The Times* before the appeasing Geoffrey Dawson and who was notoriously a bitter opponent of any concession to the Germans, could write to me as late as 6th August 1939 discussing the possibility of peace:

'In principle I agree that we should have a peace programme—which is not necessarily the same things as "peace proposals"—and that we should make it known after it has been very carefully worked out and considered. . . .

'In a couple of hours I shall be driving to Cambridge, where I have to take the chair tomorrow at Benes's lecture on "The Future of Democracy". Meanwhile, I have to think out very carefully what I shall say. He has (*strictly between ourselves*) been given a hint to avoid anything that might look like an "abuse of hospitality". Before hearing this, I had already decided that we must on no account use him as a stick to beat the "Umbrella Man" with. The work Beneš is doing is far too important for us to endanger it by giving the Wilson-Chamberlain people a pretext for hitting back at him.

'Now I cannot conceive of any tolerable "peace proposals" that would entail compromise with Nazism or Fascism. To hint at compromise or negotiation would be to ruin our position in advance. But to say, bluntly and now, that we will not compromise or negotiate might appear to give Hitler and Goebbels the knife by the handle. I have no fear of the "encirclement" cry. We have got to make the Germans understand that they will be progressively isolated and "encircled" as long as they submit to Hitler. How best to do this is the very question your letter raises.

'I have got a number of German "Aryans" working on this very problem—Rauschning and Höllarmann among them—for it is, psychologically, a German problem. Last week I put Rauschning into touch with Beneš. Tonight I shall meet Beneš at Cambridge. So, on the whole, I think I had better hold my hand for the moment. We must be very careful not to waste our ammunition, and to hit the bull's eye when we do shoot.'

If Wickham Steed was still considering the possibility of a way out of the war by the right propaganda, Keynes (like Beaverbrook) continued to believe to the very last minute that war over Poland would somehow be avoided, as it had been over Czechoslovakia. He wrote to me on 14th August 1939:

'I did not feel inspired to write anything in response to your incitement. Nor, as far as I can make out, were those of your correspondents who did respond. There is really nothing to say at this juncture. If there were any legitimate grievance to deal with, it would be another matter. As there is none, it seems to me that we have to rely on improvising something when chance and fate send the unpredictable opportunity.

'It is difficult to see how some sort of appearance of a crisis in the next month can be avoided, but I shall be extremely surprised at a warlike conclusion. Hitler's argument that he must get to Danzig, because it does not really matter either to him or to anyone else seems to me unanswerable. In due course, Danzig will be incorporated in the Reich, with an agreed formula, e.g., making it a demilitarised zone, which will leave the defective situation substantially what it is.

'I am extremely well, doing quite a lot of work and taking much exercise. Yesterday, for the first time for three years, I took quite a long walk on the top of the Downs. Tomorrow, however, we are leaving for France, for a three-weeks' cure at Royat, a bath-place, much recommended for my complaint. We must see you after we are back.'

Keynes was mistaken. We honoured, at least nominally, our impossible guarantee to Poland, though we could do nothing to save it from destruction. With the Soviet Union taking part in the spoliation of Poland and France and Britain able to do nothing, the war seemed a kind of madness and perhaps even a continuation of the Munich swindle.

The Phoney War—from 3rd September 1939 until the disastrous Norwegian campaign in 1940—was a miserable period. It is commonly presented as a time of preparation and rearmament during which everyone publicly assumed that fighting would soon begin in earnest, but in fact many people still thought Britain might keep out of the war. The evacuation of women and children into the country, arriving with gas-masks round their necks and often shocking country people by their slum habits of hygiene, by the lice in their hair and by their ignorance of everything that grows in a garden, was as neatly accomplished as a military operation can be when there is no enemy to upset the timing. We had to watch the destruction of Poland; our promises of aid to Eastern Europe were what Lloyd George called 'demented guarantees'. The more serious newspapers talked about war aims and often discussed the future as if we had already won. But what would these aims be? There was much talk of federal union, which seemed as far off as Mount Everest from the South Downs. There was a constant underlying belief that the war was not real and the B.B.C. permitted Middleton Murry to give a series of six pacifist broadcasts. The King's Christmas radio talk began, 'A new year is at hand. We cannot tell what it will bring. If it brings peace, how happy we shall all be.' Liddell Hart, a brilliant soldier, who had been more right than anyone else about the technique of modern warfare, was still arguing that conscription would be the worst policy for Britain and that we ought to defend ourselves if we were attacked, but in no circumstances to do anything to provoke the enemy. I always longed to agree with him, but could not. He was so sympathetic to pacifism since the First World War that I felt he could not be the right person to go to for military advice.

The Ministry of Information, set up on a grand scale in Blooms-bury, had become a stock joke; Tommy Handley on the B.B.C. ragged it unmercifully as 'The Ministry of Misinformation and Twerpery'. I remember one recruit who left after a year's experi-ence saying that belonging to the Ministry of Information was 'like having an affair with an elephant; it was not pleasant and would not have any result in the usual two years'. In the early days the Ministry was a singularly gentlemanly affair; the British had not got round to the idea of propaganda. The story is told of Frank Pick, famous as the originator of the then London Transport Board's attractive posters, being asked by Churchill to start a line of propa-ganda which he thought immoral. Indeed, he told the Prime Minister that he had never consciously deceived the British public, whereupon Winston rang up the Minister of Information to say that he never wanted to see that 'impeccable busman' again. The Minister of Information afterwards was Brendan Bracken, a delight-ful, if less scrupulous, public servant. He was unusual to look at, ruddy of countenance, with his head covered with a tight frizz of red curls. A journalist who suspected that he was being led up the garden said, 'Everything about you, Minister, is phoney; even your hair, which looks like a wig, is really your own!'

Some day we may learn from documents and memoirs, which no one yet seems keen to write, about the peace feelers which were undoubtedly proceeding on various levels in the Phoney War period.[1] We cannot judge now how far any of them were serious and how far they were diplomatic ploys with the object of gaining time. I think there is no doubt that the Finnish War, for which we (like the French) prepared battalions of troops equipped for arctic conditions, was regarded by some of our leaders as a hopeful oppor-tunity for changing the war against the Germans into one in which we should be fighting against the Russians.

Most people were, of course, totally unaware of our plight and

1. Interesting information about this curious period is collected by Lawrence Thompson in *1940—Year of Legend, Year of History* (Collins, 1966).

England carried on much as usual. Every kind of sport that could be continued in spite of the blackout flourished; the *New Statesman and Nation* was bejewelled by wonderful examples of rich people reluctantly deciding to give up their second footman or, if they were unusually timorous, moving to parts of England where bombs seemed less likely to fall. The blackout was, of course, a disadvantage, but it was only with difficulty enforced. I remember the Chinese Ambassador saying that some of the less-respectable areas of London were slow to disguise themselves and, when an air-raid warden in one street complained that 'a chink was showing in an upstairs window', he was met with an indignant retort from the Madame: 'No, sir, it is not a Chink, but a gentleman from the Japanese Embassy.'

The blackout was the one real inconvenience and expense; we all sympathised with the old lady who was heard to say, 'There's this to be said for the Blitz—it does take your mind off the blackout.' Barrage balloons were another reminder that there was supposed to be a war; they gave work to a few of the countless men and women who had volunteered for war service and merely found themselves unemployed. The soldiers in the camps were immeasurably bored. Everywhere they began to talk among themselves about responsibility for the war and the demand for political and social reading-matter mounted fast. Titled soldiers were still in charge of the Army and Leslie Hore-Belisha's attempts to introduce democratic reform were deeply resented. His dismissal at the end of the year was one of the few exciting political events. Only Churchill's presence at the Admiralty suggested we were seriously at war; it seemed as demented as Lloyd George had suggested.

In 1939 Harold Macmillan, in the second volume of his *Memoirs*, rightly says that there was a smell of peace in the air. After the destruction of Poland, Lloyd George began a campaign against the Phoney War and met with much support. There was serious discussion about the possibility of an international conference in which the United States would take part. Bernard Shaw wrote a long letter to the *New Statesman and Nation* urging that we ought to give up the pretence of war and leave the Russians and Germans to

come to terms. It happened that I had a proof of this letter in my
pocket when I was with Maynard the night before we went to press.
Now that the war had actually started, he had thrown aside his
doubts. He threatened to have the issue of the N. S. & N. stopped by
the Censor if I was determined to print the letter. I left his house
without argument. The next morning I found a note from him on
my desk:

> 'My opinion is:
> (1) That the whole article is mischievous and that your edi-
>   torial judgement should be against accepting it; I think it
>   would do harm both ways—both to the chances of success
>   in peace and the prospects of success in war. And
> (2) That in any case, you ought to take the advice of the
>   Censor before publishing it (this applies not to the whole
>   of the article, but to one or two extensive passages in it).
> 'If, after re-reading it, you want to proceed with publication, I
> agree with you that others should be consulted—the available
> members of the Board immediately and the other two as soon as
> possible. I should also attach importance to the opinions of Lloyd
> and Raymond.[1] If I am in a minority, I still reserve my liberty of
> action, but should, if I used it, resign from the Board.
> 'From your own standpoint, I believe the article would do
> great harm.'

I recall my hesitation. Was Maynard right? Would Shaw's letter
do harm? In the end I consulted my friend Charles Peake at the
Foreign Office. He was strongly in favour of publication and said
that the censorship would place no difficulty in the way of publishing Shaw's views. He wrote to me next day that 'he was reflecting
the views of the Secretary of State for Foreign Affairs, who of course
agrees that, so far as the limits of public policy allow, the opinions
of all responsible writers in this country should be given the opportunity of expression'.

1. C. M. Lloyd, the Foreign Editor, and Raymond Mortimer, the Literary
Editor.

I decided to publish Shaw's letter, omitting only one passage which was unnecessarily offensive and did not alter his argument. He wrote, warmly thanking me, and asked me on the phone whether Keynes, who had also had a long telephone argument with him, was 'punch-drunk'. He wrote off to Lady Astor saying that the war was over, as she could see if she dashed out and bought the current *New Statesman and Nation*. The story is fully told from Shaw's point of view in Hesketh Pearson's biography. Keynes said no more about it, but the issue whether we ought not to attempt to end a war which we were not in a position to fight was taken up by many correspondents and Keynes came back with a letter which has since been much quoted. It was primarily an answer to Shaw and to all those who were opposed to making war on Hitler and the Soviet Union at the same time. It read:

'Sir,
   'The Intelligentsia of the Left were loudest in demanding that the Nazi aggression should be resisted at all costs. When it comes to a showdown, scarce four weeks have passed before they remember they are pacifists and write defeatist letters to your column, leaving the defence of freedom to Colonel Blimp and the Old School Tie, for whom Three Cheers.'

Shaw wrote characteristically, remarking that:

   'As I am a born coward, and dislike extremely all this blackout business and ruinous taxation and the rest of it, I shall still want to know what I am fighting for. Mr. Chamberlain has cleared up that question, to a certain point. He declares that we are not out for territorial conquest or material acquisitions of any sort. This means that the war is a purely ideological one. That is, we will not cease from military fight, nor shall our swords sleep in our hand, until we have forcibly smashed National Socialism in Germany and Communism in Russia, and replaced both by the British Constitution. . . .'

Keynes wrote in reply that he could not agree that a compromise peace on terms which were 'reasonably satisfactory' could now be made. He added a truly remarkable sentence: 'For myself, I am not yet ready to rule out the ideal peace. It may fall within our grasp in ways which we cannot foresee.'

For my part, the war still seemed to me phoney and I reported to Keynes my conversations with Cabinet Ministers who thought we ought 'to cease fighting Hitler and join with Germany against Stalin'. One of these Ministers was Sir Samuel Hoare, with whom I had two interviews, the other I don't recollect. No one held this view so strongly as Joseph Kennedy, the father of the assassinated President of the United States: as a millionaire who thought he would be ruined by the war, he took every step he could to persuade Roosevelt to keep America clear of it. He was persuaded that Britain would lose, and that she would inevitably be conquered by the Nazis before becoming Communist. I once met him at a party and was rude enough not to stand up when he came to speak to me. To my astonishment, several people came up to me afterwards to congratulate me on snubbing him. His biography is incidentally very revealing.[1] He quotes Churchill as saying that the Government would never quit fighting 'even if Britain is burnt to the ground' and would 'move to Canada and take the Fleet and fight on'.

This reference to the Cabinet's plan to evacuate to Canada, if necessary, recalls to me a strange controversy at a Board meeting of the *New Statesman and Nation*. When the Germans were overrunning France in May 1940 one or two directors as well as Maynard Keynes and myself were discussing the desperate situation. I remarked that I had just been informed that the Government had decided to go to Canada and carry on the war from there if Britain was occupied. In that case we should be blockaded by the British Navy and presumably bombed by British aeroplanes, like the rest of occupied Europe. In this I was correct and Maynard perhaps uninformed. He turned on me furiously and said that people who talked like me ought to be in prison. After that we had a great argument—in a taxi, I think. I held that the small nations would not

1. Richard J. Whalen, *The Founding Father* (Hutchinson, 1965).

seriously resist Hitler and Maynard denounced me as a defeatist. I am sure we both exaggerated. Maynard was angry; I was depressed and stubborn in my unhappiness.

A few days later I spent a few days in Ireland and wrote in a singularly black mood, apologising for my gloom, but supporting my case. I also suggested that I had better do something useful of a practical kind. Perhaps I had better put on a uniform? I meant as a weekend Civil Defence worker or something of that kind. Keynes took this to mean that I was suggesting my resignation:

> 'Your letter raises more matters and more intense ones than one can well deal with in a letter. I am coming back to town tomorrow and expect to stay until Friday, with plenty of free time. Meanwhile—
>
> '(1) I am sure you are doing your most useful work where you are at present. I have felt that the paper has been useful, and it may very well get more and more useful as time goes on and the opportunities for independence diminish themselves. It is good for you to work off more gloomy and desperate feelings on your friends, and they must not complain if you do so! I am *quite clear* that it is your duty to continue where you are. . . .
>
> '(2) My objection to discussing remote (or I would rather say unclothed, since I do not mean very improbable) hypotheses is that it is absolutely useless and simply paralyses one for more urgent and necessary activities. It is absolutely useless because one has to know all kinds of unknown details in order to arrive at any decision of the slightest interest. You must not suppose, because other people do not spend their time discussing the worst, that such thoughts do not pass through their minds. Of course they do—but not, in my case, at any rate, with that clarity in detail that makes them a proper subject for reasonable judgement.
>
> '(3) You are really deceiving yourself in supposing that you have prophetic insight into all that is going to happen. If,

in private talk, one has predicted every conceivable disaster, the imagination can conceive, when things go wrong
something or other which happens can hardly help bearing
some resemblance to one of the predictions. The particular
one of which you remind me where I said I thought your
fears were absurd has in fact turned out not correct, as you
now seem to think, but exactly the opposite of the truth.
You told me, if you will throw your mind back, that the
governments of all the neutrals were, to put it truthfully,
pro-German, and that, at the first serious threat, or even
without it, would allow themselves to be dictated to by
the Germans. Indeed, you went so far as to say that even
their sympathies were often pro-German. In fact, exactly
the opposite happened. Norway, Holland and Belgium
have come in on our side (which remains true even though
they surrendered). Surely you will remember that my
reaction was that these neutrals might be terrified, might
be blackmailed, might be defeated, but to say that they were
not sympathisers with the Allied cause was the absurdity.

'(4) Of course, gaol is not the right remedy for people like you.
That is to say, so long as it is only to me that they talk. If
you put it all in the paper, it might be another matter! The
right chastisement for people like you is to write every
week with candour and encouragement, leaving your
public feeling instructed, with fewer illusions and yet with
more resolution.

'There is one point I wish you would think over before we
meet—the question of an additional Director. What would you
say to Leonard?'[1]

I replied to Maynard on 8th June 1940, on my return from
Ireland:

Life has become much more tolerable as the real danger has

1. Leonard Woolf became a Director in 1941.

appeared. Reality is never too difficult, because action removes fear and doubt. The almost intolerable thing is the doubt, conflict, sense of guilt and responsibility, above all the muddle of a period during which some leadership is required and there seems no escape from direction which leads to a terrible, if not necessarily a completely disastrous conclusion. . . . As regards the paper, there is no doubt at all about its influence. Just because it has endlessly discussed the problems and conflicts, been partly pacifist and Left, etc., it has been more responsible for converting more people of the pacifist and Left way of thinking than anything else—except Hitler.

Comic at Liverpool the other day. I arrived to find that the C.I.D. man in charge and the Immigration Officer had just had an argument about who should read the *N.S.* first. The Immigration Officer kept my passport back till last until I was wondering why. The reason was that he wanted a chance to speak to the editor of the paper he called his Bible!

As to the question of gloom and prophecy, it is of no importance and egotistic to discuss it. Possibly I'll amuse myself by writing about it at some length in a memo sometimes. You have not, I think, quite understood about it. It is not that I have claimed any special foresight or that I have foretold all disasters in order to be right, as you suggest. The point is that it has for a long time seemed to me certain, not hypothetical, that Germany would overrun Europe if permitted, but that the result of pressing for resistance would be too late—that is, when it would be desperately dangerous and appallingly destructive for civilisation. Chamberlain would obviously *never* do the things we asked—collective security, Russia and the democratic appeal to the anti-Nazis everywhere—and the result of our asking these demands would be to force him into a war with a minimum of allies and on the worst possible terrain. This is what has haunted my mind —that we who opposed him would not get the action we wanted in time and should be, indirectly at least, responsible for the war. It was this I got desperate about, because so few of my friends seemed to feel this and I could see it almost as a certainty. They

T

were right not to worry about it, I suppose, because there was no alternative line of action. I, for my part, was always searching for a way out.

War did come, just like that, and I felt and feel a ridiculous amount of guilt about it. Similarly, about the neutrals. You, as always, were extremely optimistic. You said things were going well and all the neutrals would rally to us. As usual, when reacting to optimism I no doubt exaggerated my case, but I knew (a) that in each neutral government there were pro-Germans—so much so, as I now know, that British Staff secrets were always passed on to Germany and (b) that people who were not pro-Nazis exactly were afraid to support us when Britain had so often failed before, and (c) that in the war of today the mass of the population of any civilised country would prefer, up to the very last minute, to avoid war if conceivably possible and (however much they may dislike the Germans), would even, like the Danes, prefer German occupation to a hopeless war. You seem to me quite deluded about the power, prestige and popularity of Britain. . . . The divisions between pro-Germans and pro-Allies or anti-Germans is no longer a real one. The point in such countries is between giving in and helplessly seeing your cities and your people destroyed on the other. I could not see that we had any right to call on small peoples to resist in such circumstances and I did not think many of them would do so effectively, if at all.

I had not suggested that I should leave my job just now. I meant that I must look for a uniform to put on over the weekend, if I could find it, so that I could not think and visualise and could finally kill in myself much that was most deep-rooted. Great excitement and much sensible organisation going on re parachutists as well as some less sensible. One is now asked for Identity Cards on every main and many side roads. All the able-bodied in this village are in arms. I think Hitler will go to France first, don't you? And then when he comes here, if he does, he will have some device and method which we have not considered—I wish our Secret Service in Germany had not been wiped out at the beginning of the war, as it was—the French, too.

This week in Ireland ended my period of gloom, partly, I think, because I had found something active to do. The reason for my visit was the hope, which may have been born from conversations with my friend J. W. Dulanty, the Irish Representative in London, that now there was a chance to end the disastrous partition of the country. Ulster was already in the war; was there not a chance of persuading Eire and Ulster to join in a new policy of mutual defence? I knew Dublin fairly well, for I had been several times asked to speak at the Historical and Philosophic Societies at Trinity College. On my first visit I made a great hit by saying that Britain 'had robbed and bullied and starved Ireland for centuries. Oddly enough, we don't bear you any ill-will on that account and can't understand why you are not similarly willing to forgive and forget. The British genius consists in forgiving those whom we have wronged.'

I had already discovered that Irish memories were long. In 1932 I called on a staunch supporter of De Valera and asked him how he justified the repudiation of the annuities which Ireland had voluntarily agreed to pay in the Treaty settlement, I said:

Let's be quite clear about this. British behaviour in Ireland has been shocking and indefensible. You can say that we have depopulated Ireland, repressed it and so treated it ever since the seventeenth century that if we gave you the British Museum and the National Gallery, we should still be hopelessly in your debt, economically, let alone spiritually. But what I want to know, leaving the past aside, is on what grounds today you justify your repudiation of the Treaty?

He replied:

'All right, we'll stick to the present situation. *When Cromwell first came to Ireland . . .*'

I also called on De Valera on the same occasion and asked him whether he felt it was legal to abolish the Oath of Allegiance, which the Irish had taken in the Treaty and which he had fought unsuccessfully to defeat. 'Yes,' he answered unhesitatingly, 'perfectly legal.' 'Then why,' I asked, 'did you have to refuse these terms when they were accepted by Michael Collins? After all, he had not wanted to go as a diplomat to England: you refused to go, sent him instead, and had a civil war rather than accept terms which you now say left you free to declare independence.' De Valera talked for twenty minutes and never succeeded in justifying that tragic contradiction. I was staying with friends who regarded him as a murderer and never forgave him for provoking the civil war which had now obviously been unnecessary.

However, I found De Valera by no means the doctrinaire and humourless monster commonly depicted in the English press. I have had many conversations with him since and always found him a reasonable and indeed fascinating conversationalist. On my 1940 visit it was wonderfully pleasant to come out of the blackout into the familiar, easy atmosphere of Dublin; there was lavish hospitality, good food and drink and endless talk. Nobody seemed much bothered by the report that a used parachute had been found in the house of a German. It was said that, in addition to the parachute, the Irish police had discovered 20,000 American dollars, some revealing documents and, rather oddly, a number of Austrian and German military medals. Arrests had been made and there was reason to believe that there was a German conspiracy centring on the legation in Dublin. I was invited to spend the weekend with the British representative, now Lord Rugby, and got also to know John Betjeman, then Public Relations Officer in Dublin. Rugby took me out to dinner with a leading Irish politician. It was an embarrassing occasion, because I sat between two leading Dublin socialites, who took delight in scoring off a British radical. As a guest of the British Representative, I could not answer back. It was some time before I realised, carefully guarding my tongue, that they were quite deliberately attempting to put themselves in the right with the Germans in case of a Nazi invasion. They wanted to be reported as being on the German side.

Next day I asked De Valera why he allowed so little of the realities of the Nazi regime to be reported in Irish newspapers. No doubt the Irish enjoyed seeing the English discomfited; but would they not be dismayed if Britain were occupied and Ireland threatened? He made a memorable reply. He answered very wisely: 'If I were to allow a free press to tell the people of Ireland the truth about the war and the Nazi regime, they would now all be committing themselves to one side or another. Many of them believe that they hate England so much that they would welcome a German victory. As it is, they are not allowed to say anything in public and if Ireland is invaded, they will all rise to the defence of their country and I shall lead a united nation on the side of the Allies.'

When I returned to the London blackout, I found that my own Dissenting past had ceased to be an obstacle to accepting the war; on the contrary, I had turned into something like a Covenanter. On 22nd June, remembering a sermon of my father's, I took as a text for a leading article, 'If not——'. It was a declaration that never must we surrender to Nazi threats and violence, 'whatever may happen on the battlefield'. Like Shadrach, Meshak and Abednego, who were thrown into the burning, fiery furnace, we had to say, 'Our God, whom we serve, is able to deliver us from the burning, fiery furnace. But *if not*, be it known unto thee, oh King, that we will not serve thy gods.'

England had at last settled down to total war. People no longer seemed unmoved because unawakened. The man in the street was determined to carry on with his allotment or his Sunday golf as long as possible, but he was no longer under any illusion that peace was just round the corner. It was his way of showing that Hitler couldn't get him down. Only occasionally in London and in the universities, where I often spoke, I saw that look of harassed anticipation of the worst which I had first seen among German intellectuals in the summer of 1931. In the long run, imagination and education are the only things that can save us, but in such a moment of crisis as the summer of 1940, these gifts made life more difficult. Most people just carry on when things happen outside their experience, but the intellectual, who has contacts with 'people in the know', lives in a

coterie of talk and tries to understand. That is his job. He proved in
the crisis of the war that his services were essential and completely
gave the lie to the often-made charge that only soldiers could run the
war.

A well-known pacifist remarked to me that he was now a victim
of the 'herd instinct', and some of my friends were astonished that I
so far put aside my anti-Imperialism and Socialism that I wrote
strongly supporting Winston Churchill. I said I had not changed any
of my views. He had been my enemy-figure; I felt I had been fighting him all my life. He had tried to make war on Russia in 1919, had
used soldiers against strikers, and nearly turned the General Strike
into a civil war. By returning to the gold standard in the twenties
he was largely responsible for the economic disasters of the thirties,
he had been precisely wrong about India and, in fine, about everything. But, miraculously in 1940, the man had matched the hour and
I had not become so decadent that I could not welcome the one man
with the qualities of leadership now that we were at war with the
Nazis.

Churchill's broadcasts that summer after the collapse of France
were of immense importance because they removed hesitations
and settled the issue once and for all. Priestley's broadcasts about
the social revolution which was necessary if people were to feel
themselves properly involved and to realise that the war was not
just a matter of survival were scarcely less important than Churchill's. Churchill was annoyed and even jealous of the success of
Priestley. He wanted no war aims apart from winning the war and
just took it for granted that everyone would share his resolution. The
masses, of course, never doubted Britain's invincibility and were
even pleased that we were now fighting without troublesome
allies. King George VI wrote to Queen Mary: 'Personally, I
feel happier now that we have no allies to be polite to and to
pamper.'

It is hard for a later generation to realise how preposterous our
situation appeared. We had no weapons to use against Hitler apart
from a quite ineffective blockade. Germany was in some sort of
alliance with Russia and it seemed merely irresponsible deliberately

to provoke a Nazi attack when Hitler did nothing but offer us conciliatory terms. When, in 1940, we did expect immediate invasion I remember walking on the terrace of the House of Commons with Sir Ralph Glyn, the Conservative M.P. who was then chairman of the Weapons Committee in the House of Commons; he told me the Home Guard had really nothing to fight with except garden-tools, because the only rifles we had were on the high seas coming from the United States. When asked how we should defend ourselves in case of invasion, Churchill was reported as answering that we should destroy as many Germans as we could on the seas and 'hit any survivors over the head with bottles as they crawled up the beaches'.

The realisation that Britain was no longer a demi-paradise or a fortress built by Nature to defend herself, but rather a vulnerable island off the land-mass of Europe, defended by no more than radar and a tank-trap—this new picture of our sceptr'd isle only began to dawn on us in 1940. Invasion was now taken for granted and occupation seemed likely. My changes of mood were, it seems, no worse than those of many other people at this period, though few of them have written candidly about them like Harold Nicolson. My reason, like his, told me that victory was 'almost impossible' and that it was only sensible to prepare some escape route if Himmler were shortly to be expected in England. One of the leading American journalists in this country called on me one day to discuss how I could best escape death by torture, and a M.P., who in 1967 is a leading member of the Labour Government, had a better idea; he told me that he planned in case of occupation to get lost as a cloth-capped worker in some factory or mine where he was not known. Harold Nicolson arranged with his wife Vita Sackville West to escape 'torture and humiliation' by procuring a poison pill from a friendly doctor.

In reviewing his book Rebecca West remarks that most of us had taken similar precautions. Personally, I carried some morphia tablets in my pocket, with the rather vague idea that they might come in handy in an extremity. I doubt, in fact, if I or Rebecca or Harold would have used them when it came to the point.

Like me, in June Harold forgot his doubts and fears and, as it
happens, I have a diary note of my own recording a conversation
with him at the doors of the Ministry of Information, where he was
Under-Secretary to Duff Cooper, in which, as his published letters
show, he was positively 'gay'. He told me that he was now 'utterly
happy', free from all doubts and expecting to die before long in the
company of his friends. We decided to get hold of a couple of old
blunderbusses and try to shoot a German or two as they marched
up Gower Street. We discussed whether this decision was based on
reason or sentiment? He compared his own peace of mind with that
of a man who, after a long period of spiritual doubt, had surrendered
to the Catholic faith. He decided that it was the path of reason to
withstand with everything in our power the rule of organised
brutality; any kind of spiritual capitulation would allow our children to be trained as janissaries to fight in Hitler's future wars. I
doubted if, in any such fundamental decision, reason played a vital
part.

I thought that Harold had now found his peace by discovering
that his real religion and ultimate loyalty was to Britain; he had been
brought up to admire this stubbornness in the British character and
in the last resort this upbringing was the decisive factor which over-
came any rational arguments. I had discovered that I, too, was a
patriot and I had made the same decision inside myself. I was not
sure whether God or the historian of the future would think that
reason had had much to do with our decision. The truth, as I saw it,
was that we were fighting, as men had in the past, not for any end
rationally conceived, but for pride in ourselves.

It may even be that in our hearts our finest hour did not materialise as we expected. We could not die as heroes, though all over the
country people were forming themselves, even before the Home
Guard officially existed, into resistance groups, often armed only
with pikes and shotguns. In the event, most people were called up
for some comparatively dull form of service and had only to show
their courage when the Blitz began in the early autumn. The
British people were not tested beyond breaking-point. We were
allowed to feel that we had won, not only because of the heroism

of fighter pilots in the Battle of Britain, but also by our own endurance. Our lonely resistance in 1940 had been essential, but our actual share of the fighting, as compared with that of the U.S. and the U.S.S.R., was on a small scale.

CHAPTER FOURTEEN

Lloyd George

ONE man at least was still unconvinced by Churchill that the war need be fought to a finish, even after bombing began. Lloyd George had been kept out of office even longer than Winston Churchill. Churchill had been too clever by half for the Conservative Party, had changed parties too often, had a disastrous record behind him. Neither Conservatives, nor Liberals, nor Labour would have anything to do with him until the eve of war. Lloyd George, the hero of the First World War, had also been a lone wolf in Parliament. Baldwin hated and feared him, and the Tory Party treated him as a brilliant back number. The Labour Party deeply distrusted him because of the Black and Tans and as the author of the Versailles Treaty. Nobody I ever knew had his skill or brilliance as a natural leader in bad times and yet he could do nothing but manœuvre, fly political kites, and live in the country where he grew the finest apples and raspberries that I ever saw anywhere.

I used to go down to see him at Churt; his billowing cloak, sheaf of white hair and be-ribboned *pince-nez* were the only external signs of his past wizardry. He continued to put forward schemes for economic reconstruction such as those on which he had fought the election of 1929. If he had been listened to, England would have been saved from ten years of miserable deflation. Walking in his orchard at Churt, he would tell me of his plans for another New Deal.

I wondered whether there were not passages in his latest manifesto which the Tories could use to their own advantage? He pulled down his lower eyelid and said, 'Do you see any green in my eye?' Then he would explain that he managed to grow his extraordinary crop of Cox's Orange Pippins in the sandy soil of Surrey because he had bought so many tons of horse manure from Aldershot. 'The only use I have ever found for cavalry,' he said. And then, returning to Parliament, he would discuss whether any of the Labour leaders had any brains. Stafford Cripps, for instance, was a K.C., but how could anyone be so foolish a politician? He himself retained a unique gift of making a House of Commons speech which somehow seemed to each individual listener made personally to him. The Labour Party found his attacks on the Conservatives useful, but I was always reminded of the song about the girl who 'was poor but honest'. It was the rich, you will remember, who got the pleasure, but the poor who got the blame. Wasn't it a bleeding shame?

> In the cottage in the country
> Where her aged parents live,
> They drink the champagne that she sends them,
> But they *never can* forgive.

No, Lloyd George's speeches fizzled out like so much flat champagne. Labour could never forgive his past or make terms with his Liberalism, even though their own leaders were less capable than he was of a policy to regenerate England and had not a tithe of his ability in opposition.

I used to hear stories of Ll.G.'s past brilliance from Tom Jones, who could talk in Welsh with him and had been his intimate when Lloyd George first brought him up to London as Assistant Cabinet Secretary. Tom Jones used to tell how at the worst moment of the war, when the Germans broke through in March 1918, he had put the Cabinet papers round the table which told their own story of an apparently desperate position. When Ll.G. was feeling deeply about anything he fell back on his own language. He threw his arms out in a familiar gesture and sang a Welsh hymn which was probably: 'When we have passed through the Valley of the Shadow, we shall be grateful to you, oh God.' He called out 'Jan, come here', and Jan Smuts arrived in military kit and wearing heavy boots, which Tom Jones said looked like a farmer's. Lloyd George again sang his Welsh hymn and though Smuts did not understand Welsh, Tom Jones's comment was that they were united, one peasant talking religion to another, which somehow made the language difficulty un-important.

Another of Tom Jones's stories was that when Lloyd George had decided to accept the substance of defeat in Ireland he summoned De Valera to see him. De Valera was claiming to be made President of the Irish Republic; Lloyd George had no intention of going beyond Home Rule. A flunkey announced to Ll.G. and Tom Jones that De Valera had arrived with another Irishman who described him-self as De Valera's Ambassador. Ll.G. replied brusquely, 'Ask Mr. De Valera to come upstairs,' and when he arrived, brushing aside the 'Ambassador', said, 'How do you do, Mr. De Valera.' De Valera produced a scroll written in the Irish language, which he did not himself understand, and said he had brought with him an English translation to facilitate discussions about the Republic. Ll.G., making play with his eye-glasses, examined the Irish document. 'This is headed "Saor Stat"—sounds rather teutonic, doesn't it? What exactly does it mean?'

' "Saor Stat" means "Free State",' said De Valera.

'And what would be the Irish for "Republic"?' Lloyd George asked.

De Valera turned to his 'Ambassador' and discussed in English what the Irish word for 'Republic' would be. Ll.G. turned to Tom Jones and said, in the living language of Wales, 'That's flummoxed him, hasn't it?'

De Valera turned and said:

'The fact is, Mr. Lloyd George, that the word for "Republic" would, I think, be "Saor Stat".'

Ll.G. replied, 'Quite so, Mr. De Valera. We Celts never have been Republicans, have we?'

And so, with half the battle won, Lloyd George and De Valera got down to the details of an Irish settlement. Since then De Valera has learned some Erse; the Irish have a word for 'republic' and a genera-tion later became republicans.

Lloyd George was haunted in the thirties by the fruits of Versailles. He always insisted that if we had carried out its intentions it would have been a good not a bad treaty. I have a letter from him dated 28th March 1936, when Hitler reoccupied the Rhineland:

Bron-Y-De,
Churt,
Surrey.
28th March 1936

PRIVATE

'Dear Kingsley Martin,

'I thought I had made it perfectly clear, not only in the *Evening Standard*, but in the speeches I delivered in the House of Commons, what my view was about the ultimate policy of appeasement in the world. I do not want to reverse the decisions of Versailles—I want them carried out honestly:

'1. As to Disarmament.

'2. As to revision of any conditions which seem to be unjust or unwise in view of subsequent events, especially permanent settlement, e.g., the allocation of the Mandates.

'3. The enforcement of provisions as to the rights of minorities.

'4. In a few cases where boundaries were not quite justly drawn.

'But I agree with you that these are mostly oddments, and do not constitute very substantial grievances. What you say about the Treaty in this vital respect is a great compliment to the wisdom and framers of the Treaty.

'If we had the Disarmament provided for in the Treaty the question of the demilitarisation of the Rhineland would never have arisen. It certainly would not if we had made the Covenant of the League a reality, and not a sham.

Ever sincerely,
D. Lloyd George.'

In September 1936 Lloyd George went to see Hitler in Germany, taking with him Tom Jones, Lord Dawson of Penn and his son and daughter. He was also accompanied by people who were in close touch with Ribbentrop and other high-ranking Nazis. He was completely bowled over by Hitler; Tom Jones has described his visit in great detail.[1] Hitler flattered Ll.G. by saying that he was proud to meet the one man who had won the World War, adding that he was determined to maintain friendship with Britain. Ll.G., says Thomas Jones, 'speaking with a tear in his throat', was deeply touched by the Führer's tribute and proud to hear it paid to him 'by the greatest German of the age'. Ll.G. wished that Chamberlain could be 'closeted with Hitler for an hour'. On his return he made the serious mistake of writing popular articles in the Beaverbrook press about this visit. He praised the Nazi regime and insisted on saying, in spite of protests from Megan Lloyd George and Tom Jones, that 'The Germans have definitely made up their minds never to quarrel with us again.'

For all his efforts at appeasement, Lloyd George always saw the importance of keeping our relations sweet with Russia. He was on close terms with Maisky, the Soviet Ambassador, and insisted that without Russian support Halifax's guarantee to Poland was mad. He went further than others in opposing the British guarantee to Eastern Europe, ran a personal campaign in the Sunday press and demanded a positive reply to Hitler's peace offer after the destruction of Poland. He proposed a Peace Conference in which Russia and the United States should be asked to take part. I supported this idea without, I am afraid, much conviction. In July, 1940 he was asked to join the Government by Churchill, but refused, perhaps not so much because Chamberlain and Halifax were, as he complained, still members of it, but because at his advanced age he no longer felt equal to the job. He said that we could not beat Germany without Russian and American assistance and that 'we have got to get something like a revolution here and a better future for the common man' if we were to fight a successful war. Neither Chamberlain nor Halifax would agree to anything of the kind, while 'Winston doesn't care either way'. Ll.G. said to me personally that 'Churchill had got his war', and in public, not so long before, he said that Churchill 'loves war as a fly does carrion'. In a House of Commons debate on 7th May 1941 he attacked the Government's policy in general, repeating that we were in no position to help Greece and other coun-

1. Thomas Jones, *op. cit.*

tries in Europe, and was constantly interrupted by Churchill. In his reply, Winston said that Lloyd George had made 'the sort of speech with which, I imagine, the illustrious and venerable M. Pétain might well have elevated the closing days of M. Reynaud's Cabinet'.

Lloyd George was deeply wounded and I think made no more interventions in the House. It was said that he was prepared to act as 'Britain's last card', that is, the man on whom the burden would fall of making the best terms he could for England if we were compelled to capitulate. In February 1941, before Russia had been brought into the war and Churchill's efforts to involve the United States had signally failed, I called on Lloyd George and asked him what he thought of our prospects. I had myself by then decided that it was no longer any good talking about a possible compromise and I had written in the paper saying that there was no alternative but to continue the war until Germany was militarily defeated. Lloyd George at once took me up on this issue and we had a long conversation of which I kept a full-length record.

February 1941

Long talk with Ll.G. He began almost at once to tackle me about our two leaders in the *N. S. & N.*, both of which said that a compromise peace with Hitler would be fatal. I said we had not necessarily ruled out the possibility at some stage, but that it was true in my view that a peace with Hitler would mean a temporary truce at best, without disarmament or the real alleviation of the war strain. Hitler, in a word, would never leave off fighting against us whether the guns were firing or not. We should therefore have the same choice as we had at Munich always in front of us. Either we should organise on a totalitarian basis for war in the near future or we should live on sufferance, finding ourselves rather in the position of Mussolini. All democracy, free criticism, etc., would have to be stopped and we should have to do what Hitler told us. We should at once lose American support. They would say we were yellow, etc. and go into isolation. Ll.G. snorted at this and I agreed that it would not be very reasonable on America's part—the U.S.A. was trying to fight her war with Hitler on our soil and without any sacrifice—but that certainly would be the result of our making peace. We should be left alone either to give in to Hitler's pressure and propaganda till we became a satellite power, behaving as the Nazis wanted us to or we should simply prepare for the war again, giving Hitler plenty of time to consolidate on the Continent.

Ll.G. did not really answer this. He said that if it was a question of survival he would fight to the last man, etc. He was no pacifist and if we could win he would want to fight it out. But he judged that we could not win. How was victory possible? Our own military article of which he complained showed that we could not. It was hopeless to rely on revolt on the Continent because revolt could not come, as history showed, until the armies had suffered severe defeats. We could not land troops; Germany would far outnumber us. Bombing would not be decisive and Germany was in a far better position to blockade us than we to blockade Germany. He took a very grave view of the shipping situation. Adding to the 3 million ton losses admitted, we had to reckon ships not mentioned because they were not sunk but put out of action. Often in present congestion it took them a year to repair and they had to be considered as total losses. Then we did not include accidents which in present conditions were terribly frequent. We were probably losing about 5 million tons. He recalled in the last war how small the figures were in Dec. and Jan; how they leapt up in Feb. and doubled in March and were worse in April and May. Some invention might turn up to do what the convoy did last time, but in view of the help now given by aeroplanes to submarines, the lack of the Irish bases this time and the German use of the French and other Atlantic bases and the greater number of submarines against us and the vast area of work which now had to be done by the British navy alone which was shared last war by the French navy now inactive, the Italian navy (now against us) the American navy (now mainly in the Pacific) and the Jap navy (now a likely belligerent against us) he could not be hopeful, especially in view of the Government's failure during recent years to develop our own agriculture to its most useful capacity. At best, he said, he saw stalemate; that was the most likely result and I was ruling it out. 'In a year's time,' he said, 'if we are both alive, you will be sitting here and I shall remind you of this conversation. We shall be weaker and Germany will be stronger. Peace will be more difficult to get, the war will have spread everywhere in the world, causing suffering and destruction beyond imagination and it will not be a whit nearer solution.'

I said, 'This is an odd conversation between you and me. In 1917 you proclaimed the knock-out blow and Lansdowne was defeated. I regarded you as the devil and I think I was right. A compromise peace with that Germany was possible and the results of victory have been what we have seen.' 'No,' he said, 'I did not proclaim the knock-out blow until I had, with Asquith's agreement, inquired from the Germans whether they were willing to evacuate Belgium. I got no answer. And the knock-out blow was justified by a rational calculation of the chances of victory. I could see how we could win and I was right. We did win. This time there is no rational calculation which shows how victory is possible.'

I did not want to waste time on the history and asked whether he thought we could now negotiate a peace. No, he thought not now, but that we should have to do so sooner or later and that it was very unwise, by what I said now, to make it impossible to support a negotiated peace when the time came. When could the time come? Probably, he thought, when we had repelled invasion. Then we could negotiate from strength. But I said, 'That is the one time when we never should. A country which has just scored a great victory will not offer peace to an implacable enemy. Especially with Winston as P.M.' He agreed that it would be difficult. 'Winston likes his war. He has always loved war and is dictatorial at heart.' He told me of a fascinating conversation with Winston who did not reply to the argument, but ended with a passionate shout that 'never, never, never' would he have conversations with Hitler or the Nazis. Ll.G. told him that he could not say such things; the situation was too grave for irresponsible
U

utterances like that. Then Mrs. Churchill, who is a quiet, intelligent little Scottish woman, looked up from her sewing and said, 'We all have the right to change our minds.' W.C. said nothing more.

'Well,' I said, 'you agree that we are unlikely to negotiate after a victory. But take the other more likely possibility. That we are not invaded. I don't think we shall be unless Hitler has already got a winning position in the air, which seems unlikely. Suppose he just blockades? How do we seek a peace then?' 'That,' said Ll.G., 'is very difficult. To negotiate from so weak a position, while our ships are being sunk. That would be very difficult indeed.'

This was where we left it. I could not see how Ll.G. had made his case because the conditions for negotiation seemed neither present nor likely to be present. He asked me earlier in the conversation how I went on talking as I did if I agreed with him that victory was highly improbable or even impossible. I said that I did agree that it was highly improbable and that I more than agreed with him about the utter catastrophe of the war, long continued, whoever won. But I saw, as I explained in the beginning, no way of making peace with the Nazis, with whom people like me would still be at war even if the government patched up a peace, and that I therefore just stuck to it. War was incalculable. Something might happen in Germany or elsewhere which would alter the whole situation. Ll.G. said that this was a cowardly attitude—just to go on against one's judgement, hoping for something to turn up.

Something *did* turn up. Alas for prophecy in politics! The conditions which Ll.G. thought essential for victory became realities at the end of 1941. Russia and the U.S.A. were both brought into the war against Hitler, and the conflict was no longer between Britain and Germany, but a world struggle in which we were no longer required to play more than a secondary role.

CHAPTER FIFTEEN

What It Was All About

I

I HAVE been writing about the intellectual and moral conflicts of a generation rather than about historical events, and what remains is to say something about what happened to the ideas we had been quarrelling about and how our hopes and fears were realised during the course of the war. It was not surprising that almost everybody, including Lloyd George, Keynes and myself, should have had moods of defeatism or despair, and that it took us a long time to accept the necessity of another national war against Germany. That was what we had all, if for slightly different reasons, sworn not to do. We did not expect civilisation to survive the war and, in any case, Britain seemed unlikely to be on the winning side. We never imagined, as so many people did in 1914, that this was a war to end war, or that any good result could come from it. We were just forced into it by Nazi Germany; there was no alternative.

First, about the Blitz. I had expected to be frightened of bombs, but I am half ashamed to confess they came as a relief to me, almost an enjoyment. I recall walking up the hill to Hampstead, with London on fire behind me, loud noises everywhere, bits of shrapnel falling on the path, and arriving in a state of something like exaltation. The responsibility of opting for this monstrous horror was over; there was no longer any choice. Fear is a complicated affair, not at all easy to analyse. I have always been a coward, afraid of the future, but there have not been many occasions when I recall being physically frightened.

Standing out in my memory is one day in the blazing summer of 1921 when I—with only one guide—climbed the Wildstrubel in Switzerland in charge of four adolescents. Many of the slopes which would normally have been covered with snow were nothing but precipices of ice. It was my first time in the Alps and I remember now my horror, knowing that if I stumbled we should all fall down many thousand feet. When I, leading the company, started to walk across the ice the guide shouted from the other end of the rope, 'Don't loiter about there; a lot of boulders are coming down this way.' The incident remains in my mind because it was the one occasion on which I recall physical fear. My fears on other occasions seem to me to have been mostly irrational guilt.

Dorothy and I were lucky in the Blitz; we were not hit, though plenty of destruction took place all round us. We were bombed out of our flat in Great James Street, on the edge of Bloomsbury; the house was surrounded by time-bombs and a policeman allowed me ten minutes in which to decide what to take away. Books? Clothes? A typewriter, of course. Everything and nothing seemed worth saving. One day after the time-bombs had been removed, Dorothy and I visited the partly wrecked flat. In the bathroom one of the floorboards gave way; Dorothy's leg went through and a rusty nail made a jagged gash in her thigh. I hurried her to a chemist in the hope of getting a makeshift bandage before we went to hospital. A sailor, who had no doubt had some elementary lessons in first aid, was standing in the shop and offered to help. Dorothy lifted her skirt and displayed her wound. The sailor fainted. She was eventually sewn up in the Westminster Hospital.

We had moved into an evacuated, very modern house in Highgate; it was built by Erno Goldfinger and was largely made of glass. There had not then been bombs in that area and a variety of friends took refuge with us at nights. It happened that when Margery Fry and the Chinese Ambassador were both sleeping on mattresses under the stairs a fire-bomb fell next door and started a wonderful blaze. Then a landmine was dropped only a hundred yards away. The windows and glass doors fell in and we had to move again. That was the occasion on which I reported in my *London Diary*, much to the general amusement, that I was bombed off the lavatory seat while reading Jane Austen. *Mansfield Park* went into the bath and I was thrown out of the door. We moved to some empty rooms in Joad's house not far off in East Heath Road, Hampstead, and stayed there until 1944, when we found a top-floor flat overlooking the Thames

at the bottom of Buckingham Street, off the Strand. It had a gorgeous view, which we could not enjoy during the last part of the war
because our windows were smashed by buzz-bombs and V-2s and
had to be boarded up.

We had always slept in our beds during the earlier raids and later
we were never bothered by the lethal danger of V-2s. If one dropped
near you, you would never know and so it wasn't worth bothering
about, but buzz-bombs, with a lateral blast, were a confounded
nuisance because it was your own fault if you, or your friends near
you, were cut to bits by flying splinters of glass. If you were sensible,
you led the way to a shelter. Night after night we would both go to
bed, and then be woken by a familiar noise in the sky. I preferred the
nights I spent fire-watching. The bomb would cut out and I would
turn over in bed and mutter, when I heard the bang, 'Oh, that's
Mrs. Smith and not us', but after two or three times I would realise
my folly, get up and find Dorothy, also in two minds, sitting on her
bed near a window. We would dress and go down to a shelter,
which we shared with Olga Katzin, and wait for the morning. In
the day I would work in the kneehole under my desk to avoid the
danger of shattered glass from the windows. I remember that children in one of the great hospitals had their faces so penetrated by glass
splinters that the doctors questioned whether their lives would be
worth saving. Glass, unlike metal, will not respond to magnets
and there was no alternative but to cut away their faces.

One morning early, when I was going to the printers in a tram
with a load of Whitehall charladies, a buzz-bomb came overhead.
I shouted in an authoritative voice, 'Get down on the floor'. They
obeyed and the bomb burst a hundred yards away. They all got up
in a flurry of petticoats, red-faced and roaring with laughter. I
realised how much better it was to take action which might prove
unnecessary than to store up one's fear; it needed a bit of courage not
to be afraid that someone would think you were frightened. The
right way was to take cover like a soldier. Sir Kenneth Clark was in
a queue waiting to buy a ticket at Waterloo Station when a buzz-
bomb cut out overhead. He shouted to the others to get down on
the ground and himself took cover behind a pillar. When he looked

up after the explosion, most of the other members of the queue
were dead. They had not heeded his warning—fearing, no doubt,
the loss of their places in the queue. Sir Kenneth tells me that he was
unhurt, but that his 'felt hat was covered with tiny spines of glass
so that I looked like a hedgehog decorated for Christmas.'

People have forgotten such details nowadays, because a younger
generation tends to assume that we were unnecessarily troubled by
air warfare. Certainly in the West End, we could 'take' the raids we
got; whether we could have survived many more like the last two
raids in the spring of 1941, when many of London's gas and water
mains were destroyed, I don't know. We might not have been able to
carry on, but bombs do not induce surrender. The Government had
miscalculated the effect of raids; the 300,000 papier mâche coffins
which were ready when the bombing began were never used
and the hospitals, which were cleared for patients who were expected to be driven mad by raids, remained empty. On the contrary, bombs tended to cure psychological maladies. Many people
who were neurotic about the prospect of war were cured by its
reality. They had too much to do to have time to be frightened.
Wendell Willkie came over from the United States to see us when
the early raids were at their height. He naively imagined everyone
would be in jitters. He told us how, after a noisy night, he asked the
chambermaid at the hotel whether she was beginning to want to
make peace with Hitler. He was surprised at her response. He took
a bus and made the same enquiry from his fellow-passengers. He
reported, with admiration, that they seemed unperturbed. The idea
that we should all be ready to give way to Hitler in 1940 seemed
merely comic. It would have been ridiculous even in the last stage of
the war. After Germany's defeat I flew over the Ruhr and saw Essen
and other great towns reduced to tangled heaps of wire and mangled
machinery. Even then the bombing of civilians had not had the expected effect and the Germans were not at all anxious to surrender.

In the late summer of 1940 German bombers for the first time
began their raids on Dockland. I was one of a small company who
went down to the East End in early mornings with Bob Boothby,
then Under-Secretary to the Ministry of Food. We took with us a

mobile canteen which provided hot drinks for people who had been bombed out. I got to know Father Groser, the happiest example of a priestly saint, who was then and afterwards beloved by co-workers of all denominations as well as by the poor he helped. I recall one morning my pleasure in being able to ring him up to say that I had just received a cheque for £1,000 to help his work in the Blitz.

Ritchie Calder wrote of the effects of the Blitz in the East End in a vivid series of articles which I published in the *N. S. & N.* The number of dead was small, but the army of refugees was larger than expected and he pointed out that, if you were homeless and had lost everything you possessed, you were, in effect, a casualty. No provision had been made for these destitute people, and Ritchie caused a sensation when he described how many of them were herded into schools which were themselves afterwards bombed. I myself wrote an article about a vast, underground food store in Stepney where hundreds of poor people took shelter among the crates of margarine, and where stacks of boxes containing London's food supply were being used as screens for unofficial lavatories. I made a frontal attack on the Home Secretary, Sir John Anderson, and the local authorities for their total failure to deal with an increasingly shocking and dangerously unhygienic situation. This article was read by General Ismay and passed on to Winston Churchill. This may have had something to do with the fact that Herbert Morrison took Anderson's place immediately afterwards. At any rate, he told me that each time he met the Prime Minister in the next few weeks Churchill would ask him whether the Stepney scandal was properly cleared. Herbert added: 'The shelters are now my job. Winston ought not to be bothering about them, his concern should be with the bombers in the sky.'

II

During the war the paper flourished; and trebled, by the end of it, to almost 90,000, which is its circulation in 1967. John Roberts and I were determined, in spite of paper rationing, to meet the rapidly increasing demand even if it meant reducing the quality of the news-print until it was fit only for lavatories. We crowded the pages with three columns of small print and found that people did not worry about the 'make-up', provided they were offered reading matter which contained hope for the future and something to argue about. The troops, most of the time in England, were insupportably bored, read it with avidity and wrote to me with a gratitude which they finally expressed by voting Labour in 1945. We ended the war with a greatly enhanced reputation. The *N. S. & N.* was naturally bombed out, and doubtless contained many mistakes and misprints, especially when the paper was written by a minute staff in the printer's offices, but we always managed to come out somehow and were pleased with our achievement.

We were, of course, understaffed, but I was lucky when Freda White joined us after baffling experiences at the Ministry of Information. George Schwartz, who has become famous as a City writer since the war, was with us for a year and, most fortunate of all, Aylmer Vallance, who was a lieutenant-colonel acting as liaison officer between the War Office and the hush-hush propaganda department, was permitted throughout the war to write about its progress in the *N. S. & N.* This suited everyone, because I was not interested in military details and he knew exactly how much he might divulge. Indeed, we were told that the Censor never had to bother about us, since we were the one paper which could be relied upon not to betray secrets by accident. In 1942 Norman MacKenzie was invalided from the R.A.F. and was able to come on to our staff. For the rest, I and H. N. Brailsford managed as well as we could. He usually wrote the leading article, while I wrote the Diary, as well as innumerable, often signed, pieces in addition to editing the paper.

In 1943 I made a valiant effort to strengthen our staff. I wrote on 17th November:

Dear Lord Beaverbrook,

I understand that Michael Foot is no longer editing the *Evening Standard*, and I am writing to ask you whether it would be possible in his new position for him to write occasional articles in the *New*

Statesman and Nation. I put the point to him today and he tells me that he is not at liberty to write for any other paper. But there has always been a convention that daily paper writers could contribute to weeklies, since weeklies do not in any way compete with their daily contemporaries. Would it be possible for you to give him permission to be an occasional contributor, signed or unsigned, in this journal?

I should regard this as a very special kindness if you are able to agree. I have been very short-handed here for a long time; my younger writers having been of course taken away for war work. Michael began his journalistic career for a short period on this paper, and I should very much like him to be, even if only occasionally, again associated with the paper. I fully realise that I am asking for a special concession, but I believe you may be generous enough to agree to it.

Beaverbrook's reply was characteristic:

PRIVATE

18th November 1943

Thank you very much for your letter.

I can well understand your desire to make use of the fine talents of Michael Foot. And I have a great deal of sympathy for you in the war-time difficulties you encounter.

But the proposition you put forward is not one that I could possibly entertain.

If the newspapers opened that door, it would swing very wide indeed.

The newspaper pays Foot nearly £4000 a year. If he were to do similar work for another paper, the directors would ask 'Is Beaverbrook losing his punch?' 'Is he going down into the valley where all the newspapermen before him have gone?'

And they may be right.

I am very sorry that this is my answer to you, but it must be so.

Yours sincerely,

Beaverbrook.

There was plenty to fight about on the home front. In the first panic of 1940 thousands of refugees were shut up in the Isle of Man and some transported to Canada. This was a silly episode about which most people felt ashamed. To intern Germans who had themselves escaped German concentration camps was cruel, foolish and unnecessary. Amongst them were many who served the Allied cause well because they best knew the lines of propaganda which were likely to embarrass the Nazis. If there were really a risk of any of the refugees being 'planted' here to help the German invasion, then women, who were not interned, should have been locked up, too. On this matter the *N. S. & N.* and a few other papers, which demanded that indiscriminate internment should at once be abolished, won a resounding victory. We kept at it week after week, far into 1941, illustrating in a hundred ways the monstrous absurdity of keeping these allies in concentration camps, and I think that the *N. S. & N.* was responsible for the release of many who proved their value to the Allies during the war. This campaign was brilliantly inaugurated by Dick Crossman, who was carried off in the autumn of 1940 into the hush-hush world as head of British psychological warfare against Germany.

In spite of many blunders by Whitehall, the military, and the police, Britain retained her liberties to a remarkable degree during the war. I had shared with other people a fear that when we were fighting fascism we should ourselves develop authoritarian tendencies. Winston Churchill was always accused of wishing to be a dictator and I had had a long interview with him in January 1939 about the preservation of civil liberty if war broke out. I went to see him at Chartwell. He came in from the garden, wearing his bricklayer's uniform. We lunched together and spent the afternoon talking. He said that there was no reason why the basic freedoms of democracy should not be compatible with efficient military organisation. Chamberlain had accused press critics of the Government of 'fouling their own nest' and I had written a pamphlet on the freedom of the Press. Winston called Chamberlain's accusation 'a convenient thesis, if a dangerous one'. He thought criticism essential, even in wartime, and remarked about the Labour Party's attitude to rearmament and the Government's resentment of their criticism, 'Naturally, if the leaders of the Conservative Government insist that all is well, one can scarcely expect the Opposition to press for increased armaments.' He did not see why preparation for defence need involve loss of liberty. Captain Liddell Hart had remarked that 'To have conscription to combat Fascism is like cutting our throats to avoid a disease.' Winston replied that if the voluntary system was inadequate he would advocate filling up the gap 'by ballot among all the young men in the country'. He did not believe 'any enemy would waste its bombs in an effort to kill ordinary citizens just out of spite, when he could obtain a much greater military result by bombing docks, factories, Government offices and the like'. We could not, as Liddell Hart has suggested, fight a purely defensive war, merely digging ourselves in, using the Channel as a Maginot Line. Passive defence was 'the theory of the turtle, which is disproved at every Lord Mayor's Banquet. If the enemy can attack us when and where he pleases without fear of reprisals, we shall become the whipping-boy of Europe. We need shelters and tunnels, but'—here Winston did an admirable piece of pantomime to illustrate fighting blindly in the dark—'crouching in a shelter is not a fighting posture.'

On the whole, Winston proved as good as his word throughout the war. He treated the House of Commons with respect and re-mained a strict constitutionalist, even when he was bitterly attacked by Aneurin Bevan and other less-effective critics. He was at his worst, perhaps, when he lost his temper with the *Daily Mirror* which Morrison threatened to ban after a bitter and, I think, misunder-stood cartoon in which Zec showed an exhausted British sailor on a raft, who, as Maurice Edelman explains, symbolised the struggle of British sailors to bring petrol to *Daily Mirror* readers through the dangerous Atlantic seas.[1] The caption was 'The price of petrol has been increased by one penny.' Zec appears merely to have meant 'Don't waste petrol, it costs lives'. Churchill bitterly resented this and many *Daily Mirror* criticisms and actually ordered that the *Mirror*'s ownership should be investigated, as well as the background

1. Maurice Edelman, *The Mirror—A Political History* (Hamish Hamilton, 1966): the incident is described at length in Chapter VI.

of Zec himself. Why Churchill should have thought that this cartoon suggested that sailors' lives were being endangered to enhance the profits of the petrol companies I am not sure, but he certainly did so, and enmity between himself and Cecil King was long maintained, and probably did not cease with the libel action which Churchill successfully brought against the *Daily Mirror* after the war.

I once had a characteristic glimpse of Winston during the period when U-boats were playing most havoc with British shipping. Newspapers were naturally anxious to let the public know what had happened to British boats and British sailors. They fully realised that if published too soon the information would be useful to the enemy, but thought there could be no harm in publication months later. Winston called a conference of editors in the Cabinet Room of 10, Downing Street, to explain that the Germans would find the information valuable, however much time had passed since such sinking occurred. He was dressed in a Teddybear suit, with the First Lord of the Admiralty, A. V. Alexander, somehow looking comically tiny beside him. (This may have been due to cartoons which always represented Alexander as a pip-squeak imitation of Winston.) Churchill made his point, and in five minutes I was satisfied that Nazi sinkings were not things to talk about. But the extraordinary thing was that Winston made his explanation last for a solid forty minutes. He told us nothing except that Goebbels could use the information. I can't recall what he said or how he managed to be interesting in saying nothing for so long. His energy and eloquence simply boiled over, although at the time he had the whole conduct of the war on his shoulders, and enough, one would have thought, to prevent him doing more than just have a D notice sent to us all. When he had finished, he turned to Alexander and said, 'Perhaps the First Lord has something to add?' Alexander said that he thought that the Prime Minister had 'very adequately covered the subject'. We agreed by our silence and this extraordinary occasion was over.

The only papers which were actually suppressed during the war were the *Week* and *Daily Worker*, when they seemed not only to be opposing the Government and the war but to be advocating 'revolutionary defeatism'. After much pressure, in which I played a part, they were allowed to reappear later when, after the Russians were brought into the war, the Communists became its keenest supporters. It happened that I was able to meet regularly at a friend's house one of the top people of M.I.5. From the beginning he was ready to listen to the argument that the Communists would in the long run be allies in the war, while the Fascists were a potential Fifth Column. He told me he had the utmost difficulty in persuading his staff that Fascists were the people who had to be watched and sometimes arrested, and he had constantly to correct idiotic, trivial persecution of the Left. The *N. S. & N.* enjoyed exposing such incidents as the arrest of a man because Left Book Club volumes were to be seen on his shelves. My M.I.5 friend told me at the beginning of the war that he hoped to end it without concentration camps, which struck me as being a good, liberal sentiment to hear from that quarter. He failed only in being compelled to enforce Regulation 18B, under which members of the Fascist party and some who were considered pro-Nazi were 'detained'. On the whole, we did well in the matter of civil liberty, even the detainees were given fair treatment, and opportunities of appeal; Mosley himself was released on grounds of health before the war was over. Conscientious objectors were not victimised or driven mad, or in effect murdered, as some were in the First World War. One reason for Britain's increased humanity was that there was less distinction between soldiers and civilians in a war in which the troops were often idle in England, and the bombs were equally lethal in and out of prison.

III

I became absorbed in the problem of increasing social equality during the war. The Army, of course, began with the same absurd spit-and-polish routine that we all remembered from the 1914 war; its senior officers had titles and it was not until after Dunkirk that the idea of a People's War began to be understood. In the winter of

1939 the Army had nothing to do and the men were grousing about
the privileges of the officer class just as I remembered them doing
twenty years before. About a score of them were billeted in my
cottage in Essex and after the troops had left for other quarters a
sergeant's wife was allotted one of my bedrooms which seemed to
her very inadequate. Our upper rooms had sloping, raftered ceilings
and she complained that there was no proper wardrobe in which to
hang her clothes. She left, saying with a sniff, 'It's not *quite*, really,
is it?'

After the Coalition had been formed, I published many articles,
particularly by Harold Laski, who urged that the Government, in
which Attlee, Morrison and Bevin all held important offices, should
introduce such Socialism as was possible during the war. Churchill
opposed social changes, but pressure was brought to bear on the
Government to obtain such a reform as the Beveridge Plan. Churchill was defeated in his opposition to an army education which
involved discussion on social questions. General Sir Ronald Adam
and Bill Williams (Sir William Emrys Williams), Professor Boris
Ford and others in charge of Army Education made a reality of
A.B.C.A. (Army Bureau of Current Affairs). How keen idle troops
in England were to ask questions and debate about post-war reform
I learnt personally in many camps where I was asked to say something which would start a discussion.

A typical letter from a young officer is still in front of me:

'Last Saturday's *New Statesman* was excellent, and I could hardly
fail to see myself in the London *Diary*. This A.B.C.A. course is
just finishing, but personally I should like another month of it.
For the first time since I joined the army I feel really and completely at home. Just for this weekend I've been able to pick up
the trend of my life where it broke off when I came down from
Cambridge and went into the army.

'There have been excellent talks on the progress of the War, on
Australia, Russia, the Nazis, etc., and we have each given a talk to
our own syndicate on some aspect of the war, as well as joining
in the numerous discussions. All of us on this course—though

soldiers with our primary duty to train to fight—all of us are keen to see that our own men do get a true picture, and are prepared for what must inevitably take place here when the war is won.

'For our men to think that we shall all be demobilised at once, that Japan will cave in when Germany surrenders, that rationing, high taxes and high prices will soon vanish, that in fact we shall return to a better version of England in 1939—that is what we must guard against. We have to create a real faith in our own cause until there is no question of personal safety or feeling. To win this war we must possess a faith in our cause as strong as that of the Germans, yet not a fanatical faith but a reasoned one. And we must prevent by early action our men having vague ideas about England after the war, which are bound to be turned into disillusionment. One of the greatest dangers to the peace will come from those who are disillusioned through their own facile thinking. Finally, we must make our men interested in democracy, in taking their own part in government. Many have not yet used the vote, and very few have any idea how local government works, or how much responsibility devolves on the individual. As I see it, A.B.C.A. can give the army a positive and constructive outlook, not through propaganda but through education, discussion, and through stimulating the mind to understand the difficulties. If, at the end of this war, England possesses a very large army—as she will—yet an army which in the main does understand the difficulty of reconstruction, and has a positive faith that these difficulties will be overcome, then we shall not repeat the tragedy of the last war. It is up to us. We have a great chance before us.'

A.B.C.A. was an innovation. My talks on social reconstruction usually led to very free and lively debate, but I do remember one hot Sunday afternoon when the men were released from other duties, carried benches into an open field and slept comfortably while I discoursed upon the future of mankind. Perhaps I should say something here about myself as a speaker. I made one of my serious mistakes in early life when I was too lazy to take elocution lessons and never learnt to produce my voice so that it would carry. I was fluent enough and seldom needed notes, even if I was speaking for more than an hour. In an audience of a few hundred, say, I spoke effectively, but at a mass meeting people would come up to me afterwards, much to my chagrin, and say that I had not been audible at the back of the hall. This was not important when I spoke to small Army audiences or groups of foreign soldiers in England. Perhaps if I had been any use at mass meetings I might have found it more difficult to avoid standing for Parliament. Anyway, I never wanted to be an M.P. I was approached by a number of constituencies—once hesitated about standing for Rugby and was for a time the Labour candidate for Cambridge University.

In 1941 many people had become restive about the results of the continued Party truce. The Labour Party had agreed not to fight in the constituencies during the war, but many people feared that politics would die of inertia, and critics who ought to be in the House of Commons would be permanently excluded if the by-election opportunities were neglected. This issue was one of many discussed by the 1941 Committee, which was founded by J. B. Priestley after his exclusion—he believed through Churchill's intervention—from the famous B.B.C. Postscripts on Sunday evenings.

The 1941 Committee was really rather a joke. Its members were individuals who had only one thing in common—a grumble against the Government for failing to carry out social reforms which were possible during the war. It met at Edward Hulton's private house, where a cold collation of unparalleled luxury for those days awaited us. After plenty of chicken and ham, we sat round a table and discussed 'projects' which didn't, in fact, ever materialise. H. G. Wells, always belligerent at committees, blew the whole show up one day because Raymond Gauntlett, the secretary, had engaged in a correspondence about the 'revolutionary neo-Christianity of the Archbishop of York'. Wells was unmercilessly ironical about this Christian revolution a couple of thousand years after the Crucifixion. It was I, I think, who gave the *coup de grâce* to the 1941 Committee. After a long debate one evening, it decided to run Independent candidates at elections and at the next meeting decided to revoke this decision. I did not want to be an Independent candidate myself, but there seemed no sense in such a self-contradictory body and I exploded; I said that if the truth were told, we were at 1941 Committee meetings only because of the excellent hospitality offered us by Hulton. I don't think I went to the Committee again—anyway, it soon died. The Common Wealth Party, which arose from the 1941 Committee, survived long enough to contest —and in some cases win—several seats in 1945 under the leadership of Sir Richard Acland and Tom Wintringham.

In December 1940 Maynard Keynes and I had again begun to write each other letters of disagreement. We exchanged small discourtesies, Maynard suggesting that, 'Some Freudian censor always forbade such good news as what is happening in Greece' reaching the level of the paper's consciousness, and I replying that there was something Freudian about the fact that when the *N. S. & N.* seemed interesting to many people, his comments were confined to complaints. He followed this up on 17th December by saying:

'You will have discovered that in the meantime I have found something I like! Your main duty is to criticise, and that makes questions of tone and balance so extraordinarily important. I so often find myself almost driven to dislike criticism, which in fact I think absolutely justifiable, and most necessary to make, by its environment, and especially by attempts to exploit the war in favour of something you want anyhow on the bogus ground that it will promote the winning of the war, when quite likely it won't. I think that the critic, if he is to be valuable in war time and pull his full weight, has to maintain an extraordinary, and possibly an impossible, urbanity of soul.'

On 6th February 1941, in a letter about the internal affairs of the paper, I told Maynard Keynes that I had found a quotation from him which I was sticking on my office wall:
'*Words ought to be a little wild, for they are the assaults of thought upon the unthinking.*'
I added, 'I have this as a permanent weapon,' and Keynes replied, 'I had forgotten this lovely quotation, yet I am not ashamed of it.'
x

In the autumn of 1941 I published a short book called *Propaganda's Harvest*. I re-read it in 1967 and found it wore better than I should have expected. It analysed Hitler's propaganda in *Mein Kampf* and dealt with his prophecy that his middle-class opponents could be easily smashed by fear, lies and violence and that abroad he could build up a 'Fifth Column' in each of the countries he intended to invade. I dealt at some length with Vansittart's *Black Record* in which he did not deny that there might be individual 'good Germans', but asserted that Germany was a 'butcher-bird' which preyed on other nations which behaved like sparrows and songbirds. My reply to him still seems unanswerable; his thesis began with Tacitus and omitted the fact that the Germans of those days were our ancestors as well as Hitler's. 'He discovered that the Teutonic Knights in the twelfth century were cruel to the Slavs and Jews. He forgets that our forefathers treated the Irish very much as the Teutons did the Slavs, and hounded such Jews as survived out of this island.' He described the cruelty of Tilly and his Germans in the Thirty Years War, though in fact Tilly was a 'Walloon at the head of an army of mixed Croats and Poles, with a few Southern German Catholics thrown in.' As an alternative to his historical mythology, I tried to explain the evil development of Germany by the catastrophe of the peasant and democratic revolts in Germany having been destroyed, in contrast to the comparative success of democratic movements in Britain. But my main point was a protest against the First World War propaganda which had had a terrible reaction. By pretending that the Germans were all wicked and had to be permanently suppressed, we had paved the way for the equally foolish reaction by which the Germans were believed to have been politically ill-treated at Versailles and now had to be cossetted by us as if it were we who ought to feel guilty. This began a long controversy with Vansittart, who never answered my historical points, but remained indiscriminately anti-German until, by one of the most remarkable of *volte-faces*, he decided after the war that it was the Russians who were the real birds of prey. He was an agreeable opponent with whom I debated on the B.B.C., and with whom I quarrelled constantly in newspaper correspondence. He was remarkable as a man of letters, but as the head of the Foreign Office he was dangerously emotional and unbalanced.

In November I sent *Propaganda's Harvest* to Maynard, who replied in a letter which contains two pieces of information of historic interest:

'I have looked through your *Propaganda's Harvest* with much interest. It is a very good little paper. One minor correction. It was not Sir Auckland Geddes who talked about the pips squeaking but *Eric* Geddes. He invented this perfect expression in an election speech at the Guildhall in Cambridge, during the Coupon Election, which was only reported in the local paper. It would have been entirely lost to fame if my mother had not cut it out and sent it to me, and it was impressed on my memory when I came to write the *Economic Consequences*.

'The phrase about the hardfaced men, which you quote, I stole from Stanley Baldwin, who invented it. I was sitting in the Chancellor's room in the Treasury having tea on the first day of the new Parliament after the Coupon Election. Baldwin, who was then Financial Secretary and had the adjoining room, poked his nose through the door, as I can see him now, to us at tea. I asked him—"What do they look like?" And he replied in the famous phrase—"A lot of hard-faced men who look as if they had done well out of the war." '

In 1942 I had become optimistic about the result of the war because it was now being waged on two fronts. From now onwards my correspondence with Maynard turned on the question whether a revolution in Europe was really desirable or not. The *N. S. & N.* had assumed from the beginning that Capitalism could not be reconstructed after the war and that one of the important factors leading to victory would be a revolutionary underground composed not only of Communists, but also of Catholics, Liberals, Democratic Socialists, and patriots of all kinds. This Popular Front actually came into existence. At the beginning of the war Dick Crossman and I had written an anonymous book called *A Hundred Million Allies if We*

Choose. We argued that the liberation of millions of anti-Fascists on the Continent was vital for victory; we took the opportunity also of attacking the Foreign Office, which was run, as it still is, largely by the Old School Tie, and was very loath to find itself in alliance, at least openly, with revolutionaries.

After Hitler's invasion of Russia, the thesis that we needed a popular underground front in Europe had become easier to maintain. I was not very optimistic, but I hoped that out of the wartime alliance some form of co-operation between Britain, the U.S.A. and the U.S.S.R. might emerge. Countries that fought a common enemy might lose some of their suspicions and animosities; their own ideologies would necessarily change and 'in the immediate post-war period, problems of frontiers and constitutions will be far less urgent than those of hunger, disease and devastation'.

I hoped that Capitalism would be changed during the war, and that Communism might be so far modified as to make collaboration between East and West possible in Europe. Britain had largely aborted revolutionary movements in Europe after the First World War and we had been left with a nationalist treaty which had made the Second World War inevitable. All Europe was being scrambled under the Nazis; was it not possible that we could make use of Hitler's idea of a united Europe, not under the Germans, but under the impulse of revolutionary egalitarianism? Dorothy made it her job to find out how real the anti-Nazi movement on the Continent really was and in 1943 we published in the *N. S. & N.* an unusually well-informed series of articles, in which she revealed much unpublished information about the beginnings of the Resistance Movement in a number of countries. The book that developed out of these articles was called *Europe Rises.*[1] It seems thin today, but in 1943 it was remarkably prophetic. I remember well the discussions on which it was based. Dorothy discovered members of each exiled embassy who had genuinely 'anti-Fascist' notions and who were not merely seeking a sheltered residence in this country during the war. Often they were willing to meet us and to provide information about the anti-Fascist movement in their own countries. There were

1. Dorothy Woodman, *Europe Rises* (Victor Gollancz, 1943).

people in the British Foreign Office who were also ready to help. Brochures giving the facts about resistance in France, Germany, Holland and Belgium, Norway, Hungary, Bulgaria, Czechoslovakia and Poland were all issued by the U.D.C. and the facts discussed in the *N. S. & N*. Dorothy was careful; I don't think we made any mistakes, and enquiries came from the hush-hush world about the possibility of using Dorothy as a propagandist. She would not have accepted such an offer, but it was, in any case, quickly withdrawn because she was regarded as far too dangerously Left-Wing.

This reminds me of an incident at the beginning of the war when I was myself approached by Quintin Hogg, then I think a major in Intelligence, who asked me whether I would take charge of propaganda against the Franco Government, which at that moment, when minds were more direct than they became afterwards, was assumed to be an enemy because it was a Fascist one. After his visit I was rung up by M.I.5, or some similar organisation, with a query about my mother's maiden name, which, as it happened, was Turberville, impeccably Norman-French. I was not, however, surprised to hear no more about the proposal.

As the war went on, Dorothy's interests became increasingly Asian. The China Campaign Committee organised a monster petition, representing some million voters, against closing the Burma Road, and we became deeply involved, not only in the struggle for Indian independence, but in the resistance movement of Burma, Indonesia and Vietnam. Many of the younger Burmese, who were assumed by British officialdom to be enemies because they accepted their Japanese conquerors as liberators from the British, were really only concerned to win independence for Burma. General Aung San and his friends of the anti-Fascist movement seized the first opportunity to co-operate with General Slim in turning out the Japanese. Dorothy and I realised the importance of Burmese nationalism during the war itself and became firm friends with many Burmese. We have remained deeply attached to Burma ever since. We were in fact the only unofficial British to be asked to Rangoon to watch the ceremonial lowering of the Union flag and the hoisting of the Burmese flag at 4 a.m. on 4th January 1948. The soothsayers thought this hour and date more propitious than they proved to be. A more complex story could be told about Dorothy's work with the Indonesian and Vietnamese resisters, whom the Dutch and the French, under the British umbrella, attempted once more to bring under colonial rule. The focus of Dorothy's and my world was to shift from Europe to Asia quite soon after the ending of the war.

In Europe, I thought the Resistance Movement was a key to any reasonably worthwhile peace and I began to argue that we should hasten a Second Front, partly to encourage and work with the Resistance and partly to avoid the danger that Russia, which never ceased to press us to invade Europe, might be forced into a separate peace. Maynard Keynes was quick to notice an element of wishful thinking in our argument. Was it true that a revolutionary movement was important for victory? Had I any right to be talking of a Second Front when I knew nothing of the technical possibilities? Did I really think that Britain was refusing to organise a Second Front because the Foreign Office was anti-Soviet?

This controversy has never been settled. It was true that I knew nothing technically, apart from such information as my friends in the War Office and the Department of Political Warfare could supply without breaking the rules of secrecy. They told me that preparations for a Second Front were constantly put off by ideological factors, which they declared played an important part in our strategy, and I noticed as a curious fact that not only U.S. high-ups, who did not share Winston's anxiety to enter Europe through the Baltic and thereby forestall the Russians, but also Beaverbrook, who could not be accused of ignorance in this matter, were also urging that there should be a Second Front in the West. Some day, no doubt, published documents will show whether I was right in believing that ideology was an important factor in deciding where and when the Second Front should take place. I am sure that I exaggerated the part that revolutionary resistance could play before it was supported by full military invasion.[1] I wrote a lengthy memo supporting my case

1. The impatience felt for a Second Front in Europe is illustrated by this story, which leaked out to me from the French Underground movement:
In the year A.D. 2000 a raffle was held in France. The prizes were a rat, a bag of

at the time, but the whole argument was blighted by the fact that the opponents of a Second Front looked forward to a Europe perhaps not so very different from that of pre-war, while I hoped that this time, in contrast to 1918, the peace would be made in alliance with revolutionaries who might include Communists, but who were very unlikely to be simple followers of Stalin.

I was right in believing that the revolutionary forces in France and Italy would eventually play a serious part in victory, but it was only in Eastern Europe, which was occupied by Russia, that the revolution was carried out. Soviet Russia and the capitalist West confronted each other and bargained. This was precisely what I hoped would not happen. I wanted one Europe, which would necessarily be Socialist rather than Communist. I got two Europes, divided by an Iron Curtain.

There was one exciting exception. The effort to maintain the old tyrannical Yugoslavia seemed to Dorothy and myself, particularly monstrous. In the later stages of the war, nightly broadcasts were made by Yugoslav colonels in support of General Mihailovich, whose chief activity by that time was to frustrate the Partisans rather than to fight against the Hungarian, German, Italian and local Fascists who controlled Yugoslavia. When three Yugoslav workers, who were arrested by the Nazis and put to work on the fortified North Wall of Germany, escaped to Sweden, they were sent on by the British to London. They got into touch with the U.D.C., which

beans and ten minutes' use of electricity. The fortunate winners were interviewed by the Press.

'What,' the first was asked, 'did you do with your rat?'

'It was admirable. We had rat steak two days running.'

'And the bag of beans?' asked the interviewer of the second prizewinner.

'Most useful. We had half of it for supper all the week and the other half I gave to my daughter for her dowry.'

'And the ten minutes' use of electricity?'

'Oh, I used that,' said the third, 'for the radio.'

'What did you hear?'

'I listened to the B.B.C.'

'Oh, yes, and what were they saying?'

'Courage, my friends. We are coming soon.'

had already become known as a centre for revolutionary refugees. I remember the excitement of interviewing them in the tiny office in Victoria Street. The article which I published as a result was, I think, the first public evidence of the Tito movement in this country. When I visited Yugoslavia in the autumn of 1945, Partisans told me that this article had been translated into Serbo-Croat and that the fact that their struggle was given publicity abroad had greatly encouraged them in their savage fight in the Serbian hills.

Soon after this visit I was informed that Vladimir Velebit and an accompanying officer were coming to England, nominally to obtain medical supplies for Tito, but actually to further his cause and persuade the British Government to switch its support from Mihailovich to the Partisans. Velebit met a large group of sympathisers in our flat, satisfied them by their answers and laid the foundation of British support for Tito. It was arranged that Velebit should see Churchill on the following Monday. On Friday I learnt that his enemies had not been idle; the Foreign Office had informed him that he would leave England by plane on Sunday night, with his mission unfulfilled. I realised that I had twenty-four hours in which I could pull strings on Velebit's behalf. I interviewed Churchill's personal secretary and sent messages to Winston through Attlee and Lady Violet Bonham Carter, whom I knew as one of the few people with constant access to the Premier. I also saw George Malcolm Thomson, secretary to Lord Beaverbrook, and urged my case to him. Having done what I could, I went down to my Essex cottage in the evening. Late, the telephone rang, and the following conversation ensued:

'This is Lord Beaverbrook speaking.'

'Oh,' I said, 'how did you find me out?'

'I have a man named Jones. If I tell him to phone you, he'll find you in Hell or Timbuktu. I had your message this morning. You'll understand that this is a Foreign Office matter that doesn't come into my department. I can say nothing at all about it.'

'No, of course, I understand that quite well, Lord Beaverbrook.'

'But I think you are quite right. Now, you understand, don't you, that I can't interfere in any way, but *I think it will be all right.*'

So it proved; Velebit saw Churchill and British propaganda began belatedly to support and aid the Partisans. It amused me later to hear from the War Office that the Russians were even slower to switch their propaganda and even sent emissaries, or other aid, first to Mihailovich in the belief that he would pass some of it on to Tito! As a footnote, I may add that Velebit (now in Geneva at the head of E.E.C.) became Ambassador to Britain after the war and has remained our close friend ever since. In 1967 Tito is still President of Yugoslavia and though much that is cruel and tyrannous has happened there, Yugoslavia has paved the way for that modification of Communism which is now to be seen in all the satellite countries and begins to be visible in the Soviet Union itself. But the story of the Cold War, which by the folly of both camps prevented collaboration in Europe, must wait for another volume.

IV

I was usually rather gloomy about the world and had no illusions that a good peace would follow the war. But a number of events combined to make me somewhat optimistic in 1945. The first arose from my friendship with Gil Winant, who was something entirely new in American Ambassadors to this country. The contrast between him and Jo Kennedy, the former U.S. Ambassador, could not have been greater. Jo was a self-centred, frightened rich man who thought only in terms of money and Gil was a modest, enquiring dedicated and selfless man who thought only of winning the war and building a more sensible world after it. I first met Winant at a party at the Chinese Embassy and learnt from him that the person he most wanted to meet in England was R. H. Tawney. I promptly took a room at an hotel where I asked Tawney and Low to join us for lunch. I arrived on that occasion just in time to persuade the hotel manager to take down a vast Stars and Stripes flag which he had pinned up on the wall in honour of his distinguished guest. Tawney remarked afterwards that Winant seemed 'too good to be true', but in fact he was good all through, even if, as his suicide afterwards suggested, deeply neurotic. His dedication to his job was absolute and was made all the more difficult by the fact that he was a shy man who found the utmost difficulty in making a speech. People like Harold Laski helped him to write his talks to the British people. He was not afraid of the Left, though, not, I think, at all Left himself. He more than once came to lunch with our group at the *N. S. & N.* and stayed on till four in the afternoon, while messages from the Embassy had to wait. He loved unconventional, undiplomatic conversation.

In 1942, with Gil's encouragement, I went to the United States. New York, humming with activity and over-spilling with prosperity, was staggering to an Englishman still blinking after the blackout. In those days, the arrival by 'plane across the Atlantic in a single night still seemed miraculous. I wanted to see the whole of the American scene, as far as I could, and I made my way by train across to the Pacific coast, though I had not enough money for my return journey. I walked about the streets of Los Angeles looking for a bed, spent an uncomfortable night in a cheap lodging-house and borrowed money for my return from the British Consul-General. I paid a call at Pasadena on that most radical and independent-minded novelist, Upton Sinclair, who, after making a great hit with *The Jungle*, bored the world by a long series of sociological novels. The Pacific War was taken much more seriously than the European, and the Japanese hated in a way that the Germans never were. If you asked a G.I. what he intended to do with the Japs the regular reply was 'Kill all the yellow bastards'.

In New York I renewed my friendships with the staff of the *New Republic* and with Freda Kirchwey of the *Nation*. I found myself meeting key members of the New Deal and by way of contrast, renewing my acquaintance with Wendell Willkie, for whom I had formed a great liking. We ate sandwiches and blueberry pie in his Wall Street office. No one was so clumsy as Willkie. He upset his entire lunch on to the floor and we had to begin again. But the most interesting thing about him at that time was that he had ceased to be the conservative lawyer who had fought against the Tennessee Valley scheme and, instead, had become the idealist who wrote *One*

World. No doubt it was partly due to Joe Barnes, who accompanied him, that he formed so hopeful a picture of the Soviet Union and so excitedly prophesied the arrival of a World State which would make political sense of the scientific advances in travel and telecommunications. I found him a most hopeful phenomenon. Similarly, I talked long to Henry Wallace, the Vice-President, who was then making bold and unorthodox remarks about the 'century of the common man'. Clearly some of the people in power in the U.S. intended the coming peace to be, if not revolutionary, at least constructive and anti-imperialist.

It so happened that I also met Henry Luce, the owner of *Time* and *Life*, which at that moment was engaged in a furious controversy with the British, cursing us up hill and down for our retention of India and our colonial attitude. The occasion was a dinner at the Stork Club; my host was J. W. Lamont, who had gathered together a group of the most distinguished journalists in New York. The editors of the *New York Times* and the *Herald Tribune* and the top representatives of the big newspaper agencies were all present. The principal guest was Lord Halifax, British Ambassador in Washington. I arrived early with Lord Halifax just behind me. 'What can I give you to drink, my Lord?' said an immaculate waiter with a strong English accent. 'Tomato juice,' said Lord Halifax, careful to make it rhyme with potato in the American manner. 'Your tom*ah*to juice, my Lord,' said the waiter, carefully reminding him how the English language is spoken.

During dinner Luce turned brusquely on Halifax and asked if he agreed with Churchill, who had just made his famous speech refusing India her independence and saying that he was not fighting the war to give away the British Empire. Halifax turned to me and said, 'Kingsley Martin has just come from England. Perhaps he can tell us something useful about the reception of this speech.' I replied, with something more than my usual tact, that I and many others had thought it a singularly unwise speech to make, in view both of Indian and American opinion. Lord Halifax took me aside afterwards and told me that he was entirely in agreement with me, but was not in a position to criticise his Prime Minister.

One afternoon I had tea with Mrs. Roosevelt in the White House. I saw her many times after the war, thought her a most lovable person, and immensely respected the way in which she managed to build an independent career of her own without saying or doing anything which would embarrass her husband. That evening I took the train straight from Washington to Chicago and said to myself, 'There's no reason to be a journalist on this occasion. Thank goodness, I'm not obliged to write about interviewing Mrs. Roosevelt. It was a private occasion.' At Chicago, someone pushed an evening paper into my hand which contained Mrs. Roosevelt's regular column entitled 'My Day'. *She* had interviewed *me*. Not that she said anything about me of more significance than anything else she said. She remarked that I was one of those up-and-coming young Englishmen whom she was happy to entertain at the White House!

I had travelled to the United States by plane; it had been easy to find space going West. Leonard Woolf had been looking after the paper for me while I was away, and I had promised to return within a month. But I could find no way of returning. Every aeroplane and boat was packed with men and supplies, and though I waited constantly on Lord Halifax, who certainly tried his best for me, several weeks passed before I hit on the right idea. Direct application to the Ambassador or the Transport authorities was useless, but a New Deal friend rang up another important New Dealer in the Pentagon and I found myself on the *Queen Mary* with, I think, two other civilians, and some 15,000 U.S. officers and G.I.s.

We travelled at great speed, zig-zagging about to avoid U-boats and there was perfunctory drill to be observed if we were torpedoed. Everyone knew that we relied on speed and that there was not a hope in Hell of being saved if we should be sunk. One walked about all day carrying a lifebelt, the decks were packed tight with G.I.s, girls in the Services and American officers; we slept five in a cabin and sat down when we were tired on our Mae Wests. This was the first time I got to know any of the G.I.s. They included a small number of mature men; one of them was Dick Meyer, who, as it happened, was afterwards posted in an American camp not far from my Essex cottage for most of the rest of the war. Dorothy and I became close friends of his and I visited him in Chicago after the war, when he had become an active politician as well as a successful businessman. Most of the other G.I.s I knew were very young, simplest men who understood nothing much about why the war was fought and who were desperately homesick. They were very nice boys, not much interested in England or other countries they fought in, childishly pleased if you knew anything of their 'home town' and anxious at the first excuse to pull out their wallets and show you photographs of their mothers, sweethearts or wives and children. They had not the British Tommy's facility, picked up in many lands, for making himself welcome on a day's leave in a local family, where he could share a meal, help with the washing-up and bath the baby. The G.Is. lived a separate existence, dated the village girls, but only occasionally made lasting friendships with British families. After all, they were the first army in history which did not live on the land, and were fed and supplied entirely by their own overseas government.

In April 1945 I flew to the San Francisco Conference with Francis Williams, who was in charge of the British press, and with General Jacob and other military high-ups. I remember this conference as one of the most extraordinary events of my life. We lived in luxury hotels with wonderful roof-gardens, where we ate and discussed the political future with anyone of any nationality who happened to be there. San Francisco is one of the few American towns with true individuality and a great beauty of its own. There was an atmosphere of intense excitement and rejoicing at the prospect of German defeat. Political interest centred on the Russians. We journalists dashed from one press conference to another, but no delegate aroused so much curiosity as Molotov. Was it possible that Russia and her Western allies would make an agreement and that a new and better kind of League of Nations would really emerge?

Roosevelt's death just before the conference opened had deflated optimism. The full implications of Yalta had not yet dawned on us, and in any case I was not inclined to be unhappy because the Russians were occupying countries which the Nazis were being thrown out of. But any hopes I had of genuine co-operation between America

and Russia were destroyed when Eden told us journalists that sixteen
Poles who had been promised a safe-conduct by the Russians in
order to discuss the future of Poland had been arrested as soon as
they emerged. The result of this breach of faith was devastating.
The future of Poland had become a main issue at the Conference
and it became obvious that the Russians, at all costs, intended to
hold on to countries they had occupied whether the Western powers
liked it or not. One of my most vivid memories of that astonishing
jamboree was being asked to debate on the air with Claud Cockburn
as a partner against two Poles with a Western outlook. We were
given vast steaks which we had no time to eat before we started in a
cavalcade with police motor-cyclists sounding their sirens across the
bridge to Oakland. We were rushed into a studio and egged on to
make a fight of it. I had sympathy with the Polish case, but never
had a chance to express it. Claud and I were better debaters than the
Poles and I felt ashamed at the end of the discussion that their case
had never been properly presented. I came away with the knowledge
that it would be very difficult to maintain an objective view of
East/West relations.

The Russians had lost twenty million people in the war and were
not much interested in codes of honour or in any form of gentlemanly behaviour. They would hold on to what they had got, and
treated with contempt the efforts of people like Henry Wallace,
who stood for co-operation between East and West, and for sharing
with the emergent countries some of the vast surplus wealth of
America. They assumed all this could be nothing but a new form of
colonial exploitation, and though they did co-operate on the World
Health Organisation and on Locust Control, they started with the
assumption that Western Capitalism was necessarily an enemy, and
they treated every economic proposal as political. This played
directly into the hands of Henry Luce and the believers in the
American Century, who thought that the U.S.A. should fill the
world Imperialist role which had been Britain's in the nineteenth
century. Fundamentally, the Communists were quite right in
believing that the United States would be at war with Communism,
even though some idealists might foolishly hope that the alliance

against Germany would continue. The conflict was not only ideological. I remember talking to an American businessman one day in a train; he said there would obviously be war with Russia soon and when I suggested that there was no real economic conflict between them, he said they had to fight each other because there would not be room for two large pike in the world fishpond.

After the Conference I wrote in the *N. S. & N.*:

So it comes about that in this hour of victory, with every prospect of a formally successful Conference, many of us doubt whether anything real is being accomplished. There was never any hope here of a World Federation, but the argument was that, since the Big Three had all the power, and since their vital interests did not clash, they might reach a genuine agreement not to quarrel and might gradually come to work together and to settle their disputes by regular meetings and with the aid of a World Organisation. This is still not impossible, but the hope diminishes. Molotov may still change the picture by a dramatic announcement. The Polish issue may pass, but confidence between the Powers will be difficult to create, and on that all hangs. The opportunity is unique, since the psychology of joint victory should be uniquely favourable. We shall never have another week of triumphs such as this—with the daily news of German surrenders; with the announcement of Hitler's death; with the joyous pictures of American and Red Army soldiers embracing each other in the hour of victory. In war we have co-operated in spite of all obstacles. After the war it will be more difficult.

German surrender was now imminent and I decided to hurry back to England. On the *Lark* (the night express train between San Francisco and Los Angeles), I found myself sitting next to Bruce Bliven, the editor of the *New Republic*. He had much the same hopes and fears as mine about the post-war world. He pointed out that a man sitting immediately in front of us was Walter Winchell, whose daily column appeared in some three hundred newspapers and whose broadcasts attracted listeners all over the United States. Walter, Bliven said, lived on scandal-mongering, but at the moment he was on the same side as ourselves and infinitely more powerful than either of us could ever be. I was introduced, and Walter at once gathered me into the select set around him. He moved into the double coach which, by a special arrangement of the buffers, could take the curves all in one piece. We sat side-by-side and word got around that the great Walter Winchell was on the train. The first-comers were a lady and her daughter who came in gasping with pleasure at meeting so great a man. 'The pleasure is entirely mine,' cried Walter, 'you are the very people I have been looking for all my life. You are Mrs. and Miss America; do sit down and have a scotch and soda.' The next to arrive was a tall sailor, just back from the war in the East. 'What can I do for you, buddy?' said Walter. 'Get me out of this good, steady job,' said the sailor. 'Oh,' cried Walter, 'what a wonderful crack! Do you mind if I use it in my next broadcast?' He then pulled out from his pocket a number of scraps of paper and, to the sailor's delight, wrote down his *bon mot*. His pocket was already half-full of remarks about Germans and the peace which I had made, and which he declared he intended to immortalise. By this time the coach was becoming full of awestruck men and women, drinking scotches at Walter's expense. I met his Public Relations Officer who seemed to have a cushy job; Walter was his own publicity man. He was much concerned about a young man on a New York newspaper who, he insisted, had maligned him the day before. 'Before starting, I rang up this paper,' he said, 'and asked whether Cyrus P. X. . . . had written this offensive paragraph. He admitted he had. "Oh," I said, "so you're the s.o.b. to whom I gave a helping hand only a week ago and now you write like this about me? Well, if it comes to kicking in the groin, I can do that too!" And so I said on my last night's broadcast this and this and this and this. Was I right?' To which the audience with one accord declared, 'You were right, Walter, you were right.'

Until about one o'clock in the morning we both signed our names across valueless currency notes from Pacific islands brought to us by scores of sailors. They had not, of course, any notion who I was, but as I was next to Walter, my signature went with his. He went on signing for several hours more after I had gone to bed. His normal routine was to sleep until late in the afternoon, when his team of research workers brought him the material they had discovered during the day. This he wove into his nightly broadcasts. He was at his brightest and most bewitching at seven o'clock in the morning when the train arrived at Los Angeles. We descended from the train on a platform kept empty so that he should not be pestered by autograph-hunters, but one large man, whom I remember as hairy and dark, was allowed on to the platform. To my astonishment, Walter raised one arm in the air and shouted: 'Communist,' and then, raising both hands, shouted even louder, '*Communist*, COM-MUNIST.' He turned to me and said, 'Did you hear me say Communist?' I admitted that I had. 'That's Orson Welles,' he said. I parted from them after a pressing invitation from Walter to come and have a Scotch with him at his hotel any day I liked, but I never saw either of them again. When I said goodbye to Walter he was already telling Orson about the s.o.b. who had double-crossed him, and Orson was being asked whether Walter had done right in saying on the radio this and that and that?

I was in the garden of the Beverly Hills Hotel when I heard the King announce the German surrender over the loudspeaker. I had only time to go with Bob Boothby to one grand party of film stars in celebration of victory before returning, this time to Baltimore, from which the flying-boats then started for England. This was the most comfortable form of travel I ever knew. It lasted another five years before it was superseded by swifter and more profitable aircraft. There was room on these boats, room to eat and move about freely, and there were couches to sleep on. We dawdled, as people nowadays would call it, for perhaps five hours a day in the air, and spent the nights in our private hotel, which rested on the water at some such interesting place as Cairo or Calcutta. We did not travel at six hundred miles an hour, but I have never really been able to see what advantage there was in crossing the Atlantic in three hours, or reaching Tokyo in seven. But it was already clear that we

Y

were coming back to a new world where all the technical advances made in the war would continue to rush ahead, making life always quicker, more anxious and more dangerous. In August I listened with cold foreboding to the announcement that an A-bomb had destroyed Hiroshima.

I must stop here, because I seem to be beginning a third volume of autobiography which, if it is ever written, must be concerned with the nuclear threat, the Cold War, racialism, mounting over-population, India, China, and the new emergent states. I shall have to report the easy victory of national madness over economic sanity in the Far East, the Middle East and indeed, in every part of the world. I must be content here to notice, with some satisfaction, after my gloom about the American-Russian confrontation, that there were three occasions on which in the years immediately following the war I threw up my hat in delight on the front page of the *N. S. & N.* One was at the proposals of the Marshall Plan (not then to be confused with martial), the second was Indian independence, and the third was when Tito broke the unity of the Communist bloc and cocked a snook at Stalin.

CHAPTER SIXTEEN

Left Illusions

IN THE prewar period, the division between Left and Right was definable. The Right accepted booms and slumps, unemployment and periodic wars as inevitable, while the Left looked forward to a Socialist government which would end unemployment and might even find a way of preventing war. Russia became the centre of controversy, not because anyone except the Communists believed in the Workers' Paradise, but because it had adopted an economic plan and had no unemployment. Moreover, an alliance with the Soviet Union, which the Tories treated as a pariah country, offered the only hope of defeating Hitler with or without war.

Every generation finds the last one naive; in the twenties and thirties we laughed at the simple political motives assumed by Gladstone and Disraeli, and the present generation scoffs at our habit of believing that everything was explicable and soluble in terms of economics. We talked psychology and assumed economics. We were not gullible ninnies who expected the League of Nations to overcome sovereignty, but we thought it the only hope and fought for it long after it was betrayed. We, not the Tories, were the realists who saw that isolated defence was an out-of-date conception and that the collective idea alone made sense. We did not think that the Labour Government would introduce Utopia, but we thought, as it turned out rightly, that given a parliamentary majority Labour could make great strides towards what we now call a Welfare State.

This is what the gradualists always hoped, but thoughtful politicians including at one period Attlee himself, were not sure whether Laski was right in thinking that a Labour Government which seriously attacked property rights would be confronted with an opposition that would not yield to normal constitutional means. The precedents were 1832, when the ruling class gave way to avoid revolution; the Liberal Government, when Lloyd George pushed

Y*

radical reforms through in spite of the Lords; and 1931, when international finance dictated policy to a Labour Government that was not even mildly Socialist. Innumerable books and articles were written on this topic in the long years while Labour was in the wilderness, but the argument was almost forgotten when in 1945, as the result of the war, Labour found itself in power, elected by a public ready for drastic change. It resigned before the issue of Socialism was really joined and when Labour came back to power in 1964 international finance again stultified its promises of Socialism.

Labour, it is true, had never thought out what it meant by Socialism and whether, for instance, it was willing for Britain to lose its status as a world power and accept that of a Scandinavian state. Labour followers, as well as Tories, cherished the picture of Britain playing a noble, international role, boldly championing the victims of aggression everywhere, but yet not running any risk of war. We jeered at Palmerston's gunboat policy, but still hoped that we could preserve the rights of the oppressed as well as look after our own interests. The net result of these confusions and disappointments, both domestic and international, has been that in 1968 what Beatrice Webb in the 1880s called 'the coming religion of Socialism' no longer evokes the old optimism or enthusiasm, the vision between political parties is blurred and the system of Parliamentary Democracy is itself in danger.

Labour also failed to solve the problem of incentives. It was natural to put this on one side when hunger and unemployment made it seem only theoretical. It was enough, in the thirties, to demand a living wage. As a matter of theory, it was possible to believe that a future Socialist government would inspire everyone to work enthusiastically for the creation of a new society. Bernard Shaw, of course, solved the problem: anyone who did not work for his living under Socialism would be shot. Characteristically he added that, although there should be complete equality of income, an exception should be made for playwrights. But the problem of how to avoid paying special salaries to ambitious tycoons and how to apply adequate incentives without any degree of compulsion in a fully-employed society, has so far proved insoluble in Socialist Russia, as in a still Capitalist Britain.

The thirties certainly under-estimated—to adopt an old Victorian idiom—Nature, and relied too much on Nurture. We were right in saying that given a better-educated society, not over-populated and reasonably homogenous, a more equal civilisation was possible, but we did not attach enough importance to colour differences or ancient national traditions, or understand how limited would be the effect of good laws, and how overwhelming the social results of world communications would be. It is dangerous to make these admissions, lest we seem to give support to ignorant racialists or to suggest that all our evils are due to Original Sin, as if one scientific or social invention such as the parliamentary vote or the water-closet had not done more to civilise society than twenty centuries of sermons. Where we went wrong was in not realising the complexity of human motives and the universality of aggressive drives. We assumed that the Affluent Society would be a satisfying one.

When I saw prostitutes lining the streets of Berlin or London, I assumed, quite correctly, that this was a disease of poverty; most of the girls were selling their bodies because they had nothing else men would pay for. But it was a mistake to leap to the conclusion that there would be no prostitution if there were no poverty; in the Affluent Society some women (and some boys) would prefer prostitution to work. In the same way, we thought that people only stole because they were in want or unemployed; in days of prosperity we learnt that some young, adventurous and neglected adolescents would prefer to form gangs, wantonly destroy telephone booths, slash railway carriages, or embark on a career of robbery and violence in preference to well-paid jobs available to them.

We certainly went too far in our belief in economic motivation. The slogan that 'Capitalism means War' sprang from a Marxist analysis which applied to the era of Imperialist societies which, at the end of the nineteenth century, were rivals for overseas markets and raw materials. Though most of these rivalries were settled between the Imperialist states without war amongst themselves, one could point to such incidents as the Fashoda crisis in 1899 or the South

African War of 1900 as examples of the Leninist theory. But the issues for which the Imperialist states fought in 1914 were long-standing European problems of frontiers and the balance of power. The Second World War was not economic; if Hitler had been an economic man and we only interested in profits, Germany and Britain would never have dropped bombs on each other. The truth is that in a state of anarchy nation states, like individuals, can go to war with each other for many reasons—dynastic, national, economic or religious. Men are aggressive animals and, like dogs, they do not only fight over a shortage of bones, but because it is their nature to bark and bite. According to Konrad Lorenz, a very great biologist, men are unique in the animal world (with the exception of doves) in preferring to fight to the death within their own species; some biologists add that men, like robins, may even have territorial limits which they are prepared to defend to the death.

The belief in economic motivation was our most pervasive illusion. Marxists held that to enforce a communal form of land ownership would create Communists, if not amongst the first generation then certainly amongst the second or third. I remember the difficulty I had in persuading my Communist guide in Moscow to admit, in the fifties, that Russia's land policy had been largely a failure; Communists had assumed wrongly that people would be willing to share work and profits on the land, as they would in the factory. In no Communist country that I have visited, from Cuba to China, has communal ownership of the land been a success. Always there has been a return to some compromise with individual owner-ship. The outstanding exception was in Israel, where communism worked in the *kibbutzim*, because the *kibbutz* was also a fortress to be defended against siege with a gun as well as a spade. And *kibbutzim* lost their communist characteristics years before the Suez war.

The greatest disappointment of all was the discovery that peoples who had been held together under Imperialist rule would not co-operate with each other when they were free. Colonial experts in the Labour Party did not make the mistake of thinking that the Imperial powers could walk out of African colonies without preparing them for independence; it was the Tories who refused to spend money on

African education and to prepare them for self-government. But very few had realised how quickly the peoples of vast areas of Africa which had been under British or French rule would disintegrate into tribes, and how urgent would be the danger of both tribal and national wars breaking out all over Africa. Much more surprising was the discovery that in other parts of the world peoples who were supposed to be on the road to modern civilisation would quarrel bitterly when the Imperialists departed. Who, for instance, could have imagined that Greeks and Turks, who had long lived together in amity in the loveliest and most potentially prosperous of islands, would today be prevented from cutting one anothers' throats only by foreign bayonets and United Nations intervention? It is true, of course, that the differences of religion in Cyprus are exploited by the mainland powers of Greece and Turkey, which are old and bitter rivals, but it is also true that only a minority of the Greeks and Turks in Cyprus itself now talk as if it were possible to tolerate each others' existence.

The most unhappy case of all is that of India, where Moslems and Hindus had everything to gain by remaining friends when the British left. Partly, no doubt, this misery is Britain's fault. Hindu and Moslem friends who spent their lives in mixed communities have told me that in the old days before the First World War they were unconscious of communal differences; that the British intensified these by the inauguration of communal voting in 1908, and that communal rivalry was increased by dyarchy after the First World War. But even those who knew India well did not realise how bitterly communal hatred had developed in the years that followed, and I recall how, in the middle of the Second World War, I accompanied two men with long experience of India on a delegation to Leopold Amery, then Secretary of State for India. We were protesting that the British were still using the excuse of Moslem and Hindu rivalry to postpone the grant of independence. We were almost overwhelmed and convinced against our will by the facts and figures Amery showed us about the undoubted reality of Hindu-Moslem hatreds. I had to admit that he proved right in the massacres of 1947 and the subsequent history of India/Pakistan relations.

I think finally we all believed too simply in the speedy triumph of reason over tradition, and, especially, of humanism over religious faith. When I first went to Moscow, I watched with pleasure the exposure of frauds imposed upon an ignorant peasantry by the Orthodox Church. Once deprived of the economic advantages which the priests reaped from fake miracles, the Communists assumed that the populace would see that the doctrines of orthodoxy were also rubbish, and that the whole paraphernalia of religion was fit only for museums. When I visited Russia twenty years later and went to a famous cathedral town not far from Moscow, I saw thousands of people, many of whom could only have been children when the Anti-God campaign was in full swing, taking the eucharist from priests, all from the same spoon, and apparently with the same belief that their fathers and grandfathers had had, and the same disregard for hygiene. I do not suggest that progress in rational thought has not grown in the U.S.S.R. as elsewhere, but only that the process of eroding tradition is far slower than any of us used to think. I realised how wrong it was possible to be when one day in 1945 I saw written upon a wall on the frontier of Communist Hungary the sentence 'We have no use for history'.

Nonsense, of course, to imagine a future that ignores the past; there can never be a Year One in human society. But 1945 was, to an unprecedented extent, the beginning of a new era, not because the Hiroshima bomb killed more people than non-atomic explosives and incendiaries killed in Dresden and Tokyo, but because it marked the beginning of a Take-over by science. An unplanned and unpremeditated Take-over, but a Take-over all the same. Nowadays, our leading biologists look forward to a day not far distant when supermen will be able to realise the fantasies of Aldous Huxley and decide, for instance, how many alpha-men of supreme intelligence are born and how many deltas will be required to carry out the menial jobs that will still be necessary in the Brave New World. Already they are promising a store of hearts, kidneys, livers and lungs, enabling them, like gods, to give life to men of their choosing and allowing others to die. We are to be guided by computers which, they tell us, will acquire the human characteristics of reason and even of emotion without the errors which now threaten mankind. That they are far from successful as yet in this field, we know because President Johnson's decisions are based upon an unimaginably, swiftly gathered, store of information about the effect of each of his escalations on the military situation in Vietnam, on the public opinion of the world and on his own chances of re-election. The only things not fed into the President's computer are imponderables, such as love, compassion and commonsense. Perhaps that is the reason why he finds it so difficult to conquer a small, quite unscientific people intent on maintaining their liberty.

Looking backward and forward today, I think we were right in the thirties in believing that the future of mankind depends on morality, personal, political and international. Very few of our new, scientific supermen seem today much concerned with the everyday issues of poverty, social misery and the threat of another world war. Einstein indeed said that the men of science have slipped so much that they have come to regard 'servitude to governments as their natural lot'. Half a century earlier another great scientist, Thomas Huxley, grandfather of Julian and Aldous and inspirer of a whole generation (including H. G. Wells), said that 'the prostitution of the mind, the soddening of conscience, the dwarfing of mankind are the worst calamities'. We shall not solve these human problems by flying to the Moon.

Index